WILLIAM KOENIG

EYE TO EYE

PUBLISHING WITH A PURPOSE

WWW.21STCENTURYPRESS.COM

Eye to Eye

Facing The Consequences of Dividing Israel

Published by 21st Century Press

Springfield, MO 65807

 Unless otherwise indicated, Bible quotations are taken from the King James Version of the Holy Bible. Requests for permissions should be addressed to:

21st Century Press
2131 W. Republic Rd.
PMB 41
Springfield, MO 65807

ISBN 0-9728899-9-X

Cover: Lee Fredrickson and Keith Locke
Book Design: Terry White

Visit our web-site at: 21stcenturypress.com
and 21centurybooks.com

For childrens books visit: sonshippress.com
and sonshipbooks.com

TABLE OF CONTENTS

Introduction -- U.S. Senator James Inhoffe (Oklahoma-R) 9

Preface -- William Koenig 21
Where does President Bush stand today? --Ari Fleischer ...23

Chapter 1
U.S. Catastrophes and Events 27
What do the following events have in common? 27
The major "land for peace" efforts and the corresponding catastrophes or events from October 30, 1991 to December 13, 2000 29

Chapter 2
U.S. Catastrophes and Events Continued 101
The major "land for peace" efforts and the corresponding catastrophes or events from March 31, 2001 to November 4, 2003 101

Chapter 3
The Major U.S. Catastrophes and Events in Perspective 153
The major catastrophes or events that transpired when Presidents Bush, Clinton and Bush were in office, beginning with the Madrid Peace Conference of October 30, 1991, to November 4, 2003 153
Top ten natural disasters ranked by FEMA relief costs ...157
The three largest insurance events in U.S. history 161
Four of the seven costliest hurricanes in U.S. history 162
Three of the four largest tornado outbreaks in U.S. history .164

Chapter 4
Eight Disruptive Periods 169
Eight Disruptive Periods When President George W. Bush is Involved with Israel's Land 192

Chapter 5
Eight Disruptive Periods - Period 7 & 8 217
5 week summary 219
Top news headlines from May 4 to May 29, 2003 220
Bush heads to Russia, Europe & Middle East 223
Rice raises objections with Sharon on the Security Fence . .228
Bush meets with Abbas at the White House 230
Review of the Bush plan and involvement 234
Bush meets with Sharon at the White House 236
The Arafat problem 243
Bush Welcomes King Abdullah II to Camp David 246
What will give? 248
Plans coming from many directions 257
New Phase - New Pressure 259
Sharon responds with his own plan 261

Chapter 6
U.S. and Israel "Land for Peace" Statements and Efforts 277
Bush Administration Middle East peace efforts that coincide with major suicide bombings 277
Statements by Israeli leaders and peace efforts that coincide with major suicide bombings and terror events 281
The cycle of violence continues 285

Chapter 7
U.S. Administrations and Middle East Leaders Involved In The Middle East Peace Process & Defining Events 287
What happened to the U.S. Presidents who were actively involved in the dividing of Israel's covenant land? 289
What happened to the Middle East leaders who were directly involved in the Middle East peace process? 297

Chapter 8
Conclusion, Addendums and Letters 301
Conclusion 301
Addendum -- Open Letter to Israel: William Koenig 304

Addendum -- Land Grant Scriptures 307
Addendum -- The Error of Replacement Theology 315
Addendum -- Resolutions, Agreement, Letters,
and Speeches 318
UN Security Council Resolution 242 -- November 22, 1967 .319
UN Security Council Resolution 338 -- October 22, 1973 .320
Remarks by President George H.W. Bush, The Madrid
Conference -- October 30, 1991 321
A Performance-based Road Map 327
Speech by President George W. Bush at Aqaba Summit
-- June 04, 2003 337
Letters to the White House and their response 341

Endnotes 355

Bill Koenig's Biography 374

INTRODUCTION

When World Leaders Pressure Israel to Divide Her Land Major Consequences Follow

In *Eye to Eye – Facing the Consequences of Dividing Israel,* we document what happens the same day or within 24 to 48 hours of Israel being pressured to divide her land. Here are a few examples found in these pages:

There were 29 record-setting catastrophes or major events during President George H.W. Bush and President Bill Clinton's presidencies;

There were 20 record-setting catastrophes or major events during President George W. Bush's first 36 months in office;

There were eight periods of disruption in the United States following the 9-11 terror events from October 1, 2001 to January 9, 2004 when President George W. Bush attempted to divide Israel's land;

There were 26 major suicide bombings in Israel that occurred at the same time President George W. Bush or one of his top-level staff and/or one of Israel's top officials were working with the U.S. on either a cease-fire agreement, a peace deal, publicly stating Israel's approval of a Palestinian state, or Israel was about to evacuate property.

The book also documents what happened to previous American Presidents (beginning with the Presidency of Richard Nixon to the present) and Middle East leaders who were actively involved in the Middle East peace process during their time in office and/or afterwards.

Eye to Eye is a profound example that the God of Israel is very serious about His covenant land and that those who continue to pressure Israel to divide her land will experience even greater consequences.

March 4, 2002

In a speech before the Senate, Senator James Inhofe stood against world opinion and offered seven reasons why Israel alone is entitled to possess the Holy Land. The following is the complete speech.

I was interested the other day when I heard that the de facto ruler, Saudi Arabian Crown Prince Abdullah, made a statement which was received by many in this country as if it were a statement of fact, as if it were something new, a concept for peace in the Middle East that no one had ever heard of before. I was kind of shocked that it was so well received by many people who had been down this road before.

I suggest to you that what Crown Prince Abdullah talked about a few days ago was not new at all. He talked about the fact that under the Abdullah plan, Arabs would normalize relations with Israel in exchange for the Jewish state surrendering the territory it received after the 1976 Six-Day War as if that were something new. He went on to talk about other land that had been acquired and had been taken by Israel.

I remember so well on December 4 when we covered all of this and the fact that there isn't anything new about the prospect of giving up land that is rightfully Israel's land in order to have peace.

When it gets right down to it, the land doesn't make that much difference because Yasser Arafat and others don't recognize Israel's right to any of the land. They do not recognize Israel's right to exist.

I will discuss seven reasons, which I mentioned once before, why Israel is entitled to the land they have and that it should not be a part of the peace process.

If this is something that Israel wants to do, it is their business to do it. But anyone who has tried to put the pressure on Israel to do this is wrong.

We are going to be hit by skeptics who are going to say we will be attacked because of our support for Israel, and if we get out of the Middle East -- that is us -- all the problems will go away. That is just not true. If we withdraw, all of these problems will again come to our door.

I have some observations to make about that. But I would like to reemphasize once again the seven reasons that Israel has the right to their land.

The first reason is that Israel has the right to the land because of all of the archeological evidence. That is reason, No. 1. All the archeological evidence supports it.

Every time there is a dig in Israel, it does nothing but support the fact that Israelis have had a presence there for 3,000 years. They have been there for a long time. The coins, the cities, the pottery, the culture--there are other people, groups that are there, but there is no mistaking the fact that Israelis have been present in that land for 3,000 years.

It predates any claims that other peoples in the regions may have. The ancient Philistines are extinct. Many other ancient peoples are extinct. They do not have the unbroken line to this date that the Israelis have.

Even the Egyptians of today are not racial Egyptians of 2,000, 3,000 years ago. They are primarily an Arab people. The land is called Egypt, but they are not the same racial and ethnic stock as the old Egyptians of the ancient world. The first Israelis are in fact descended from the original Israelites. The first proof, then, is the archeology.

The second proof of Israel's right to the land is the historic right. History supports it totally and completely. We know there has been an Israel up until the time of the Roman Empire. The Romans conquered the land. Israel had no homeland, although Jews were allowed to live there. They were driven from the land in two dispersions: One was in A.D. 70 and the other was in A.D. 135. But there was always a Jewish presence in the land.

The Turks, who took over about 700 years ago and ruled the land up until about World War I, had control. Then the British conquered the land. The Turks entered World War I on the side of Germany. The British knew they had to do something to punish Turkey, and also to break up that empire that was going to be a part of the whole effort of Germany in World War I. So the British sent troops against the Turks in the Holy Land.

One of the generals who was leading the British armies was a man named Allenby. Allenby was a Bible-believing Christian. He carried a Bible with him everywhere he went and he knew the significance of Jerusalem.

The night before the attack against Jerusalem to drive out the Turks, Allenby prayed that God would allow him to capture the city without doing damage to the holy places.

That day, Allenby sent World War I biplanes over the city of Jerusalem to do a reconnaissance mission. You have to understand that the Turks had at that time never seen an airplane. So there they were, flying around. They looked in the sky and saw these fascinating inventions and did not know what they were, and they were terrified by them. Then they were told they were going to be opposed by a man named Allenby the next day, which means, in their language, "man sent from God" or "prophet from God." They dared not fight against a prophet from God, so the next morning, when Allenby went to take Jerusalem, he went in and captured it without firing a single shot.

The British Government was grateful to Jewish people around the world, particularly to one Jewish chemist who helped them manufacture niter. Niter is an ingredient that was used in nitroglycerin, which was sent over from the New World. But they did not have a way of getting it to England. The German U-boats were shooting on the boats, so most of the niter they were trying to import to make nitroglycerin was at the bottom of the ocean. But a man named Weitzman, a Jewish chemist, discovered a way to make it from materials that existed in England. As a result, they were able to continue that supply.

The British at that time said they were going to give the Jewish people a homeland. That is all a part of history. It is all written down in history. They were gratified that the Jewish people, the bankers, came through and helped finance the war.

The homeland that Britain said it would set aside consisted of all of what is now Israel and all of what was then the nation of Jordan--the whole thing. That was what Britain promised to give the Jews in 1917.

In the beginning, there was some Arab support for this action. There was not a huge Arab population in the land at that time, and there is a reason for that. The land was not able to sustain a large population of people. It just did not have the development it needed to handle those people, and the land was not really wanted by anybody. Nobody really wanted this land. It was considered to be worthless land.

I want the Presiding Officer to hear what Mark Twain said. And, of course, you may have read "Huckleberry Finn" and "Tom Sawyer." Mark Twain--Samuel Clemens--took a tour of Palestine in 1867. This is how he described that land. We are talking about Israel now. He said:

> A desolate country whose soil is rich enough but is given over wholly to weeds. A silent, mournful expanse. We never saw a human being on the whole route. There was hardly a tree or a shrub anywhere. Even the olive and the cactus, those fast friends of a worthless soil, had almost deserted the country.
>
> Where was this great Palestinian nation? It did not exist. It was not there. Palestinians were not there. Palestine was a region named by the Romans, but at that time it was under the control of Turkey, and there was no large mass of people there because the land would not support them.

This is the report that the Palestinian Royal Commission created by the British, made. It quotes an account of the conditions on the coastal plain along the Mediterranean Sea in 1913. This is the Palestinian Royal Commission. They said:

> The road leading from Gaza to the north was only a summer track, suitable for transport by camels or carts. No orange groves, orchards or vineyards were to be seen until one reached the Yavnev village. Houses were mud. Schools did not exist. The western part toward the sea was almost a desert. The villages in this area were few and thinly populated. Many villages were deserted by their inhabitants.

That was 1913.

The French author Voltaire described Palestine as "a hopeless, dreary place."

In short, under the Turks the land suffered from neglect

and low population. That is an historic fact. The nation became populated by both Jews and Arabs because the land came to prosper when Jews came back and began to reclaim it. Historically, they began to reclaim it. If there had never been any archaeological evidence to support the rights of the Israelis to the territory, it is also important to recognize that other nations in the area have no longstanding claim to the country either.

Did you know that Saudi Arabia was not created until 1913, Lebanon until 1920? Iraq did not exist as a nation until 1932, Syria until 1941; the borders of Jordan were established in 1946 and Kuwait in 1961. Any of these nations that would say Israel is only a recent arrival would have to deny their own rights as recent arrivals as well. They did not exist as countries. They were all under the control of the Turks.

Historically, Israel gained its independence in 1948.

The third reason that land belongs to Israel is the practical value of the Israelis being there. Israel today is a modern marvel of agriculture. Israel is able to bring more food out of a desert environment than any other country in the world. The Arab nations ought to make Israel their friend and import technology from Israel that would allow all the Middle East, not just Israel, to become an exporter of food. Israel has unarguable success in its agriculture.

The fourth reason I believe Israel has the right to the land is on the grounds of humanitarian concern. You see, there were 6 million Jews slaughtered in Europe in World War II. The persecution against the Jews had been very strong in Russia since the advent of communism. It was against them even before then under the Czars.

These people have a right to their homeland. If we are not going to allow them a homeland in the Middle East, then where? What other nation on Earth is going to cede territory, is going to give up land?

They are not asking for a great deal. The whole nation of Israel would fit into my home State of Oklahoma seven times. It would fit into the Presiding Officer's State of Georgia seven times. They are not asking for a great deal. The whole nation of Israel is very small. It is a nation that, up until the time that claims started coming in, was not desired by anybody.

The fifth reason Israel ought to have their land is that she is a strategic ally of the United States. Whether we realize it or not, Israel is a detriment, an impediment, to certain groups hostile to democracies and hostile to what we believe in, hostile to that which makes us the greatest nation in the history of the world. They have kept them from taking complete control of the Middle East. If it were not for Israel, they would overrun the region. They are our strategic ally.

It is good to know we have a friend in the Middle East on whom we can count. They vote with us in the United Nations more than England, more than Canada, more than France, more than Germany--more than any other country in the world.

The sixth reason is that Israel is a roadblock to terrorism. The war we are now facing is not against a sovereign nation; it is against a group of terrorists who are very fluid, moving from one country to another. They are almost invisible. That is whom we are fighting against today.

We need every ally we can get. If we do not stop terrorism in the Middle East, it will be on our shores. We have said this again and again and again, and it is true.

One of the reasons I believe the spiritual door was opened for an attack against the United States of America is that the policy of our Government has been to ask the Israelis, and demand it with pressure, not to retaliate in a significant way against the terrorist strikes that have been launched against them.

Since its independence in 1948, Israel has fought four wars: The war in 1948 and 1949--that was the war for independence--the war in 1956, the Sinai campaign; the Six-Day War in 1967; and in 1973, the Yom Kippur War, the holiest day of the year, and that was with Egypt and Syria.

You have to understand that in all four cases, Israel was attacked. They were not the aggressor. Some people may argue that this was not true because they went in first in 1956, but they knew at that time that Egypt was building a huge military to become the aggressor. Israel, in fact, was not the aggressor and has not been the aggressor in any of the four wars.

Also, they won all four wars against impossible odds. They are great warriors. They consider a level playing field being outnumbered 2 to 1.

There were 39 Scud missiles that landed on Israeli soil during the gulf war. Our President asked Israel not to respond. In order to have the Arab nations on board, we asked Israel not to participate in the war. They showed tremendous restraint and did not. Now we have asked them to stand back and not do anything over these last several attacks.

We have criticized them. We have criticized them in our media. Local people in television and radio often criticize Israel, not knowing the true facts. We need to be informed.

I was so thrilled when I heard a reporter pose a question to our Secretary of State, Colin Powell. He said:

Mr. Powell, the United States has advocated a policy of restraint in the Middle East. We have discouraged

Israel from retaliation again and again and again because we've said it leads to continued escalation--that it escalates the violence. Are we going to follow that preaching ourselves?

Mr. Powell indicated we would strike back. In other words, we can tell Israel not to do it, but when it hits us, we are going to do something.

But all that changed in December [2001] when the Israelis went into the Gaza Strip with gunships and into the West Bank with F-16s. With the exception of last May [2001], the Israelis had not used F-16s since the 1967 6-Day War. And I am so proud of them because we have to stop terrorism. It is not going to go away. If Israel were driven into the sea tomorrow, if every Jew in the Middle East were killed, terrorism would not end. You know that in your heart. Terrorism would continue.

It is not just a matter of Israel in the Middle East. It is the heart of the very people who are perpetrating this stuff. Should they be successful in overrunning Israel--which they won't be--but should they be, it would not be enough. They will never be satisfied.

No. 7, I believe very strongly that we ought to support Israel; that it has a right to the land. This is the most important reason: Because God said so. As I said a minute ago, look it up in the book of Genesis. It is right up there on the desk.

In Genesis 13:14-17, the Bible says:

> The Lord said to Abram, "Lift up now your eyes, and look from the place where you are northward, and southward, and eastward and westward: for all the land which you see, to you will I give it, and to your seed forever... Arise, walk through the land in the length of it and in the breadth of it; for I will give it to thee."

That is God talking.

The Bible says that Abram removed his tent and came and dwelt in the plain of Mamre, which is in Hebron, and built there an altar before the Lord. Hebron is in the West Bank. It is at this place where God appeared to Abram and said, "I am giving you this land," -- the West Bank.

This is not a political battle at all. It is a contest over whether or not the word of God is true. The seven reasons, I am convinced, clearly establish that Israel has a right to the land.

Eight years ago on the lawn of the White House, Yitzhak Rabin shook hands with PLO Chairman Yasser Arafat. It was a historic occasion. It was a tragic occasion.

At that time, the official policy of the Government of Israel began to be, "Let us appease the terrorists. Let us begin to trade the land for peace." This process continued unabated up until last year. Here in our own Nation, at Camp David, in the summer of 2000, then Prime Minister of Israel Ehud Barak offered the most generous concessions to Yasser Arafat that had ever been laid on the table.

He offered him more than 90 percent of all the West Bank territory, sovereign control of it. There were some parts he did not want to offer, but in exchange for that he said he would give up land in Israel proper that the PLO had not even asked for.

And he also did the unthinkable. He even spoke of dividing Jerusalem and allowing the Palestinians to have their capital there in the East. Yasser Arafat stormed out of the meeting. Why did he storm out of the meeting? Everything he had said he wanted was offered there. It was put into his hands. Why did he storm out of the meeting?

A couple of months later, there began to be riots, terrorism. The riots began when now Prime Minister Ariel Sharon went to the Temple Mount. And this was used as the thing that lit the fire and that caused the explosion.

Did you know that Sharon did not go unannounced and that he contacted the Islamic authorities before he went and secured their permission and had permission to be there? It was no surprise.

The response was very carefully calculated. They knew the world would not pay attention to the details.

They would portray this in the Arab world as an attack upon the holy mosque. They would portray it as an attack upon that mosque and use it as an excuse to riot. Over the last 8 years, during this time of the peace process, where the Israeli public has pressured its leaders to give up land for peace because they are tired of fighting, there has been increased terror.

In fact, it has been greater in the last 8 years than any other time in Israel's history. Showing restraint and giving in has not produced any kind of peace. It is so much so that today the leftist peace movement in Israel does not exist because the people feel they were deceived.

They did offer a hand of peace, and it was not taken. That is why the politics of Israel have changed drastically over the past 12 months [since March 2001]. The Israelis have come to see that, "No matter what we do, these people do not want to deal with us...They want to destroy us." That is why even yet today the stationery of the PLO still has upon it the map of the entire state of Israel, not just the tiny little part they call the West Bank that they want. They want it all.

We have to get out of this mind set that somehow you can buy peace in the Middle East by giving little plots of land. It has not worked before when it has been offered.

These seven reasons show why Israel is entitled to that land.

PREFACE

In the Bible, God speaks to Abraham, father of the Jews and the nation of Israel, and directs him to the land of Canaan. In the first book of the Bible, God says to Abraham, "I will make of thee a great nation, and I will bless thee and make thy name great; and thou shalt be a blessing. And I will bless them that bless thee and curse him who curseth thee: and in thee shall all the families of the earth be blessed" (Genesis 12:2-3).

Later in the same book, God promises Abraham, "Unto thy seed have I given this land, from the river of Egypt unto the great river, the river Euphrates" (Genesis 15:18).

And two chapters later, God tells Abraham, "And I will establish My covenant between Me and thee and thy seed after thee in their generations for an everlasting covenant to be a God unto thee and to thy seed after thee" (Genesis 17:7).

The Bible also says Israel must be mindful of God's covenant with Abraham, "O ye seed of Israel his servant, ye children of Jacob, his chosen ones. He is the LORD our God; his judgments are in all the earth. Be ye mindful always of his covenant; the word which he commanded to a thousand generations; Even of the covenant which he made with Abraham, and of his oath unto Isaac; And hath confirmed the same to Jacob for a law, and to Israel for an everlasting covenant, Saying, Unto thee will I give the land of Canaan, the lot of your inheritance" (I Chronicles 16:13-18).

America is now experiencing the consequences (curses) of Middle East policies, which have been opposed to God's Word and to the preservation of His covenant land. Ever since the Madrid Conference of October 1991, the United States participation in Israel's destiny has been flawed when put in context of Holy Scripture.

The events of September 11, 2001, were a national wake-up call. However, if this nation continues to support the Road Map, affirming a "land for peace" approach, America can expect to experience the further lifting of the Lord's protective hand in an even greater measure.

"I will also gather all nations, and will bring them down into the valley of Jehoshaphat, and will plead with them there for my people and for my heritage Israel, whom they have scattered among the nations, and parted my land" (Joel 3:2).

It is a fact that Israel's very existence is in grave danger, because of our nation's sponsorship of "land for peace" plans, which have led her to the brink of war.

What is happening in the world, and especially in the Middle East, these days is truly remarkable. But then again, Bible believers shouldn't be surprised, because the Old Testament prophet, Zechariah, pre-warned us about these times over 2,500 years ago:

"And in that day will I make Jerusalem a burdensome stone for all people: all that burden themselves with it shall be cut in pieces, though all the people of the earth be gathered together against it" (Zechariah 12:3).

"And it shall come to pass in that day, that I will seek to destroy all the nations that come against Jerusalem" (Zechariah 12:9).

The Bible is very clear that our loving and fair God will always warn His people before judgment comes.

—William Koenig
Watch.org

Where does President Bush stand today? -- Ari Fleischer

In the White House Press Briefing of June 9, 2003, Ari Fleischer, White House Press Secretary, was asked the following questions:

QUESTION: Ari, there are millions of conservative supporters of the President who have signed letters protesting this Road Map for peace. Does the President see these letters, and does he give any consideration to this important constituent base of his?

MR. FLEISCHER: There's no question the President is aware of the risks to the Road Map. And the risks of the Road Map come principally from both edges of the debate. And, of course, within Israel there will be many people who oppose the dismantlement of these illegal outposts. But these are the actions that are required to be taken for Israel and Palestine to live side by side in peace and security.

And never stop asking yourself the question when it comes to the Middle East, how much longer can Israel and the Palestinian Authority live the way they are, with violence, with killing, with retaliation. Israel has the right to defend itself. But is there a better way? Is there a way that Israel and a Palestinian Authority can finally, at long last, live side by side as Israel and as a Palestinian state?

There have been Arab nations that have made peace treaties with Israel, and have honored them -- Egypt has, Jordan has. Why does anybody have to assume that the Palestinian people don't want the same thing? There are terrorists who don't want it. And the terrorists are the enemy, not only of peace, but also of the creation of a Palestinian state. And that's why the President welcomes the words and is now looking for the results in the actions of the new Palestinian leader, as well as Prime Minister Sharon.

QUESTION: Do you know if President Bush plans a direct response to these letters or plans to meet with any of these conservative leaders?

MR. FLEISCHER: The President's response is widely known. The President is dedicated to implementing the Road Map.

QUESTION: Okay. Since the Palestinian Authority has done no more to fulfill its obligations to the Road Map than it did for the Oslo Accords, and since yesterday's [June 8, 2003] killings of five Israeli soldiers, my question is, can you cite any reason why, with the Road Map completely road blocked, that the President should not end his exemption of Palestinian terrorists from his promise of war on all terrorists?

MR. FLEISCHER: The Road Map is just beginning. The Road Map is just being implemented.

QUESTION: What have they done? What have the Palestinians done to fulfill any of the requirements of last month for the Road Map?

MR. FLEISCHER: When you take a look at the statements that have been made by the Prime Minister of the Palestinian Authority, this President --

QUESTION: Statements? That's --

MR. FLEISCHER: This is exactly how the Road Map was designed to begin. The Prime Minister of the

Palestinian Authority is determined to work with the United States and the Arab nations to rebuild their security forces so that he can, indeed, live up to the terms of the Road Map, which involve cracking down and dismantling terrorism. The President has confidence that over time, with the help of the United States and the help of the Arab nations and the help of Israel, that Prime Minister Abbas is the best hope for implementing the terms of the Road Map.

This is an issue that has always been fraught with extremists who seek to derail the Road Map. What is important now is that the Palestinian Authority is led by someone who is not an extremist, but somebody who is dedicated to implementing the Road Map. And the President will continue to work with both the Israelis and the Palestinians, despite the recent violence, to help them to implement the peacemaking sides of the Road Map. [This was stated prior to Palestinian Prime Minister Mahmoud Abbas's resignation on September 6, 2003.]

CHAPTER 1

U.S. CATASTROPHES AND EVENTS

What Do the Following Events Have in Common?

- Twenty-nine major U.S. catastrophes and events from October 20, 1991, to January 28, 2001 (during President George H. W. Bush and Bill Clinton's terms)
- Twenty major catastrophes and events from March 31, 2001 to November 4, 2003 (during President George W. Bush's term)
- Largest terrorism event in U.S. and world history
- The three largest insurance events in U.S. history
- Seven of the top ten FEMA events in U.S. history
- NASDAQ's peek followed by a major sell off, U.S. and Israeli companies were devastated
- The two largest weekly Dow Jones sell offs in U.S. history
- The Perfect Storm
- The Perfect Fire
- The Perfect Political Storm
- The Perfect Tornado
- 88 tornadoes in 48 hours
- 412 tornadoes in ten days
- Three of four largest tornado outbreaks in U.S. history
- Four of the seven costliest hurricanes in U.S. history
- The largest tornado in Maryland history

- The largest tornado in Oklahoma history
- The largest tornado in Kansas history
- The largest forest fire in Colorado history
- The largest forest fire in Arizona history
- The largest ice storm in North Carolina history
- The largest tropical rain producer in U.S. history
- The largest hurricane evacuation in U.S. history

All of these events transpired on the same day or within 24 to 48 hours of Presidents George H. W. Bush, Bill Clinton or George W. Bush applying major pressure on Israel to:

1. give up her covenant land, or,
2. when one of their top-level officials was in active negotiations with the Israelis and Palestinians, or lastly,
3. when they stated their approval of a Palestinian state.

Also:

- The U.S. experienced eight "disruptive periods" beginning on October 1, 2001.
- Seventeen major suicide bombings occurred in Israel from December 1, 2001 to January 29, 2004, the same day or within 24 hours of major U.S. peace initiatives with Israel.
- Nineteen major suicide bombings or terror events occurred between October 2001 and January 29, 2004, the same day or within 24 hours of Israeli leadership participating in active negotiations with the Palestinians on Israel's covenant land or stating Israel favored a Palestinian state or releasing Palestinian prisoners.

Message: God's covenant land is Israel's and not to be traded for promises of peace and security. Furthermore, those nations who sponsor and promote the "land for peace" efforts will continue to be judged and pay the consequences (Joel 3:2).

Solution: The U.S. should stop the sponsorship of the "land for peace" effort and tell the world community that the U.S. will stand with Israel to help insure her future and that her land is not to be given to the Palestinians, Syrians or any other Arab nation. If the United States doesn't do this, further devastation will come to America and any other nation that continues exerting pressure on Israel to participate in the "land for peace" process.

The Major "Land for Peace" Efforts and the Corresponding Catastrophes or Events from October 20, 1991 to December 12, 2000

Catastrophe #1
October 20, 1991: Oakland Firestorm – Estimated $2.5 (3.5) billion damage/costs

Friday, October 18, 1991, Secretary of State Baker, at a news conference in Jerusalem, says President Bush and Soviet President Gorbachev are inviting Israel, the Arab states, and the Palestinians to attend a Middle East peace conference to be held beginning October 30 in Madrid. Baker says the conference is to be followed by "direct negotiations to achieve real peace."

Sunday, October 20, 1991, will be remembered as the date of one of this nation's most costly fires, the worst fire involving loss of life and property since the Great San Francisco Earthquake and Fire of 1906. The Oakland fire began within 48 hours of the Bush Administration's announcement of their Madrid "land for peace" conference, which was to call on Israel to divide- God's covenant land in return for promises of peace and security.

Oakland Fire

The "Tunnel Fire" magnitude and scope, of what is simply referred to as, is far beyond the experience of any living American firefighter. According to one fire official, only those who fought the Chicago Fire last century or battled the Great Fire in San Francisco would be able to identify with this conflagration and firestorm.

The 1991 drought affected the entire western U.S. Less than average rainfall caused the area to become unusually dry. Hardest hit was California, where numerous wildfires broke out across the state. Particularly devastating was the Oakland fire.

The unusual weather conditions were described in FEMA's Hazard Mitigation Report as follows: "...an unusual east wind, at speeds in excess of 65 miles per hour, that raced down from the crest of the Oakland-Berkeley Hills. Coupled with record high temperatures well into the nineties, the hot, dry winds gusted and swirled through five years of drought-dry brush and groves of freeze-damaged Monterey pines and eucalyptus trees. All the conditions for a major disaster were present that morning of October 20, 1991."

Catastrophe #2

October 30-November 1, 1991: Perfect Storm

When the Gulf War ended in 1991, President Bush Sr. began a process to formulate a Middle East peace plan involving Israel, the Palestinians, and the countries surrounding Israel.

The current phase of the Middle East peace process was launched at the Madrid conference convened by the United States and the former Soviet Union October 30-November 1, 1991. Former Secretary of State James A. Baker III reached agreement on the conference in a series of trips to the Middle East region between March and October 1991. (As stated in Catastrophe #1, the decision was finalized on October 18 in Jerusalem.)

President H.W. Bush made it clear to the Israelis, with cancellations of loan guarantees on September 6, 1991, that America did not accept the permanent occupation of the West Bank and Gaza.

Bush stated, "Throughout the Middle East, we seek a stable and enduring settlement. We've defined what this means. Indeed, I make these points with no map showing where the final borders are to be drawn. Nevertheless, we believe territorial compromise is essential for peace."

The co-sponsors' letter of invitation to the conference laid out the framework for the negotiations, including:

- A just, lasting, and comprehensive peace settlement based on UN Security Council Resolutions 242 and 338;
- Direct bilateral negotiations along two tracks--between Israel and the Arab states and between Israel and the Palestinians; and
- Multilateral negotiations on region-wide issues, such as arms control and regional security, water, refugees, environment, and economic development. These talks would complement the bilateral negotiations.

The bilateral negotiations were split into four separate negotiating tracks: Israel-Syria, Israel-Lebanon, Israel-Jordan, and Israel-Palestinian.

Perfect Storm

It was later termed the "perfect storm" and was described by meteorologists as one of the most powerful storms ever! Extremely rare weather patterns, which happen only about once every 100 years, came together to create this weather monster, and record-breaking ocean waves were measured over 100 feet high. This storm ran down the East Coast into the Carolinas, causing millions of dollars in damage. It affected the entire East Coast from Maine to Florida.

The "perfect storm" heavily damaged the Bush family home in Kennebunkport, Maine. Eyewitnesses said that waves as high as 30 feet smashed into the President's seafront property. The President had to cancel speaking engagements in order to go and inspect the damage done to his home.

The front page headlines of *USA Today* on November 1, had the stories of the Madrid conference and the "Perfect Storm" next to each other! One article was titled, "One-on-one peace talks next." The article touching it was titled, "East Coast Hit Hard By Rare Storm." The connection between dividing the land of Israel and judgment on the nation causing it was tied together on the front page of America's largest national newspaper.

Catastrophe #3
August 23-24, 1992: Hurricane Andrew - Estimated $27. 0 (35.6) billion damage/costs

On August 24, round six of the bilateral peace talks resumed in Washington D.C. until September 3. On August 24, Prime Minister Rabin canceled 11 deportation orders against PLO activists. Israel presented a detailed autonomy plan, defining the role of the Palestinian Administrative Council controlling civilian matters.

That same day, Hurricane Andrew -- a phenomenal category five storm with top winds recorded at 177 miles per hour -- smashed into southern Florida and became the worst natural disaster ever to hit America. It was described by the National Hurricane Center as a 25-to-30-mile-wide tornado, and it left 180,000 people in Florida homeless and another 25,000 in Louisiana. Damage was estimated as high as $30 billion.

On August 24, the front pages of both the *New York Times* and *USA Today* contained adjacent headlines about Hurricane Andrew and the reconvened Middle East peace talks which reportedly resumed "on a positive note." In addition, the newspapers that day also ran stories about President Bush's ratings collapsing in the polls, falling behind Bill Clinton by a substantial margin. Only a year before, President Bush, who initiated the Madrid Conference, had a tremendous approval rating as high as 92 percent.

Three major events converged on the same day. The Madrid Conference convened for the first time on American soil; Hurricane Andrew became the worst natural disaster in American history; and the popularity of the George H. W. Bush presidency was vanishing in the popularity polls. The timing was breathtaking.

Event #4

October 1 to November 3, 1992: Perot Candidacy Helps Cost Bush Reelection

H. Ross Perot's Dislikes George H.W. Bush

Reportedly, Perot came to loath George Bush because he believed Bush did not do enough to search for POWs in Vietnam. Perot's hatred for President Reagan's vice president grew during Bush's run for president in 1988. Perot, a native Texan, learned that Bush, the son of a senator from Connecticut, was a resident of Texas only because he rented a hotel suite in Houston.

Four years later, Bush's popularity was temporarily high after Desert Storm and a second Bush term seemed inevitable.

In early 1992, Bush faced a serious challenge from Pat Buchanan, who received 37 percent of the New Hampshire primary vote. Buchanan's prime time "cultural wars" speech at the Republican convention became a media scandal for Bush. His convention had been poorly run because he had insisted that his Secretary of State, Jim Baker, resign and run his campaign. Baker resented returning to politics and refused to manage the convention. Also, Bush had lost his brilliant and ruthless campaign manager -- Lee Atwater -- to a premature cancerous death, and was left without top-drawer campaign advice and operations.

In February 1992, Perot appeared on Larry King's CNN TV talk show and said he would consider running against Bush if volunteers could get his name on all fifty state ballots. Millions of U.S. citizens responded by signing petitions, which put Perot on the ballots of all 50 states by September 12.

On April 28, a Washington Post/ABC News poll finds Bush at 36%, Clinton at 31% and Perot 30%. The poll was deemed especially significant because it was the first one that puts Perot within striking distance of the major party candidates.

Perot began appearing on more talk shows and produced his own half-hour TV infomercials to explain his positions on national issues, particularly on deficit reduction.

By attacking Bush as an independent, he, in the words of Democratic political operative Paul Tully, "departisanized the critique of Bush," thus giving credibility to Clinton's campaign attacks.

On July 16, Perot quits the presidential race, saying he decided to withdraw because the Democratic Party has "revitalized" itself. (Perot's supporters continue their efforts to place his name on all state ballots.)

Ross Perot Reenters Presidential Race; Bush Loses Election Thirty-four Days Later

On October 1, Perot re-enters presidential race as an independent; makes the announcement at a Dallas press conference.

On October 11, he debates Clinton and Bush in St. Louis, the first of three nationally televised debates. Perot's opening line at the first presidential debate, "Well, they've got a point, I don't have any experience running up a $4 trillion dollar debt," reminded voters why they had initially supported his maverick candidacy. Prior to the debates, Perot earned only 5% of voter support in the polls. His performance at the three debates along with network broadcasts of his highly rated infomercials helped him win 19 percent of the popular vote on Election Day. It was the best showing of a third party candidate for president since Theodore Roosevelt's run in 1912 with the progressive Bull Moose Party.

Bill Clinton, with the help of H. Ross Perot, had defeated President George H.W. Bush. Republicans criticized Perot, believing that his conservative platform appealed to Republican and swing voters and effectively gave the election to Bill Clinton. Moreover, with the election loss, President Bush would no longer be actively involved in the Middle East peace process that he had initiated twelve months earlier in Madrid, Spain.

FEC documents state Perot spent $65.6 million of his personal fortune on the 1992 campaign.

Catastrophe # 5:
February 26, 1993: World Trade Center Bombing – Estimated Damage $750 million

In the first trip to Israel by a Clinton Administration official, U.S. Secretary of State Warren M. Christopher visited eight Middle East nations from February 18-25, 1993.

Upon his arrival in Israel, Secretary Christopher reconfirmed the special relationship, based on shared democratic values and common interests that exist between Israel and the United States. Citing President Clinton's determination to make the ties binding our two countries "even stronger and more resilient," the Secretary also reaffirmed the United States' unalterable commitment to Israel's security and its qualitative military edge, a commitment based on our recognition of Israel's continuing security challenges.

The Secretary observed that real security for Israel can

only be brought about by real peace - not just the absence of war but peace reflected in lasting treaties, normalized relations, and genuine reconciliation with her neighbors and with the Palestinians. To that end, and recognizing that obstacles still existed, he reiterated the US commitment to the role of full partner in a reinvigorated peace process.

World Trade Center Bombing

On February 26, 1993, a car bomb exploded underneath the World Trade Center in New York City. The immense blast happened at 12:18 PM local time in the Secret Service's section of the car park underneath and between what were New York's tallest buildings. It ripped through three floors of concrete, scattering ash and debris and set off a fire that sent choking smoke and flames up through one of the 110-story "Twin Towers." The resulting explosion killed six people and injured more than a thousand. More than 50,000 people were evacuated from the Trade Center complex during the hours immediately following the blast.

The bombing shocked America, which had seemed immune from acts of terrorism that have plagued other parts of the world.

An emotional Mario Cuomo, New York's state governor, told journalists: "We all have that feeling of being violated. No foreign people or force has ever done this to us. Until now we were invulnerable."

Catastrophe #6
March 12-15, 1993: Storm of the Century -
Estimated $3. 0–6.0 (3.8– 7.6) billion damage/costs

On March 10, 1993, at a news conference at Washington, D.C., the following is an excerpt of an opening statement of what was made by the United States

Secretary of State Mr. Warren Christopher:

President Clinton has asked me to make an announcement today on our efforts in the Middle East. Events in the Middle East have historically captured the attention of the world. Unfortunately, too often this has been because of war. This is a region that since 1948 had known five Arab-Israeli wars. And every time there has been a war, the world has held its breath because the risk of a super-Power confrontation was ever present.

I believe we now have an opportunity to promote peace that will serve the interests of Israel, the Arab States, the Palestinians, and the entire community. A passive American role is not enough. What is called for is an active, positive effort that will take advantage of what many believe to be a historic moment in that region.

We must now seize this opportunity to play the role of full partner, just as we did in the achievement of the Israeli-Egyptian peace 14 years ago. We have been repaid in full over the years by strong friendship and ties with both Israel and Egypt. The visits to Washington by [Israeli] Prime Minister Rabin this week and by [Egyptian] President Mubarak in April are testimony to the enduring nature of the relationships that were forged out of this negotiation.

It is time for the people in this region to set aside violence and work together for reconciliation and peace. The important steps taken at the Madrid conference have opened up a wide vista of possibilities. Over the years, Arabs and Israelis have sat together - that is, over the course of the last year they have sat together - in bilateral negotiations, seeking to achieve a comprehensive settlement based upon UN Security Council resolutions 242 and 338.

The resumption of bilateral and multilateral negotiations, which we are announcing today, is important but not an end in itself.

And so we must now all roll up our sleeves to make 1993 a year marked by real progress toward peace and reconciliation. The United States is prepared to do its part, and now the other parties must be prepared to do theirs.

Israeli Prime Minister Yitzak Rabin visited the United States from March 15-17, 1993. On May 15, President Bill Clinton and Prime Minister Rabin spoke on the unique bond between the U.S. and Israel in a news conference following their meeting in the White House. The two leaders discussed issues in U.S.-Israeli relations, including U.S. aid to Israel and peace negotiations in the Middle East. Prime Minister Rabin also visited Secretary of State Warren Christopher and Secretary of Defense Les Aspin, Congressional leaders, the media and Jewish leaders.

Storm of the Century

A storm that was called the "Storm of the Century" battered the eastern U.S. from March 12-15, 1993 with tornadoes, high winds, record low pressure and very heavy snows. On the Saffir-Simpson hurricane scale it would have been a category 3. The storm affected 26 states impacting the lives of nearly 100 million people, approximately half the nation's population. At one point, the storm covered 1/3 of the U.S. Damage was recorded from Texas, to Ohio Valley and Maine

There was $3-6 billion ($3.8 to $7.6 billion in 2003 dollars) in damages and 270 deaths attributed to the storm over land with 48 more missing at sea. Fifteen tornadoes in Florida killed 44 while 6 inches of snow fell on the Florida Panhandle. Hurricane force winds were reported from Louisiana all the way to Florida, and up the East Coast to New York and New England. The western coast of Florida received hurricane force winds up to 120 mph with ten-foot storm surges. Winds over 100 mph were reported on the Dry Tortugas (west of Key West, Florida) and Flattop Mountain in North Carolina, with peak wind speed of 99 mph recorded at a drilling station off the coast of Louisiana.

Mount LeConte in Tennessee received 56 inches of snow. Syracuse, New York received 43 inches, Albany, New York 20 inches, Chattanooga, Tennessee 20 inches, and Roanoke, Virginia 16 inches.

Every airport on the east coast was closed at one time or another for the first time ever, canceling 25% of the United States' flights for two days. Snow fell at 2-3 inches per hour. On the west coast of Florida, along the outer banks of North Carolina, and on Long Island homes fell into the sea or received wind or wave damage. Fallen tree limbs and power lines left 3 million people along the storm's path in the dark.

Catastrophe #7
May–September 1993: Midwest Flooding - Estimated $21. 0 (26.7) billion damage/costs

After intense "behind-the-scenes" contacts and negotiations from April 27 to September 13, 1993, between Israeli and Palestinian negotiators in Oslo, an agreement was achieved between Foreign Minister Shimon Peres and PLO Chairman Yasser Arafat. The Declaration of Principles on Interim Self-Government Arrangements was signed on the South Lawn of the White House on September 13, 1993. Here is the declaration:

> The aim of the Israeli-Palestinian negotiations within the current Middle East peace process is, among other things, to establish a Palestinian

Interim Self-Government Authority, the elected Council (the "Council"), for the Palestinian people in the West Bank and the Gaza Strip, for a transitional period not exceeding five years, leading to a permanent settlement based on Security Council Resolutions 242 and 338.

It is understood that the interim arrangements are an integral part of the whole peace process and that the negotiations on the permanent status will lead to the implementation of Security Council Resolutions 242 and 338.

September 13, 1993

A new page in the history of the Middle East was turned at the White House, as Israeli Prime Minister Yitzhak Rabin and PLO Chairman Yasser Arafat met and watched Israeli Foreign Minister Shimon Peres PLO Executive Council Member Abou Abbas sign the agreement. President Bill Clinton, former presidents George Bush and Jimmy Carter, and 3,000 dignitaries witnessed the signing – on the same desk used in the signing of the Camp David accords 15 years earlier.

The Great Midwest Flood of 1993

The Great Midwest Flood of 1993 was the "most devastating flood in modern United States history" with economic damages near $21 billion. More than 50,000 homes were damaged or destroyed. The area extent, intensity, and long duration of the flooding makes this event unique in the 20th century (National Oceanic and Atmospheric Administration, 1994). At least 38 people lost their lives as a result of this extreme flood (Interagency Floodplain Management Task Force, 1994).

From May through September of 1993, major and/or record flooding occurred across North Dakota, South

Dakota, Nebraska, Kansas, Minnesota, Iowa, Missouri, Wisconsin, and Illinois. Hundreds of levees failed along the Mississippi and Missouri Rivers.

The magnitude and severity of this flood event was simply over-whelming, and it ranks as one of the greatest natural disasters ever to hit the United States. Approximately 600 river forecast points in the Midwestern United States were above flood stage at the same time. Nearly 150 major rivers and tributaries were affected.

Putting this into perspective, the Middle East peace efforts intensified in the last days of April and early May and throughout the summer, with an eventual agreement signed at the White House on September 13. At the signing ceremony, President Clinton pledged continued direct engagement of the United States in the peace process. Moreover, the top news in the American newspapers throughout the summer had been the status of the Oslo Middle East peace talks and the history making Midwestern U.S. floods. As the heartland of Israel was being negotiated, the heartland of America was being devastated with record rains and floods costing $21 billion dollars.

Catastrophe #8
January 16, 1994: Northridge Earthquake - Estimated $15.3 (18.9) billion damage/costs

On January 16, 1994, at Geneva, President Hafez al-Assad of the Syrian Arab Republic and the United States President Bill Clinton made the following opening statements at their joint news conference:

President al-Assad

"Syria seeks a just and comprehensive peace with Israel as a strategic choice that secures Arab rights, ends the Israeli occupation and enables our peoples in the region to live in peace, security and dignity. In honor we fought, in honor we negotiate, and in honor we shall make peace. We want an honorable peace for our people and for the hundreds of thousands who paid their lives in defense of their countries and their rights.

"There is hardly a home in Syria in which there is no martyr who fell in defense of his country, nation and of Arab rights. For the sake of all those, for their sons, daughters and families, we want the peace of the brave - a genuine peace which can survive and last - a peace which secures the interests of each side and renders all their rights."

President Clinton

"During our meeting, I told President Assad that I was personally committed to the objective of a comprehensive and secure peace that would produce genuine reconciliation among the peoples of the Middle East. I told him of my view that the agreement between Israel and the PLO constituted an important first step by establishing an agreed basis for resolving the Palestinian problem. I also told him that I believe Syria is the key to the achievement of an enduring and comprehensive peace that finally will put an end to the conflict between Israel and her Arab neighbors.

"President Assad, as you have just heard, shares this objective - not just an end to war, but the establishment of real and comprehensive peace with Israel that will ensure normal, peaceful relations among good neighbors. Crucial decisions will have to be made by Syria and Israel if this common objective is to be achieved. That is why President Assad has called for a "peace of the brave.". And it is why I join him now in endorsing that appeal.

"Accordingly we pledge today to work together in order to bring the negotiations that started in Madrid over two years ago to a prompt and successful conclusion. Critical issues remain to be resolved, especially the questions relating to withdrawals, to peace and security - excuse me, the question of relating withdrawal to peace and security. But, as a result of our conversation today, I am confident that we laid the foundations for real progress in the negotiations between heads of delegations that will begin again next week in Washington.

"President Assad and I also discussed the state of relations between the United States and Syria and agreed on the desirability of improving them."

Northridge Earthquake

Less than 24 hours later, a powerful 6.9 earthquake rocked southern California. This 15 billion dollar earthquake was centered in Northridge, about 25 miles from Los Angeles. This quake was the second most destructive natural disaster ever to hit the United States, second only to Hurricane Andrew, and it also occurred at ground zero of the U.S. pornography industry.

Catastrophe #9
October 17-21, 1994: Texas Flooding - Estimated $1.0 (1.2) billion damage/costs

On October 17, 1994, Prime Minister Rabin and Prime Minister Majali initialed the text of a peace treaty. Jordan and Israel signed the full peace treaty in an October 26 ceremony in the Arava. President Clinton's participation in the signing ceremony underscored the U.S. commitment to the peace process. Israel and Jordan had continued their work to complete the various agreements called for in their peace treaty.

Southeast Texas Flooding

The worst flooding to impact southeast Texas on record. occurred. Lake Livingston recorded a record height on the 17th of October and a record flow of 110,000 cfs. Liberty recorded 30 inches of rainfall in less than 48 hours, and much of the city went underwater due to a failed levee system. Spring Creek and Lake Houston set new flood crest records. Several major highways into and out of Houston were flooded including I-45 north of Houston and US 59 northeast of Houston. Four fuel pipelines ruptured on the San Jacinto River, causing a massive fuel spill and widespread fires. An estimated 22,000 homes were flooded across southeast Texas during this event, with $900 million in damage reported. Seventeen fatalities resulted from the floods.

Catastrophe #10
September 27 – October 5, 1995: Hurricane Opal - Estimated $3. 0 (3.6) billion damage/costs

On September 28, 1995, the Israeli-Palestinian Interim Agreement on the West Bank and the Gaza Strip was signed in Washington, DC. The agreement contained 31 articles and seven annexes (redeployment and security, elections, civil affairs, legal matters, economic relations, cooperation programs, and prisoner release). Following the signing, President Clinton hosted a summit attended by King Hussein, President Mubarak, Prime Minister Rabin, and Chairman Arafat. The leaders reviewed progress toward a comprehensive peace and ways to reinforce and accelerate that progress.

On September 29, 1995, Secretary Christopher, Foreign Minister Peres, and Chairman Arafat convened the first meeting of the U.S.-Israel- Palestinian Trilateral Committee. The parties agreed: to promote cooperative efforts to foster economic development in the West Bank and Gaza; to explore the means to increase the availability and more efficient use of water resources; to consult on matters of mutual interest; and to promote cooperation on regional issues.

Under the U.S.-Jordan-Israel Trilateral Economic Committee, Israel and Jordan had completed the first phase of the Jordan Rift Valley (JRV) Joint Master Plan.

The second phase, an 18-month Integrated Development Study of the JRV, began in October 1995. The parties had outlined a number of projects dealing with the environment, water, energy, transportation, and tourism. They agreed to established a tourism development initiative around the Dead Sea and a Red Sea Marine Peace Park with assistance from the U.S. Government. They also agreed to explore the establishment of a free-trade zone in Aqaba-Eilat, with a view to making it an economic hub for the northern peninsula of the Red Sea. Israel and Jordan, together with the United States, are also agreed to conduct feasibility studies on expanding the Aqaba airport and developing telecommunications.

Hurricane Opal

After drifting over the Yucatan Peninsula and the southwestern Gulf of Mexico from September 27 to October 2, Hurricane Opal turned northeast toward the Florida peninsula. National Hurricane Center advisories and satellite imagery from the Louisiana State University Earth Scan Laboratory indicated that the system significantly intensified as it passed over the central Gulf, attaining category 4 status on the Saffir/Simpson scale by 6:00 a.m. Eastern Standard Time on October 4.

On October 4, 1995, over 1000 miles of coastline stretching from southwest Florida to Louisiana was struck by storm-generated waves as Hurricane Opal moved northward across the Gulf of Mexico toward landfall east of Pensacola Beach, Florida (Figure 1). Approximately 12 hours before landfall on October 4, Opal neared category 5 strength (measured on the Saffir/Simpson scale) with sustained wind speeds of over 65 meters per second. Storm surge levels of about 5 meters were estimated across the Northwest Florida shelf by the National Hurricane Center (NHC), resulting in the overwash of most of Santa Rosa Island, the most affected section of coast in the Gulf.

Opal ranked the strongest of the eighteen hurricanes that have struck the Pensacola area since 1900, and it was the most devastating. According to the NOAA Hurricane Opal produced $3 billion damage/costs and 27 deaths.

Catastrophe #11
March 1-2, 1997: Mississippi and Ohio Valley Flooding and Tornadoes – Estimated $1.0 (1.1) billion damage/costs

In early 1997, the Israeli government had begun to build 6,500 Jewish housing units in East Jerusalem, a section of the city that was claimed by the Palestinians. Yasser Arafat, Chairman of the Palestinian Liberation Organization, was upset, and he asked for a meeting with U.S. President Bill Clinton to discuss this issue.

PLO Chairman Yasser Arafat arrived in Washington D.C. Sunday, March 2, for meetings with President Clinton.

Clinton told reporters March 3, that he would have preferred if Israel had not decided to build the Har Homa housing project in East Jerusalem.

"The important thing," he said, is for Arabs and Israelis "to be building confidence and working together. And so I would have preferred the decision not have been made, because I don't think it builds confidence, I think it builds mistrust, and I wish that it had not been made."

Clinton made the remarks in response to reporters' questions as he began a meeting in the Oval Office with Palestinian leader Yasser Arafat.

The new settlements, Arafat said, are "to squeeze and to isolate Jerusalem."

Asked about U.S. views on Jerusalem, Clinton said "I do not believe, now that the parties have reached the agreement that they reached in 1993 and they have made this a final status issue, that the United States can serve any useful purpose by saying or especially by doing anything which seems to prejudge what should be a final status issue between the parties. I think that would be a big mistake."

As Arafat left the White House, the Palestinian leader told reporters that he and Clinton had "fruitful, positive, constructive talks.... We discussed everything in detail and the most important thing is the very good Palestinian-American relations, including the joint Palestinian-American committee," Arafat said.

Mississippi and Ohio Valley Flooding and Tornadoes

On March 1, 1997, a severe weather situation with tornadoes and very heavy rainfall erupted along a nearly stationary front from Texas to West Virginia. At mid-afternoon on Saturday, an outbreak of strong to violent tornadoes in Arkansas, northern Mississippi, and western Tennessee resulted in 29 deaths, including 26 in Arkansas. Several of the tornadoes have been estimated as F4 intensity, with winds in the 207-260 mph range. This was the deadliest U.S. outbreak since March 27, 1994, when 42 were killed in Alabama, Georgia, and South Carolina. Fortunately in this outbreak, the National Weather Service issued tornado warnings from 10 to 32 minutes before the tornadoes struck, using NEXRAD radar to provide much more lead time than previously possible. As of May 28th this year, 67 tornado-related deaths have been reported for 1997 vs. 24 for all of 1996.

This event also produced unusually heavy rainfall from northeast Arkansas through western Tennessee and southeast Missouri, and into much of Kentucky, southern

Indiana and Ohio, and West Virginia. In many areas, the rains fell on nearly saturated ground left by the snows and rainfall of the past few months. In parts of northern Kentucky, rainfall rates averaged at least one inch per hour for a 12-hour period on March 1.

A total of 67 deaths were attributed to this event, and damages were $1 billion overall. The last significant flooding along the Ohio River occurred in 1964, resulting in 11 deaths and about $50 million damage. Prior to 1964, the "great flood of 1937" was even more severe, with some towns erecting floodwalls shortly thereafter. These floodwalls (including one protecting Louisville) prevented the flooding from taking an even greater toll.

Chairman Arafat was using America as a platform to promote the dividing of Israel, and President Clinton warmly received him! The President's own home state was devastated by the tornadoes, and the nation was ravaged by storms and floods soon after!

The connection was again captured and documented by the New York Times on March 4, 1997. The front-page headlines reported, "In Storms Wake, Grief and Shock" adjacent to a photo of President Clinton with Arafat with the caption reading, "President Clinton Rebukes Israel." The New York Times linked the judgment so clearly!

Catastrophe #12
April 1- May 14, 1997: Northern Plains Flooding – Estimated $3.7 (4.1) billion damage/costs

Clinton Tries To Get Mideast Peace Process On Track

President Clinton said he and Israel's Prime Minister Benjamin Netanyahu had "a very specific, frank, candid and long talk" April 7 on the stalled peace process in the Middle East.

The two met for nearly two hours in the Oval Office,

the first 90 minutes with a small group of their foreign policy advisers present, followed by about twenty-five minutes of one-on-one conversations.

It's best not to say too much about what was said, Clinton said, and work very hard on moving the peace process forward, "and that's what I'm going to do, I'm going to do my best to get it back on track."

Later in the day, the White House announced that the president had invited Netanyahu back to the White House for coffee at 9:00 p.m. (Washington time).

White House Press Secretary Mike McCurry characterized the earlier meeting as "profoundly important" coming at "a very important juncture in the peace process itself."

He said Clinton presented the Prime Minister with "some serious things to think about" and Netanyahu had some ideas too.

Clinton noted that he had been "heavily involved" in the Middle East peace process from the day he became President and would continue to be heavily involved and wouldn't rule out any reasonable opportunity to make a positive contribution.

Flooding of the Red River Valley and Tributaries

Substantial flooding occurred in the Northern Plains of the United States and southern Manitoba, Canada during April - May 1997, with many rivers reaching record high levels during the month.

Residents of the upper Midwest were digging out Monday, April 7 from a spring blizzard that began as rain and changed to heavy snow over the weekend. The April 5, blizzard added much to the weather woes in the upper Midwest.

For parts of Minnesota, the spring snows brought a

double whammy to a region already battling floods caused by runoff from melting winter snow.

"We've been planning for the flood since January, so the planning has frankly paid off," said Minnesota Gov. Arne Carlson. "But the combination of snow and ice along with melting and rain has really hurt us. Many people say this is the worst they've ever seen."

The primary cause of this flooding was a highly abnormal thaw during March and April of substantial winter snow and river ice. Abnormal characteristics of the thaw included its timing, duration and a real extent, as well as the diurnal temperature changes during the periods of substantial snow and ice melt.

In the Red River Valley of eastern North Dakota and west-central Minnesota flooding persisted from early April through mid-May. At Fargo, North Dakota the Red River peaked at more than 6.6 m above flood stage during this period, a level reached only once previously in the past 100 years. Farther north, river levels at East Grand Forks also peaked at more than 6.6 m above flood stage, slightly exceeding the 500-yr statistical recurrence interval at that site. Record flooding also occurred in all major tributaries of the Red River during April, including the Wild Rice River and the Maple River (a record 1.8 m above flood stage), the Sheyenne River (a record 2.5 m above flood stage) and the Buffalo River (a record 1.1 m above flood stage).

The Red River crested at 39.5 feet, 22.5 feet above flood stage at Fargo, N.D. on Thursday, April 17, breaking a 100-year-old record. The crest then surged into Grand Forks, N.D., and East Grand Forks, Minn., pushing water levels to 54.2 feet April 21; flood stage is 28 feet. The Red River in Canada crested in Manitoba's Capitol city of 660,000 early May 4, causing the worst flooding the region has seen since 1852.

The Red River, which borders North Dakota and

Minnesota and flows north toward Lake Winnipeg in Manitoba, Canada, finally fell below flood levels in the USA in early June of 1997. The James River, which flows southward into the Mississippi River, also saw major flooding in 1997

1997 Red River Flooding At A Glance

- EVACUATIONS: Estimated 80,000 people in North Dakota, Minnesota and Manitoba, including 47,500 of the 50,000 residents of Grand Forks. Some people have been returning home for limited periods since Thursday in Grand Forks, and East Grand Forks, Minn., opened to some limited visits Sunday.
- SCHOOLS: Thousands of displaced children enrolling in schools elsewhere in North Dakota and Minnesota.
- DEATHS: Five flood-related deaths in the two states and Canada.
- CAUSE: Record winter snowfall, more than 100 inches in many areas, followed by a quick thaw and then an April 5 blizzard.
- LAND: Area is so flat that locals say any heavy precipitation is like pouring water on a tabletop. Water spreads out, creating a shallow lake up to 25 miles wide, and even wider where the flood joins existing pools of standing water.
- WATER: Despite the flatness of the land, water rushed by at 10 feet per second as it passed Grand Forks. River crested there at 54.2 feet late Monday, 26 feet above flood stage.

Event #13

July 1997–October 1998. Foreign Financial Contagion–Loss of hundreds of billions of dollars and other currencies worldwide

The UN General Assembly, meeting in an emergency

special session April 27, 1997, condemned Israel for the Har Homa building project and demanded an immediate halt to the construction of the "new settlement in Jebl Abu Ghneim."

Israel immediately attacked the resolution and the UN session that produced it.

"Israel categorically rejects the one-sided resolution adopted by this session, which stands in contradiction to the peace process and its principles," David Peleg, the Israeli charge d'affaires, said Friday.

Although the votes of the assembly are not binding, they indicate the depth of international anger and unease with the Har Homa housing project. The tally was 134-3, with 11 abstentions. The US and Micronesia joined Israel in opposing the resolution, which also called for the "cessation of all forms of assistance and support for illegal Israeli activities" in the "occupied Palestinian territory."

The April 27 vote, the second on Har Homa in the assembly since March 13, came from an emergency session that was requested by Qatar on March 31. It was the first such session since 1982 and only the 10th since the Korean War.

Peleg said it was unwarranted. "There was no procedural or substantive justification for the convening of the 'special emergency session' ...concerning the construction of a residential neighborhood in Jerusalem," he said.

The US does not support the Har Homa project, but had objected to the session on grounds that Israeli-Palestinian disputes should be resolved through direct negotiations. Further, said US Ambassador Bill Richardson, the debate "can only harden the positions of both sides and make their work even more difficult." Richardson said the resolution set "a dangerous precedent" by infringing on the council's authority.

The UN debates began over the building of 6,500

housing units. Once the debate opened, however, it was not confined to Har Homa.

The resolution recommended that the permanent-status talks on Jerusalem reach an agreement that includes "internationally guaranteed provisions to ensure the freedom of religion and of conscience of its inhabitants" as well as "permanent, free and unhindered access to the Holy Places by the faithful of all religions and nationalities."

Again, the UN General Assembly on July 15 condemned Israel's failure to comply with its demands that it immediately cease building a new settlement at Jebel Abu Ghneim in East Jerusalem and demanded that it immediately cease and reverse all illegal actions taken against Palestinian Jerusalemites.

By a vote of 131 in favor to 3 against (Israel, Federated States of Micronesia, United States), with 14 abstentions, the Assembly also demanded that Israel, the occupying Power, make available information about goods produced or manufactured in the settlements, including Jerusalem.

The UN also demanded that Israel reverse immediately all illegal actions against Palestinian Jerusalemites. The Assembly recommended that the High Contracting Parties to the Geneva Convention on the protection of civilians in time of war convene a conference on measures to enforce the Convention in the occupied territories, including Jerusalem, and to ensure respect for it.

The Assembly was meeting in a resumption of its tenth emergency special session on Israeli activities in East Jerusalem and the rest of the West Bank territory. In adopting the resolution, it also recommended that Member States actively discourage activities that directly contribute to the construction of or development of Israeli settlements in the occupied territories.

Speaking for the European Union and associated States, the representative of Luxembourg Mr Wolzfeld reiterated that settlements in the occupied territories contravened international law, constituted a major obstacle to peace and violated the Fourth Geneva Convention.

What is Financial Contagion?

It is the transmission of economic shocks from one country to others, through trade or other economic connections. Financial interdependence can transmit a crisis from one country to another, for example if countries borrow from the same creditors. Faced with a crisis in one country, banks and other lenders may lose their nerve and start recalling loans made to borrowers in the region, creating a credit

Foreign Financial Contagion

The Asian economic collapse of 1997 sent shivers through world markets throughout 1998, threatening even the vigorous U.S. economy, financial experts blamed corrupt governments, unregulated banking systems, fickle investors, and the International Monetary Fund. The turmoil also led the world's financial elite to debate the need for capital controls in an age when global capital flows evidently can wreak havoc on national economies.

The Asian financial crisis, which erupted in July 1997 in Thailand, awoke the world to "contagion," a new peril inherent to highly interconnected financial markets. Spreading quickly within and outside the region, the crisis brought the world's 11th largest economy, Korea, to the brink of bankruptcy and led to the defaults by Russia and Brazil.

This crash originally threw up the term contagion. Following years of stellar performances, Thailand, Malaysia, Indonesia, the Philippines, and South Korea experienced a plunge in the value of their currencies and a sudden reversal of private capital flows from June 1997.

Investors had poured massive amounts of funds into

Asian countries until the first half of 1997, and then drastically reversed course as hot money streamed out at a staggering pace. The ensuing $100 billion net capital flow delivered a huge shock to the region.

Russia's Crisis

Meantime, the contagion created by the Asian crisis of 1997 and 1998 made investors risk averse and made them reassess their investment in the rest of the emerging economies began to pressure Russian financial markets. As a result, international capital began to leave Russia and interest rates in all emerging economies raised. Russian asset market plummeted, and speculation on the ruble developed. In addition, Russia's problematic banking sector due to the falling asset prices triggered capital outflows from Russia. Russia found themselves unable to service the debt.

By July 1998, the Russian government was unable to rollover treasury bills maturing before the end of 1999. The IMF had approved a financial rescue package of $11 billion to support Russia. Yet, within a month, on August 17, 1998, Russia abandoned to defend the exchange rate peg and declared unilateral default on $40 billion in short-term domestic treasury debt, of which about one third was held by foreign investors. Moreover, Russia had defaulted on much of its Soviet-era foreign debt of $40 billion to the Paris Club of government creditors on April 29, 1996 and of $20 billion to the London Club of commercial creditors at the end of 1998.

Brazil's Crisis

Brazil's fiscal deficit had continued to be very large, thus the IMF Plan had to rely on tight monetary policy. The Asian crisis of mid 1997 and the Russian crisis of August 1998 caused investors to be highly risk averse in the emerging economies, which resulted in high interest rates in worldwide. Brazil increased the money market rate from 22% in October 1997 to 43% in November 1997 and 19% in August 1998 to 42% in October 1998. In addition, Brazil had spent about $35 billion dollars of the foreign reserves from April 1998 to October 1998 to defend the crawling peg.

After the failure of the rescue package to Russia, the IMF, on November 13, 1998, approved a three-year financial rescue package of $41.5 billion to Brazil, which was designed to stop global financial turmoil from spreading to Latin America. The package was anchored by the IMF with $18 billion, the Inter-American Development Bank with $4.5 billion, the World Bank with $4.5 billion, the US with $5 billion, and Japan, Germany, Britain, France, Spain, Italy, and the other wealthy nations with $9.5 billion. The IMF financial package added on to Brazil's existing debt, and the total external debt by the end of 1998 is estimated to be around $305 billion or about 35% of GDP.

As the nations of the world were calling on Israel to make painful concessions to a terrorist state and instructing them on how to conduct their internal business; shortly thereafter the nations began experiencing an enormous, worldwide financial crisis, which caused these countries to incur hundreds of billions of dollars in losses (and losses in their own currencies) in an unprecedented financial crisis.

Catastrophe #14
January 4-9, 1998: Northeast Ice Storm - Estimated $1.4 (1.5) billion damage/costs

Special Middle East Coordinator Dennis Ross told the press on January 7 in Jerusalem that he is in the region now to help "prepare the ground" for the upcoming meetings in Washington. Ross said he had good meetings with President Weizman ... "and we are going to keep working towards what is our objective of trying to find a way to put the process back on track."

Following is the transcript of Ross' remarks, provided by USIS Tel Aviv:

I just had a chance to speak with President Weizman, part of the effort that I am engaged in out here right now, as I help to prepare the ground for the upcoming meeting. We had a good discussion. I am going to have more discussions and we are going to keep working towards what is our objective of trying to find a way to put the process back on track.

President Weizman outlined his views and obviously would be part of our efforts to, as I said; prepare the ground, to see how best to move forward as we look to the meetings in Washington.

Northeast Ice Storm

One of the most long-lived and damaging ice storms to hit the Northeastern United States this century struck the week of Jan. 4-9, 1998. Weather conditions favored the formation of thick icing unusually far north, into the northern parts of New York and Vermont, across New Hampshire and in most of Maine. Much of southeastern Canada also was locked in the freezing rain's icy grip all week; about 4.5 million people lost power as the worst natural disaster in Canada's history unfolded.

Event #15

January 20-26, 1998: Lewinsky Scandal

On January 20, President Clinton and Israeli Prime Minister Benjamin Netanyahu met at the White House in yet another effort to break a one-year impasse in Mideast peace talks. Netanyahu was expected to propose a relatively modest Israeli pullback on the West Bank that would fall far short of Palestinian demands.

On January 21, several news organizations report the alleged sexual relationship between Lewinsky and Clinton. Clinton denies the allegations as the scandal erupts.

In his continuing effort to revive the stalled Middle East peace process, President Clinton met with Palestinian Authority Chairman Yasser Arafat in the Oval Office January 22, two days after his meetings at the White House with Israel's Prime Minister Benjamin Netanyahu.

"I am very pleased to welcome Chairman Arafat back to the United States as our partner in the peace process. As I did with Prime Minister Netanyahu, I want to emphasize what a critical time this is in the process and the importance of both parties meeting their obligations," Clinton said as the two leaders sat down to talk in the morning

"I'm going to give Chairman Arafat a little report on my meeting with Mr. Netanyahu, and then we're going to go to work," Clinton said.

Clinton outlined for reporters the principles of the peace process: "Mutual obligations and the concept of land-for-peace so that Israelis can live in security recognized by all their neighbors, and the Palestinians can realize their aspirations to live as a free people."

"If we can focus on these principles, I'm convinced we can make some progress," the President said.

"I hope that Mr. Netanyahu will understand that peace is not only a Palestinian need. It's an Israeli need, it's a Palestinian need, it's an Arab need, it's an international need," Arafat said. "And I hope that Mr. Netanyahu will turn his words to deeds and comply with the agreements."

Chronology from CNN:

January 22: Clinton reiterates his denial of the

relationship and says he never urged Lewinsky to lie. Starr issues subpoenas for a number of people, as well as for White House records. Starr also defends the expansion of his initial Whitewater investigation. Attorney Vernon Jordan holds a press conference to flatly deny he told Lewinsky to lie. Jordan also says that Lewinsky told him that she did not have a sexual relationship with the President.

January 23: Clinton assures his Cabinet of his innocence. Judge Susan Webber Wright puts off "indefinitely" a deposition Lewinsky was scheduled to give in the Paula Jones lawsuit. Clinton's personal secretary, Betty Currie, and other aides are subpoenaed to appear before a federal grand jury. Ginsburg says Lewinsky is being "squeezed" by Starr and is now a target of the Whitewater investigation.

January 24: Clinton asks former Deputy White House Chief of Staff Harold Ickes and former Commerce Secretary Mickey Kantor to return to the White House to help deal with the controversy. Talks continue between Starr and attorneys for Lewinsky over a possible immunity agreement.

January 25: Ginsburg says Lewinsky will "tell all" in exchange for immunity. Clinton political adviser James Carville says "a war" will be waged between Clinton supporters and Kenneth Starr over Starr's investigation tactics.

January 26: Clinton forcefully repeats his denial, saying, "I did not have sexual relations with that woman, Miss Lewinsky." Ginsburg offers Starr a summary of what Lewinsky is prepared to say to the grand jury in exchange for a grant of immunity from the prosecution.

Netanyahu came into the Clinton meeting with the possibility that his government might be toppled. How ironic that, literally, right after the meeting, it was President Clinton's own administration that was in trouble. The President was humiliated and faced legal action against him. Netanyahu returned to Israel as a "conquering hero" because he did not give away any land.

From this point on Bill Clinton was in a fight for political survival.

Catastrophe #16
January – February 1998: Southeast Severe Weather – Estimated $1.0 (1.1) billion damage/costs

President Clinton stated he believed Israel wanted peace and a resolution of the current Middle East crisis, and that "it's very much in the interests of the Palestinians and Mr. (Yasser) Arafat to seek to resolve it."

The President said he's found that "more often than not, you ultimately have success if you stay at something and keep working at it in good faith."

He gave this assessment during an Oval Office question and answer session with Israeli Prime Minister Benjamin Netanyahu just before their January 20 meeting on the status of the Israeli-Palestinian peace talks.

Clinton also reaffirmed "the strong support of the United States for Israel and the strong support of the United States for the security of Israel and a peace process that proceeds within that commitment."

Albright To Try Again To Jump-Start Mideast Peace

Secretary of State Albright planned to stop in Israel, the West Bank and Gaza in an effort to get the Middle East peace talks back on track.

During a press conference at the State Department January 28, Albright said that during these visits she would attempt to measure whether and how much each side has "absorbed" the ideas President Clinton presented to Israeli Prime Minister Benjamin Netanyahu and Palestinian Authority Chairman Yasser Arafat when they visited Washington the week of January 19.

"I will carry forward the ideas offered by the President and emphasize the urgent need for progress on the four-part agenda, which includes security, further redeployment, a time out on unhelpful unilateral steps, and launching permanent status negotiations," she said.

Albright acknowledged that at this point she was "neither optimistic nor pessimistic about the future of these negotiations.

"I cannot be optimistic," she explained, "because leaders in the region remain reluctant to make the hard decisions and to offer the flexibility required to reach an agreement.

"I cannot be pessimistic, because I'm convinced the majority of all faiths and communities in the region desire peace and that a basis exists for an Israeli-Palestinian agreement and, over time, a comprehensive Israeli-Arab settlement."

"The United States remains committed to seeking progress towards Middle East peace, but it's up to the Palestinians and Israelis to make the decisions that would put the process back on track," according to Secretary of State Madeleine Albright.

She told the Senate Foreign Relations Committee February 10 that the Clinton Administration has urged those involved "to rise above the zero-sum thinking of the past, and to embrace the reality that cooperation by all will yield for all a future of greater prosperity, dignity and peace. That is certainly our message in the Middle East, where we continue to seek progress towards a just, lasting and comprehensive settlement."

The Secretary acknowledged, "1997 was not a good year for the peace process." Mutual trust, respect, and recognition had been "rubbed away," and so "what we have been trying to do is to rebuild those bonds of confidence."

1998 off to a very warm, wet start in USA

The first two months of 1998 were the warmest and wettest in the 104-year record of temperatures and precipitation measurements for the contiguous 48 states, according to preliminary data compiled by the Commerce Department's National Oceanic and Atmospheric Administration.

"During the period January-February the national average temperature was 37.5 degrees Fahrenheit compared with a normal of 32.1. The previous record was 37.0 in 1990. For precipitation, 6.01 inches fell, compared with a normal of 4.05. The previous record was 5.7 inches in 1979," said William Brown of NOAA's National Climatic Data Center.

NOAA reports that California and North Dakota had their wettest February on record. Florida, Maryland, Nevada, Rhode Island and Virginia had their second wettest February since 1895. The warmest February on record took place in much of the upper Midwest and parts of the East, including Minnesota, Wisconsin, Illinois, Michigan, Ohio, Pennsylvania and Connecticut.

"These are the patterns one would typically expect during a strong El Niño event," said Ants Leetmaa, director of NOAA's Climate Prediction Center in Camp Springs, Maryland.

During the month of February 1998, California was struck by a series of storms due in part to the affects of El Niño. The current estimates indicate over $550 million in damages for the state, and17 storm-related deaths for the winter. 35 counties were declared federal disaster areas. Clear Lake in northern California reached its highest level since 1909, flooding portions of Lakeport, about 90 miles north of San Francisco.

During the late evening of February 22 and early morning of February 23, 1998, a series of tornadoes ripped across central Florida. At least one of the tornadoes reached an estimated F4 intensity. Forty-two fatalities occurred, over 800 residences were destroyed, another 700 were left uninhabitable, over 3500 were damaged to some extent, and 135,000 utility customers lost power at the height of the storms. Damages from the tornado outbreak exceeded $60 million, and Florida's overall storm damage total since last fall is approximately $500 million. Hardest hit locations in the tornado outbreak were Winter Garden, Altamonte Springs, Sanford, and Campbell. Overall, 54 of Florida's 67 counties were declared federal disaster areas due to storms over the past few months.

Some areas report at least 20 inches of rain. About 12 inches of rain fell overnight in Waller County, and nearly all roads in the county were flooded at some point.

Some communities reported receiving 20 inches of rain by Sunday morning, swelling creeks and rivers in the Texas Hill Country near Austin and southward to San Antonio.

Event # 17

May 1 - June 5, 1998: U.S. - China Technology Scandal

"I came here not only to celebrate Israel's achievements, but also to restate our iron-clad commitment to Israel's security and well-being in its next half-century and beyond," Vice President Al Gore said May 1 in Jerusalem.

"There is no distinction between our continued commitment to Israel's security and well-being on the one hand, and our commitment to helping Israel achieve a comprehensive, just, and lasting peace between Israelis and Arabs on the other," the Vice President said at a joint press conference with Israeli Prime Minister Benjamin Netanyahu.

"These two commitments are complementary, and the United States is intent on doing all that is within our power and imagination to help fulfill both."

Gore said "a moment exists for moving the process forward" and noted that the U.S. has done its best to facilitate progress in the negotiations among the parties themselves. He expressed "high hopes that the process will yield fruit: peace with security."

Asked if the London Round is "the end of the line," Gore responded that the May 4 meetings in London between Secretary of State Madeleine Albright and the Israeli and Palestinian leaders present an opportunity for potentially significant progress. "I don't wish to entertain any hypothetical based on the assumption that progress will not be made there. I am hopeful that progress will be made there. The efforts to secure peace with security are never ending and do not have an end," he stated.

In a joint statement following their meetings, the two leaders pledged to cooperate fully in the search for just and lasting peace in the Middle East based on Security Council Resolutions 242 and 338 and the concept of land for peace. Further, they agreed that the best way to achieve the peace so greatly desired is by full implementation of each side's obligations made at the Oslo and Washington accords.

Jerusalem

On the issue of a united Jerusalem, Gore repeated the U.S. position: "It has always been and is now in favor of a united Jerusalem. There are many questions that could be referred to the final status negotiations. The question of whether or not Jerusalem will be united is a settled question in our view."

Jeddah, Saudi Arabia

Vice President Al Gore and Saudi Arabia's Crown Prince Abdullah Bin Abdulaziz met May 1 and 2 to discuss topics of mutual interest and concern.

In a joint statement following their meetings, the two

leaders pledged to cooperate fully in the search for just and lasting peace in the Middle East based on Security Council Resolutions 242 and 338 and the concept of land for peace. Further, they agreed that the best way to achieve the peace so greatly desired is by full implementation of each side's obligations made at the Oslo and Washington accords.

Clinton Under Fire

As the Clinton Administration was increasing their pressure on Israeli Prime Minister Benjamin Netanyahu, Congressional Republicans stated on May 6 that they planned a series of hearings to investigate whether President Clinton's policy on the export of commercial satellites to China had allowed the Chinese to acquire technology to improve the accuracy of their nuclear missiles.

The hearings were to focus on Clinton's decisions to allow two U.S. aerospace companies, Loral Space and Communications Ltd. and Hughes Electronic Corp., to export satellites to be launched atop Chinese rockets. The Justice Department has been investigating a report that Loral improperly gave China advice to upgrade the guidance systems on its rockets after a failed launch in 1996 destroyed a Loral satellite.

Both House Speaker Newt Gingrich (R-Ga.) and Senate Majority Trent Lott (R-Miss.) took an active interest in the congressional probes, in part because the aerospace firms had been major contributors to the Democratic Party. Loral's chief executive officer, Bernard L. Schwartz, was the single largest donor to the Democratic Party in 1996.

Republican lawmakers were attempting to find a link between the financial contributions and a decision by Clinton in February 1998 that they say effectively undercut the criminal investigation of Loral. The decision allowed Loral to launch another satellite and to provide

China with the same type of information that was the subject of the Justice Department inquiry.

The Chronology of Clinton Administration's Pressure on Israel – May 1998

May 1, 1998: Vice President Al Gore, Netanyahu toasts at lunch in Jerusalem.

May 1-2, 1998: Vice President Al Gore and Saudi Arabia's Crown Prince Abdullah Bin Abdulaziz met to discuss topics of mutual interest and concern.

May 3, 1998: Vice President Gore holds talks with Netanyahu in London on the Middle East peace process. He also meets with President Mubarak.

May 4, 1998: Netanyahu and Arafat meet separately with Prime Minister Blair in London and then with Secretary Albright. Israel offers informally the idea of 3% Area C in addition to 10% FRD.

May 5, 1998: Netanyahu and Arafat continue their talks with Albright. She invites them to Washington on May 11 for talks on 13% FRD and to start final status talks. Arafat accepts the invitation. Netanyahu says he must consult his Cabinet.

May 6, 1998: Hillary Clinton states an eventual Palestinian state is important for Mideast Peace.

May 6, 1998: Netanyahu briefs his Inner Cabinet on the London talks. Israel asks for a visit by Special Envoy Dennis Ross. 21 Members of the U.S. House of Representatives call on Clinton not to pressure Israel on the FRD plan.

May 8, 1998: Netanyahu holds talks with Envoy Ross, and announces he cannot attend the Washington summit due to lack of time to prepare for the talks. The meeting in Washington is cancelled. Foreign ministers of the G-8 nations call on Israel to accept the U.S. 13% FRD plan.

May 10, 1998: Netanyahu proposes new ideas for the

FRD to Ross. The PA rejects the ideas.

May 12, 1998: Albright hopes permanent status talks still possible.

May 13, 1998: Prime Minister Netanyahu meets in Washington with Secretary Albright. He also meets congressional leaders, addresses the AIPAC convention and briefs the media. No visible progress is achieved.

May 14, 1998: Another Netanyahu - Albright meeting yields no progress.

May 15, 1998: In a meeting with Envoy Ross, Netanyahu proposes a two-stage 13% FRD.

May 18, 1998: Secretary Albright briefs Arafat on the latest Israeli ideas. He rejects them.

May 23, 1998: A U.S. congressional delegation in Israel to celebrate Israel's Jubilee and Jerusalem Day, headed by Speaker Gingrich, cancels plans to lay cornerstone for the proposed U.S. embassy building in Jerusalem.

May 25-29, 1998: Prime Minister Netanyahu visits China.

The Chronology of Clinton's Chinese Scandal in May 6 – June 5, 1998

May 6, 1998: Congressional Republicans plan a series of hearings to investigate whether President Clinton's policy on the export of commercial satellites to China has allowed the Chinese to acquire technology to improve the accuracy of their nuclear missiles – and whether that policy was influenced by campaign contributions.

May 12, 1998: Congress's two top Republicans are demanding that the White House provide documents on whether China's nuclear missile capability was aided by an administration policy on exporting commercial satellites.

May 16, 1998: Democratic fund-raiser Johnny Chung has told Justice Department investigators that a Chinese military officer who is an executive with a state-owned aerospace company gave him $300,000 to donate to the Democrats' 1996 campaign.

May 17, 1998: The Justice Department's campaign finance task force has begun to examine whether a Clinton administration decision to export commercial satellites to China was influenced by contributions to the Democratic Party during the 1996 campaign.

May 18, 1998: President Clinton said no foreign policy decisions by his administration affecting China were influenced by political contributions.

May 19, 1998: Loral Denies Benefits in Return for Donations: The major U.S. aerospace company denied that it requested or received "political favors or benefits of any kind" in exchange for campaign donations.

May 20, 1998: House Speaker Newt Gingrich announced that he would create a select committee to probe allegations that China illegally obtained missile technology from a U.S. company that received favorable treatment from the administration.

May 21, 1998: In a series of nearly unanimous votes, the House said President Clinton failed to act in "the national interest" earlier this year when he gave permission for a Chinese satellite launch to a U.S. aerospace firm with close Democratic ties, and moved to block him from approving similar exports.

May 22, 1998: The White House intends to send to the House documents that officials said will show there was nothing nefarious about a controversial Chinese satellite launch for a U.S. aerospace firm headed by a top Democratic donor.

May 23, 1998: President Clinton gave the go-ahead in February to a U.S. company's satellite launch in China despite staff concerns that granting such approval might be seen as letting the company "off the hook" in a Justice Department investigation of whether it previously provided unauthorized assistance to China's ballistic missile program.

May 23, 1998: Officials from a Chinese satellite launching company denied that they had received any sensitive technology with military applications from U.S. firms.

May 24, 1998: Liu Chaoying, the daughter of China's most powerful military official, brokered deals for missile components one day and Sonoma Valley Cabernet the next. Johnny Chung, a glad-handing entrepreneur who boasted of his White House access, became her California business partner in 1996.

May 25, 1998: Bernard Schwartz says the "confluence" of his own increased contributions and the Clinton administration's favorable treatment of his company was "just coincidence."

May 31, 1998: The evidence so far does not amount to a credible case that China's military rockets are better prepared to strike at American cities as a direct windfall from U.S. participation in its satellite launching business, according to many independent specialists on Chinese forces.

May 31, 1998: A reconstruction of the administration's handling of the waiver for a 1998 U.S. satellite launch in China reveals a complicated, and in many ways mundane, picture of a bureaucratic process propelled by a policy forged in the Reagan and Bush administrations.

June 3, 1998: Senate Majority Leader Trent Lott (R-Miss.) said Congress does not intend to use its China investigations as a political club against the Clinton administration.

June 5, 1998: CIA Director George J. Tenet refused to discuss with the Senate Intelligence Committee a secret report about an unauthorized U.S. transfer of information to Chinese missile officials, citing a last-minute request by Attorney General Janet Reno to reserve comment on the case.

Catastrophe #18
September 24-28, 1998: Hurricane Georges-Estimated $5.9 (6.5) billion damage/costs

On September 24, 1998, President Clinton announced he was going to meet with both Yasser Arafat and Benjamin Netanyahu, when they came to New York City to address the United Nations. The purpose of the meeting was to discuss the stalled peace plan in which Israel was to give away an additional 13 percent of its land. On the same day, the headlines of the national newspapers said that Hurricane Georges was gaining strength and heading toward the Gulf of Mexico. The headlines of *USA Today* stated, "Georges Gaining Strength, Killer Storm Zeros In On Key West."

On September 27, Secretary Albright met with Chairman Arafat and Prime Minister Netanyahu on the margins of the UN General Assembly in New York City in preparation for the meeting with President Clinton. The same day, Hurricane Georges slammed into the Gulf Coast with 110 mile-per-hour winds and gusts up to 175 miles per hour. The eye of the storm struck Mississippi and did extensive damage eastward into the Florida panhandle, before stalling and then moving very slowly inland, dumping huge amounts of rain and causing extensive flooding.

On September 28, Prime Minister Netanyahu and Chairman Arafat met at the White House with President Clinton, who announced that Secretary Albright would return to the region for a further push to get direct Israeli-Palestinian negotiations back on track. The three agreed to meet again on October 15 to formally announce the agreement of the land giveaway. That day, the headlines of *USA Today* stated, "Georges Lingers," and the article adjacent was titled, "Meeting Puts Mideast Talks Back In Motion." The *New York Times* also had the two stories together on the front page.

Hurricane George

Later that same day, Arafat addressed the United Nations and made a blatant bid for approval of an independent Palestinian state by May of 1999. He was given a rousing and sustained ovation as he addressed the General Assembly, but as he was speaking, Hurricane Georges was smashing the Gulf Coast causing $1 billion in damage! When Arafat finished his speech and left America, Hurricane Georges began to dissipate.

Event #19
October 17-22, 1998: Massive Floods and Tornadoes in Texas – Estimated $1. 0 (1.1) billion damage/costs

On October 15, 1998, Arafat and Netanyahu gathered at the Wye Plantation in Maryland to continue the talks held on September 28. These talks were scheduled to last five days and were centered on Israel giving away 13 percent of the West Bank land. Negotiations stalled, and President Clinton pressured them to continue until a settlement was reached. The time frame was extended and continued until October 22, when Israel agreed to give away the land for assurances of peace by Arafat.

Floods and Tornadoes

On October 17, awesome rains and tornadoes hit southern Texas. The San Antonio area was deluged by 20 inches of rain in one day, causing flash floods and destroying thousands of homes. Rivers swelled to incredible size. The Guadalupe River, normally 150 feet wide, ranged from three to five miles wide. The floods were so powerful that entire small towns were nearly swallowed. These rains and floods continued until October 22 (the end of the Middle East talks) and then subsided, after ravaging 25 percent of Texas and causing over $1 billion in damage. On October 21, President Clinton declared this section of Texas a major disaster area, and directed the Federal Emergency Management Agency (FEMA) to assist in the relief for the flood-ravaged families. This was a record flood that hit Texas.

For almost the entire time of the Middle East talks, these storms were smashing Texas. The national newspapers once again had the Middle East talks and the weather related disasters together on the front pages for all to see. President Clinton was forced to declare a section of America a disaster area; at the exact time he was orchestrating a Middle East "land-for-peace" agreement that would carve up God's covenant land in Israel!

Event #20

November 30, 1998: Mideast Donors Conference

On November 30, President Bill Clinton announced that he will be seeking an additional $400 million in U.S. aid to assist the Palestinian people.

The President made the announcement at the second Conference to Support Middle East Peace and Development held at the State Department. Representatives from some 50 countries and international organizations attended.

"I intend to work closely with our Congress on developing a package to provide an additional $400 million to assist the Palestinian people," Clinton said.

"This amount is in addition to the regular annual contribution provided by the United States, which will reach $100 million next year," he said.

State Department sources told USIA that the Administration intended to request from the U.S. Congress $100 million in aid for the Palestinians plus $400 million in a supplemental request for Fiscal Year 1999. The Administration intended to also request $100 million for each year for the remaining four years of the five-year "cycle" (1999 through 2003) covered by this donors conference.

Initial pledges at this donor's conference came to more than $3 billion, Secretary of State Madeleine Albright told the press at the conference's conclusion.

As President Clinton was meeting with Arafat that day, the stock market was tumbling, and the Dow Jones average fell 216 points. Media news reports on November 30 and December 1 had the Arafat declaration and the stock market selloff as the featured stories.

Arafat also announced that--in May of 1999--he was going to declare a Palestinian state with Jerusalem as the capital.

On December 1, the European stock markets experienced the third largest selloff in history. How ironic that, as the nations of the world met to promise $3 billion dollars in aid for a Palestinian state, their own financial markets lost hundreds of billions of dollars of market capitalization, literally to the day for the United States and on the very next day for Europe.

Event #21

December 11-19, 1998: Clinton Impeachment

On Saturday, December 11, the House Judiciary Committee approved impeachment articles I, II and III, which accused the President Clinton of perjury in the Paula Jones deposition, perjury in his grand jury testimony and obstruction of justice in the Jones case.

The President arrived in Israel the evening of December 12 on a mission to insure the Wye Agreement was implemented.

On Sunday, December 12, the headlines in major newspapers trumpeted both the impeachment process and Clinton's trip on their front pages, while radio and television news broadcast the stories back to back. The Associated Press reported that the President went to Israel "under an impeachment cloud." Ironically, the first President to be impeached in 130 years was in Israel pressuring the Jews to give away God's covenant land!

On December 13, Clinton and Netanyahu held bilateral meetings. Netanyahu was pressured to begin implementing the Wye River Accord signed in the U.S. in October.

On December 14, Clinton arrived at the Palestinians' newly opened international airport, and got the full red-carpet treatment. Arafat's Force 17 - a unit involved for decades in PLO terrorism -provided an honor guard, which played the "Star Spangled Banner" and a strongly nationalist Palestinian anthem, "Biladi," which means "My Homeland."

Everywhere, thousands of U.S. and Palestinian flags were flying and posters informing Clinton: "We have a dream - free Palestine."

The airport itself, which Clinton was asked to dedicate, is a symbol of the statehood Arafat has repeatedly asserted he will declare in May 99, unilaterally if necessary.

Later that day the Palestinian National Council reaffirmed the cancellation of articles in the Palestinian National Charter that refer to the destruction of Israel by a show of hands that took place in Gaza in the presence of Palestinian President Yasser Arafat and U.S. President Bill Clinton.

The issue of the Charter was one of the sticking points in the implementation of peace agreements, as earlier Palestinian statements had not satisfied Israel that the charter items in question had been made null and void in 1996.

Clinton said that the Palestinian decision today "issued a challenge" to the Israeli government to move ahead with the peace process. Netanyahu has maintained that the Palestinians have not done enough. Israeli Defense Minister Yitzhak Mordechai's media advisor said that Mordechai welcomed the vote, stating that it represented the implementation of a Palestinian responsibility within the Wye River accord. However, Mordechai called for further Palestinian compliance, especially in the area of security.

Clinton said on Tuesday, December 15, that the Mideast peace process is "back on track" after a meeting with Israeli Prime Minister Benjamin Netanyahu and Palestinian President Yasser Arafat at the Israel-Gaza border. However, the summit failed to win an Israeli commitment to withdraw on schedule from more West Bank land.

Prime Minister Benjamin Netanyahu told his Cabinet that Israel would not withdraw troops from the territory -- a move certain to further damage the peace process.

Israel's position frustrated President Bill Clinton and angered the Palestinians. But Netanyahu was under intense domestic political pressures and was struggling to save his government from collapse.

"The Prime Minister (said) that he cannot at this stage report to the government that the Palestinians have carried out their part and that we will be able to implement the withdrawal on the 18th of the December," a Cabinet statement said.

At the same time, both Clinton and Netanyahu faced critical challenges: Clinton faced possible impeachment and Netanyahu was trying to survive a right-wing no-confidence vote prompted by the Wye deal.

Following Tuesday's visits in the Mideast, Clinton returned to the United States, where he resumed his struggle against impeachment. He arrived in Washington D.C. on Wednesday.

On Thursday, December 17, the House delayed debate on articles of impeachment while the United States launches military strikes against Iraq.

President Clinton's National Security Advisor Samuel R. "Sandy" Berger said Saddam Hussein's claim of victory in the aftermath of the "Desert Fox" aerial offensive against him "was a bit of whistling past the graveyard."

The operation "clearly has been a blow," Berger said during a December 20 interview on CNN. He said the "substantial strike" involved more cruise missiles than in the Gulf war and more than 300 air sorties against over a hundred targets.

On December 19, the House on articles I and III, perjury and obstruction of justice, impeached Clinton.

On Monday, December 21, the Israeli Knesset voted to dissolve and hold early elections after Prime Minister Benjamin Netanyahu failed to win support for his peacemaking policy with the Palestinians.

Event #22
March 24- June 10, 1999. Kosovo War Begins – War cost estimated at $3 billion

On March 23, Yasser Arafat met with President Clinton again in Washington, D.C. to discuss carving up Israel to create a Palestinian state with Jerusalem as its capital. The same day, the stock market took its biggest tumble since the previous November 30, the last time that Clinton and Arafat met in Washington, falling 219 points. The next day, Arafat went to the United Nations to discuss Palestinian statehood, and Clinton authorized the attack on Serbia, resulting in hostile relations between America and both Russia and China.

The U.S. led NATO forces bombed the Chinese Embassy in Belgrade, Yugoslavia on May 7, 1999.The Clinton Administration blamed the event on outdated maps. China stated it was a deliberate provocation and refused to accept apologies. Ironically, they [China] used this to turn the intense focus off of them for alleged illegal technology transfers and back on to the U.S.

Catastrophe #23

May 3-4, 1999. Oklahoma – Kansas Tornadoes – Estimated $1.6. (1.7) billion damage/costs

May 3, 1999: Highest Wind Speed in U.S. History

On May 3, 1999, the most powerful tornado storms ever to hit the United States raged through Oklahoma and Kansas. The wind of one tornado was officially measured at 316 mph, making it the highest ever recorded. The storms included many F-4 and F-5 tornadoes. (F-5 tornadoes have winds over 260 miles per hour, which are extremely rare.)

The damage from these storms was incredible. In Oklahoma City alone, more than 2,000 homes were destroyed, and the town of Mulhall, Oklahoma, ceased to exist. Thousands of automobiles and vehicles were destroyed, and total damage was in the billions of dollars. The National Oceanic and Atmospheric Administration stated, "This is an outbreak of historic proportions, no doubt about it." Oklahoma governor Frank Keating said, "This is the most calamitous storm we've ever seen."

The storm warnings were sounded that day at 4:47 p.m. (CST). In Israel, this would have been about 1 a.m. on May 4, the date that Yasser Arafat had been scheduled to declare a Palestinian state with Jerusalem as its capital. This declaration was postponed until December 1999 at the request of President Clinton, who also stated that the Palestinians should have their own state, that Jerusalem was negotiable, and that he even refused to move the United States embassy to Jerusalem.

On May 4, President Clinton had to declare parts of Oklahoma and Kansas as federal disaster areas, before sending a letter to Yasser Arafat, in which he encouraged Arafat's aspirations for his "own land." Clinton stated that the Palestinians had a right to "determine their own future on their own land," and that the Palestinians deserved "to live free, today, tomorrow, and forever."

On May 6, 1999, going beyond U.S. policy, Hillary Rodham Clinton told a youth conference on Mideast peace that she supports the eventual creation of an independent Palestinian state. While the Clinton administration officially distanced itself from the first lady's remark, a top aide to Palestinian Authority President was pleased.

"I hope this becomes official policy," Ahmed Abdel Rahman said in Gaza on Thursday. "There can be no peace, stability or security in the Middle East without a Palestinian state."

"I think it will be in the long-term interests of the Middle East for Palestine to be a state," she said. The first lady said this would be "very important for the Palestinian people" and for the "broader goal of peace in the Middle East."

White House press secretary Mike McCurry reiterated that.

"She was not reflecting any administration policy," he said. "She was responding to some very heartfelt concerns raised by the young people who were on the program. She was reflecting a personal view."

The policy of her husband's administration is that the issue of a Palestinian state is a matter for Israelis and Palestinians to work out for themselves.

The U.S. consulate in Jerusalem, which acts as Washington's diplomatic channel to Yasser Arafat's government, distanced President Clinton's administration from the first lady's statement.

"These remarks are her own personal view. The administration's position on this matter has not changed," the consulate said.

Arafat originally planned to announce a Palestinian state on May 4, 1999. Bill Clinton told him not to, but encourage him with some very positive comments. Hillary stated she favored a Palestinian state on May 6, within 48 hours of May 4. Was this Bill and Hillary's way of appeasing Arafat while knowing a current declaration would be politically incorrect? The timing of Hillary's pro-Palestinian state statement certainly makes one believe that was the intent.

Catastrophe #24
August 24- September 7, 1999: Hurricane Dennis – Estimated $1. 0 (1.1) billion damage/costs

Secretary of State Albright traveled to Morocco, Egypt, Israel, the West Bank/Gaza, Damascus and Beirut to consult with regional leaders on developments in the peace process, and attended the signing of the Sharm El-Sheikh accord on September 4. The purpose of Albright's visit was to jump start the Wye Accord, reached in October of 1998, which had stalled. Albright, Arafat, and Barak agreed to resume the talks on September 13 and to conclude them within a year with a final agreement.

In late August, Hurricane Dennis began to affect the American east coast. This Category 2 hurricane contained copious rainfall as it moved very slowly up the seaboard, drenching the states of Florida, Georgia, South Carolina, and North Carolina. Dennis lingered off the coast of North Carolina nearly a week, traveling in a bizarre path. At one point it actually reversed itself, and at another time, it was heading away from the coast. This hurricane was literally doing circles in the Atlantic Ocean until the meeting in Israel.

At the time that Albright was meeting in Israel, Hurricane Dennis finally came ashore! This storm did not do tremendous damage, but it did drop enormous amounts of rain, a fact that would prove to be extremely significant less than two weeks later.

Catastrophe #25
September 7-17, 1999: Hurricane Floyd – Estimated $6. 0 (6.5) billion damage/costs

On September 13, the Israeli Foreign Minister and one of Arafat's deputies met to work out arrangements for what was called the "final status" of Israel's giving away land in exchange for peace. They agreed to present outlines for the borders of the new Palestinian state, plus the status of Jerusalem and Jewish settlements in the West Bank and Gaza Strip by February 15, 2000.

That same day, Hurricane Floyd strengthened into a very dangerous Category 5 storm with sustained winds of 155 miles per hour. Forecasters at the National Hurricane Center were astonished at how quickly Floyd grew in size and strength in one day. Their actual statement was, "Floyd grew unexpectedly into a monster of a storm on Sunday." On September 16, a huge Hurricane Floyd slammed into North Carolina, extending hurricane force winds 150 miles and causing the greatest evacuation in the history of the United States. However, the most destructive force of this storm came from rains of 20 inches or more over the entire eastern part of North Carolina, where the rivers were still swollen and the land was soaked from Hurricane Dennis less than two weeks before.

While Israeli officials were meeting with the Palestinians to make plans for giving away God's covenant land, a huge section of America's east coast was being ravaged by a monster hurricane, resulting in some of the greatest property devastation in the nation's history. The timing coincided exactly with the implementation of President Clinton's plan to have Israel give away her covenant land in exchange for peace.

Catastrophe and Events #26
October 14-15, 1999: Hurricane Irene, Hector Mine Earthquake, and a Major Stock market sell off costing hundreds of billions of dollars

During the week of October 11, Jewish settlers on 15 West Bank hilltops in Israel were being evicted as part of the ongoing "land-for-peace" process, actively being supported by President Clinton. The settlers resisted this eviction, and the confrontation was reported in the national media during the week.

While Israel was forcing the settlers off the covenant land, the stock market was melting down, with the Dow having its worst weekly drop since 1989. On October 15, the market lost 266 points! But also that same day, Hurricane Irene hit North Carolina, and the next morning, the powerful Hector Mine 7.1 earthquake rocked the Southwest, the fifth largest earthquake to hit America in the twentieth century. Neither the hurricane nor the earthquake caused major damage or casualties, but their stories, along with the stock market melt down, shared the nation's front pages with the reports of Jewish settlers being evicted from God's covenant land in Israel!

Catastrophes and Events #27
January 1- July 1, 2000: Trillion dollar NASDAQ loss, Record Fire Season and Major Drought

January 3-9, 2000: Israel and Syria hold negotiations in Shepherdstown, near Washington D.C., with President Bill Clinton's active participation

The latest round of Syrian-Israeli negotiations, conducted in Shepherdstown, West Virginia, from January 3-9, quickly became mired in procedural disputes. The Syrian delegation led by Foreign Minister Farouk al-Sharaa insisted that the question of borders be addressed first, while the Israeli delegation led by Prime Minister

Ehud Barak demanded that the initial negotiations consider security arrangements and the normalization of bilateral relations. The United States eventually finessed the issue by suggesting that informal talks on the border issue precede formal talks on security issues, after which both issues would be addressed simultaneously.

This procedural impasse, which almost derailed the talks on the second day, reflected a fundamental disagreement: Syria insists rigidly on the unconditional return of all of the Golan Heights, while Israel maintains that it cannot commit to a total withdrawal from the region until it ascertains what kind of security arrangements and peace would follow. With prompting from Washington, working groups were formed to address four sets of crucial issues: the delineation of the border, security arrangements, the normalization of bilateral relations, and water rights.

Clinton Pressures Israel While Nasdaq Collapses

It was all but a given that the Nasdaq was going to eventually collapse. But the fascinating coincidence was Nasdaq's three worst trading days and/or periods on record occurred at the very same time Bill Clinton and/or one of his top staff were in meetings on Israel's covenant land.

The first record-setting Nasdaq drop occurred on Monday, January 4, 2000, while Israeli Prime Minister Ehud Barak was at Shepherdstown, West Virginia meeting with Syrian Foreign Minister Farouk al-Sharaa over the Golan Heights. That same day the stock market plummeted with the Dow dropping 359 points for its fourth worst one-day decline, and the Nasdaq falling 229 points for its worst drop ever (at that point). The combined losses in money for one day amounted to $600 billion.

On March 26, Bill Clinton held a summit with Syrian President Haffez Assad in Geneva to discuss the stalled peace talks with Israel over the Golan Heights. In the second major correction from March 25 - April 1, 2000, the Nasdaq fell six of seven sessions and was off 17 percent from its record high of 5,048.62 set just three weeks earlier. In the last week of the first quarter 2000 the Nasdaq lost 8% of its value.

U.S. Defense Secretary Cohen held talks in Israel from April 3-4. On April 3, 2000 the Nasdaq suffered its largest point drop (349.15) in history and its fifth largest percentage (7.6%) drop.

The fourth major correction, which ended up being the worse one-week loss in the 29-year history of Nasdaq, occurred the week Clinton met with Barak at the White House. Clinton had summoned Barak for a lengthy April 11 meeting, at which time he told Barak that he was ready to make an even greater personal commitment to the peace process. The Nasdaq loss for the trading week of April 10-14 was a record-crushing $2.1 trillion dollars.

"Year of the Wildfires"

The unprecedented number of wild land acres that burned throughout large stretches of the West, the Southwest, and Florida caused the summer of 2000 to be remembered as the "Year of the Wildfires." Fire season started in January, two months earlier than usual. By March, over 40,000 acres had already burned. By September 10, 2000, there had been close to 93,000 fires this year, burning just less than 7 million acres. The 10-year averages for this same period was 63,600 fires burning 3 million acres. Two major factors combined to contribute to the severity of the situation: extreme drought conditions due to La Niña and decades of management policy of fire suppression.

"That's one of the hallmarks of the 2000 season, the geographical breadth of it," said Don Smurthwaite, a spokesman for the NIFC in Boise. "There were times when we had active fires burning from the crest of the Rocky Mountains to the Pacific coast and from our border with Canada to our border with Mexico.

"Another reason the 2000 season will be remembered was the duration of it," Smurthwaite added. "The first wildfire began burning on Jan. 1, 2000, and there were still fires burning into December. It was a long, long season."

The 2000 fire season was the most expensive fire year in history. The federal government spent a record $1.6 billion in 2000 fighting the worst wildfires the U.S. had seen in decades, according to a new report by Taxpayers for Common Sense (TCS), a national budget watchdog organization.

The $1.6 billion figure was nearly double the cost of severe fire years in the past. It was also significantly more than the $1 billion estimated in the fall of 2000 by the Forest Service.

Warmest January to May on Record

The spring season (March-May) of 2000 as well as the year-to-date (January-May) was the warmest on record for the United States, according to statistics calculated by NOAA scientists working from the world's largest statistical weather database. The electronic database at NOAA's National Climatic Center, in Asheville, N.C., goes back through 106 years of record keeping.

For the three-month period, over 64 percent of the country averaged much warmer than normal while less than one percent averaged much cooler than normal.

During this spring season, every state in the continental U.S. was warmer than its long-term average. It was the warmest spring on record for Texas, second warmest spring since 1895 for New Mexico, and the third warmest spring on record for Nevada. Twenty additional states ranked within the top ten warmest spring seasons on record.

The extremely warm temperatures contributed to

worsening drought conditions in many areas of the country. Parts of the Southeast, Midwest, and Southwest experienced severe to extreme drought, causing crop damage and creating the need for water rationing in many areas. Twelve states averaged drier than normal for the spring season. Florida reported its fourth driest spring on record while Missouri had its eighth driest spring since 1895.

The U.S. drought impacted 30 of 48 contiguous states registering from moderate to extreme drought.

Chronology of events January 3 - June 10, 2000

- January 3-9, 2000: Israel and Syria held negotiations in Shepherdstown, near Washington D.C., with President Bill Clinton's active participation
- January 4, 2000: Nasdaq plummeted 229 points and Dow was off 359 points
- January 10, 2000: The Israel-Syria talks ended after the US proposes a draft agreement
- January 17, 2000: The US announced freezing of the Israel-Syria talks due to fundamental differences
- January 19, 2000: Syria said it will not resume talks with Israel unless Israel pledges to withdraw to the June 5, 1967 lines.
- January 25, 2000: Israel canceled plans to send experts to Washington, D.C. to discuss a working paper on Syria.
- March 8, 2000: Barak and Arafat met with U.S. Special Envoy Ross in Ramallah.
- March 8, 2000: State Department Spokesman Jamie Rubin said U.S. Special Middle East Coordinator Dennis Ross reported to Secretary of State Madeleine Albright March 8 that the U.S. had agreed to host negotiations between the Israelis and Palestinians in Washington after the Eid al-Adha, which began March 16. Rubin called this "an important development and Secretary Albright welcomed this development because

it is an indication of a willingness to sit down together with us to try to move us closer to the kind of blueprint that a framework agreement would provide for the permanent peace." The Spokesman added, "We want to accelerate the process. This is a way to hopefully do that. At the same time we recognize that the issues are extraordinarily difficult."

- March 10, 2000: Nasdaq reached its all-time high of 5,048.62. Soon after that it began tumbling and eventually losing 3,500 points. Israel, as a nation, had the third most publicly traded companies on Nasdaq. The major drop cost Israel billions of dollars and has become their greatest economic setback in history.
- March 21-26, 2000: Palestinian-Israeli talks commenced at Bolling Air Force Base near Washington, DC and lasted one week. The U.S. facilitates discussion of permanent status issues in an effort to help the parties reach a comprehensive agreement by September 13, 2000.
- March 26, 2000: President Clinton met Syrian President Hafez Assad in Geneva, Switzerland
- March 25 - April 1, 2000: Nasdaq fell six of the last seven sessions and was off 17 percent from its record high of 5,048.62 set just three weeks earlier. The last week of the first quarter resulted in Nasdaq's losing 8% of its value.
- April 3, 2000: The Nasdaq suffered its largest point drop (349.15) ever and its fifth largest percentage (7.6%) drop.
- April 4, 2000: U.S. Defense Secretary Cohen held talks in Israel. U.S. demanded that Israel cancel the Phalcon deal with China.
- April 4, 2000: In a wild trading day, and Wall Street's busiest on record, the Nasdaq recovered nearly all of a 574-point, 13.5 percent tumble that would have been the index's biggest percentage drop in history - ahead

of the 11.3 percent plunge on Oct. 19, 1987 – Black Monday.

The Nasdaq ended down 74.79, or 1.8 percent, to 4,148.89. The Dow Jones industrial average nearly emerged from its own deep hole, a 504-point drop that almost matched the tumble of October 1987. The Dow fell 57.09, or 0.5 percent, to 11,164.84.

- April 11-12, 2000: President Bush summoned Israeli Prime Minister Barak to the White House for a four hour April 11 meeting. Barak met with other Clinton Administration officials on April 12.
- April 10-14, 2000: It was the worst one-week decline ever posted by a broad U.S. market index. It was worse than the legendary Black Friday week in 1929, worse than the week of the 1987 crash that sent the Dow industrials down 22.6 percent in a single day. The week ended with an especially tough note on Friday, with stocks losing an amazing $1 trillion of market value, which Wilshire Associates said was the biggest one-day market loss since money was invented. That raised the week's losses to a record $2.1 trillion. Nasdaq, for the week ending April 14, had fallen 25.3%.
- April 20, 2000: President Clinton stated: I am very, very glad to have Chairman Arafat back here at the White House, and I'm looking forward to our talks. We've reached a very serious time in the peace process. He and Prime Minister Barak have set for themselves an ambitious timetable to reach a framework agreement as soon as they can, and then a final agreement by the middle of September. So we're working hard on it and I think we'll get some things done today.
- May 7, 2000: Barak and Arafat met in Ramallah. Barak said that Israel will shortly cede three West Bank villages near Jerusalem to Palestinian control.
- May 15, 2000: The cabinet, and later the Knesset,

approved the transfer of Abu Dis, Izariyah and Sawarah al-Sharquiya to Area A
- June 1, 2000: President Clinton and Barak met in Lisbon, Portugal.
- June 5, 2000: Secretary Albright and Envoy Ross held talks in Israel and Gaza with Barak and Arafat to prepare for a Clinton-Barak-Arafat summit.
- June 6 – Secretary Albright announced an Arafat-Clinton meeting on 14 June. Israel-PA teams to resume talks in Washington, D.C. on 12 June to prepare for a summit at the end of June.
- June 7 - The Knesset adopted by 61-48, 11 absent, a preliminary motion to dissolve itself.
- June 10 - President Assad of Syria died; his son Bashar succeeds him

Event #28
July-August, 2000: Drought/Heat Wave - Estimated $4. 0 (4.2) billion damage/costs

At the urging of Israeli Prime Minister Barak, U.S. President Clinton announced on July 5, 2000, his invitation to Prime Minister Ehud Barak and Palestinian Authority Chairman Yasser Arafat to come to Camp David to continue their negotiations on the Middle East peace process.

On July 11, the Camp David 2000 Summit convened.

Between July 11 and 24, President Clinton, Prime Minister Barak and Chairman Arafat met at Camp David in an effort to reach an agreement on permanent status. While they were not able to bridge the gaps and reach an agreement, their negotiations were unprecedented in both scope and detail. Building on the progress achieved at Camp David, the two leaders agreed on the following principles to guide their negotiations:

1) The two sides agreed that the aim of their negotiations is to put an end to decades of conflict and

achieve a just and lasting peace.

2) The two sides commited themselves to continue their efforts to conclude an agreement on all permanent status issues as soon as possible.
3) Both sides agreed that negotiations based on UN Security Council Resolutions 242 and 338 were the only way to achieve such an agreement and they undertook to create an environment for negotiations free from pressure, intimidation and threats of violence.
4) The two sides understood the importance of avoiding unilateral actions that prejudge the outcome of negotiations and that their differences would be resolved only by good faith negotiations.
5) Both sides agreed that the United States remains a vital partner in the search for peace and would continue to consult closely with President Clinton and Secretary Albright in the period ahead.

The Year of the Drought and Wildfires
Weather Log - July 11-20th, 2000 (NOAA)

It was very hot in parts of south central U.S. and into the western states. Media sources report that the heat wave blanketing the southern United States was responsible for at least 12 deaths in Texas, 10 in Alabama, and an additional 7 are being investigated as heat-related in Louisiana. Arizona, New Mexico, Oklahoma, Arkansas, Mississippi and Kansas are also suffering from the 100+ temperatures that had lasted for more than a week. An emergency health alert was announced for the Dallas-Fort Worth region, and water restrictions were implemented in 120 cities and towns throughout Texas due to drought conditions.

Weather Log - July 21-31st 2000

Fires Raging in Western U.S.: The worst fire season in years continued to worsen as 50 active fires in the western U.S. had consumed over 500,000 acres as of July 31, 2000. Two of the fires had burned over 60,000 acres each--one in the Sierra Nevada/ Sequoia National Forest area of California, and another in Nevada about 60 miles north-east of Elko. An estimated 3 million + acres have burned in fires in the U.S. thus far this year, with overall damage/cost estimates not yet available.

A story that dominated the headlines throughout the summer was wild land fires, burning out of control throughout the southeastern, southwestern, and western United States.

In the meteorological record books, summer 2000 will be remembered for the devastating wildfires that scorched more than 6.8 million acres across the nation, the searing temperatures and drought that plagued parts of the West and South, the historic string of rain-free days in Texas, which rivaled the Dust Bowl of the 1930s, and the cooler-than-usual temperatures in the East. For example, the Washington, D.C. area had its coolest summer since 1972, and the San Francisco Bay Area, by contrast, had hotter-than-usual temperatures, including a heat wave with record temperatures of up to 110 degrees.

States in the inter-mountain West were especially hard hit, with hot and persistently dry conditions giving rise to the worst wildfire season in the past 50 years.

On a national scale, by the end of August over a third (35%) of the contiguous U.S. was experiencing severe to extreme drought as measured by the Palmer Drought Index. This was a rapid increase over the last three months, nearly doubling from about 20% at the end of June (see graphic below left). Based on a real extent, the summer 2000 drought is as widespread as the 1988 drought but ranks behind the more extensive droughts of the 1950's and 1930's.

As Bill Clinton was applying enormous pressure on dividing God's covenant land, the land of the United States was experiencing one of the worst droughts and wildfire season in history. As Clinton, Barak and Arafat were meeting at Camp David much of the Western United States was on fire. As the land of Israel was placed at risk so was the land of the nation who was attempting to divide Israel's land.

Event #29

October 30 – December 13, 2000: U.S. and Israel Political Crisis; Mitchell Committee Appointed; Clinton Trying to Rush Through Last-Minute Middle East Deal; Political Chaos in Israel and the U.S.

Former U.S. Senator George Mitchell, who brokered a peace agreement for troubled Northern Ireland in 1998, was selected to head an international commission investigating six weeks of intense violence between Palestinians and Israeli security forces.

The White House announced Mitchell's appointment -- along with that of fellow commission members U.S. Senator Warren Rudman, former Turkish President Suleyman Demirel, European Union foreign and security affairs chief Javier Solana and Norwegian Foreign Minister Thorbjoern Jagland -- on Tuesday.

The announcement was made on the same day Americans went to the polls to select the man who was to follow President Bill Clinton in office, and two days ahead of planned meetings between the Clinton and PLO Chairman Yasser Arafat.

Yasser Arafat met with Clinton on November 9. Israeli Prime Minister Ehud Barak's scheduled meeting for November 13 was canceled due to terror events in Israel.

After Palestinian Authority President Yasser Arafat's meeting with President Clinton, he headed to the United Nations to seek support for a proposed UN protection force in Gaza and the West Bank.

Speaking Thursday night November 9, to the Council on Foreign Relations in Washington, Arafat said the force proposal "was one of the major points I presented to, and requested from, President (Bill) Clinton" when the two met Thursday at the White House.

Seeking to counter Israel's refusal to consider such a buffer force, Arafat said: "Between Israel and Egypt there is an international force. Between Lebanon and Israel there is an international force. Between Israel and Syria there is an international force."

Israel is opposed to the idea because such a force would "reward" Palestinian violence, Israeli Prime Minister Ehud Barak said.

The White House said that as long as Israel is opposed to such a force, the two sides should focus on where they agree.

The Bush – Gore 2000 Election Crisis

It was the concession speech that never came.

Campaign officials for Vice President Al Gore released an official blow-by-blow account on Wednesday, November 8, 2000, of the Democratic presidential candidate's contacts with his Republican rival, Texas Gov. George W. Bush, and his plans to concede following network news projections of a Bush victory in Florida and nationwide.

Here's the Gore camp's account of what happened, and when:

- Between 1:30 a.m. and 1:45 a.m. CST, Gore calls Bush to concede the election. Gore's call comes after the media report that Gore is losing Florida by 50,000 votes and after TV networks call the state -- and the election for Bush.
- Gore leaves his hotel in Nashville, Tennessee, and begins the short motorcade drive to War Memorial Plaza, where he will address supporters gathered there.
- When the motorcade is about two blocks from War

Memorial Plaza, traveling chief of staff Michael Feldman is paged by field director Michael Whouley. Whouley tells Feldman that only 6,000 votes in Florida separate Gore from Bush at that time, according to the Florida secretary of state, with a significant number of votes outstanding.

- Feldman calls Gore campaign chairman William Daley and gives him the latest numbers from Florida. Daley informs Gore.
- By the time Gore's motorcade reaches War Memorial Plaza, the difference in Florida is fewer than 1,000 votes.
- Gore, Daley and other campaign advisers meet in the vice president's holding room at the plaza to discuss the situation.
- About 2:15 a.m. CST: Daley calls Bush campaign chairman Don Evans.
- Between 2:30 a.m. and 2:45 a.m. CST, Gore calls Bush again, and the two candidates speak for a few minutes. The conversation's "contents are private," the Gore camp says, but officials tell CNN that Gore retracted his earlier concession.
- Gore leaves War Memorial Plaza to return to his hotel. He does not speak to the crowd.
- Daley addresses the plaza crowd. "Our campaign continues," he says, until a winner is officially declared in Florida. The few hundred people remaining in the plaza cheer: "Stay and fight!" and "Don't give up!"
- Gore meets with staff until 3:45 a.m. CST and then goes to bed.
- Bush and President Clinton scrap planned public statements for now.

With Florida's election returns in enough of a state of flux to send both major party presidential campaigns into a frenzy early the next morning, Republicans took some measure of comfort in their ability to retain control of both houses of Congress in this general election year.

Texas Gov. George W. Bush, estimated early Wednesday by CNN and other major news organizations to have secured his new home at 1600 Pennsylvania Avenue in Washington, saw his award stripped away -- at least temporarily -- later, when discrepancies in the Sunshine State's return numbers were brought to the fore.

CNN retracted its estimate of a Bush win when Florida state officials announced a statewide vote recount. With more than 5 million votes counted in the state, Gore and Bush would appear to be separated by approximately 220 votes.

Florida holds 25 electoral votes -- enough to boost either of the two over the required 270-vote total needed for an unquestionable win in the Electoral College.

Florida held the future of the presidency in the balance.

The campaign of Texas Gov. George W. Bush has, as promised, opened a variety of legal offensives in a fevered move to counter the effects of the ruling by the Florida Supreme Court -- with an appeal placed on file with a federal appeals court in Atlanta, and one under preparation for the U.S. Supreme Court.

To the chagrin of the Bush campaign, Vice President Al Gore lived to fight his White House battle for at least another day, and probably several more, with the state high court's ruling that manual recounts of thousands of disputed ballots must begin immediately.

Supreme Court's Decision

On December 9, the U.S. Supreme Court, in a 5-4 ruling, halted the manual recounts in Florida and set a hearing on the matter two days later.

On December 11, Bush's lawyers argued before the U.S. Supreme Court in that the Florida high court again overstepped its bounds by ordering a manual recount of undervotes in Gore's election contest. Gore's lawyers argued that the U.S. Supreme Court has no reason to intervene in the state court contest.

After stopping the Florida recount two days earlier, the U.S. Supreme Court convened to hear oral arguments on whether the Florida Supreme Court overstepped its bounds in ordering a statewide recount of undervotes.

Audiotapes of the historic Supreme Court argument aired nationally. The long wait for the decisive decision began.

A committee of the Florida House voted 5 to 2 to approve a resolution to name presidential electors for George W. Bush. A half-hour later, a Florida Senate committee approved a similar resolution by a 4-to-3 vote.

On Tuesday, December 12, the Associated Press reported that the Florida House had voted to approve 25 electors for George Bush. Just two Democrats joined the 79-to-41 vote.

The U.S. Supreme Court, in a 5-to-4 ruling split along ideological lines, stepped in to end the election and Al Gore's quest for a final recount. It reversed the Florida Supreme Court decision ordering a statewide recount of undervotes, stating, in the per curium section of its opinion, that differing vote-counting standards from county to county and the lack of a single judicial officer to oversee the recount violated the equal-protection clause of the Constitution.

Al Gore Calls Bush To Concede The Presidential Race

Vice President Al Gore conceded the 2000 presidential election Wednesday night December 13, 2000, effectively concluding an election that was supposed to have ended five weeks earlier.

"Tonight, for the sake of our unity of the people and the strength of our democracy, I offer my concession," Gore said in televised address from Washington's Old

Executive Building, adjacent to the White House.

Barak Resigns and then Is Defeated

A two-hour meeting Sunday, October 29, 2000, between Israeli Prime Minister Ehud Barak and Ariel Sharon, the right-wing leader of the opposition Likud party, failed to produce an emergency government designed to strengthen Barak's shaky hold on power.

An alliance between Barak and Sharon was bitterly opposed by Palestinians because of Sharon's hard-line stance on the peace process. Including Sharon in the government could avert a call from Barak's political opponents to dissolve parliament and call for new elections for prime minister.

Barak held only 30 seats in the 120-member Knesset and an alliance with Sharon's party would have given him enough added support to maintain power. Barak worked to bring the hawkish opposition Likud party into his coalition, but they refused to give Likud leader Ariel Sharon the control he wants over peace talks with the Palestinians.

Barak told the legislators on November 28, just before they voted overwhelmingly to dissolve parliament and hold elections two years ahead of schedule that he was prepared for such an event.

Barak's announcement came just before an overwhelming majority of MKs were poised to vote for the first reading of opposition legislation calling for dissolving the 15th Knesset and holding early elections. The first of the five bills passed by 75-1 with 29 abstentions from One Israel and Meretz MKs. The third passed by 79-1.

"I see that the Knesset wants elections, and I am willing for general elections for the prime minister and Knesset to be held," Barak said.

Coalition and opposition leaders began talking about setting an election date.

The dissolution bill headed to the Knesset Law Committee, set the exact date for the elections and sent the final draft back to the plenum for its second and third readings.

Sharon slammed Barak for blaming the Knesset for bringing about early elections. "The person who is responsible for the situation that has been created is you, you, you," Sharon said.

Shinui leader Yosef Lapid made a last-ditch effort to bring Barak and Sharon together through a document of joint principles, but primarily Barak rejected his overtures, since the plan would have given Sharon a veto on security and other matters.

After holding hours of consultations, Barak reached the conclusion that he did not have the option of postponing the vote through a no-confidence motion or calling an immediate confidence vote, since he was very likely to lose in both scenarios.

In a stunning surprise move, Israeli Prime Minister Ehud Barak announced his resignation on Saturday, December 9, apparently pre-empting the Knesset's push for an early general election and opening the door to a vote only for the premiership.

Barak said he would stand for re-election, effectively asking for a vote of confidence from the Israeli people.

"Due to the emergency situation the country is in ... and the need to continue reducing the violence and moving forward the chances of peace negotiations, I have decided to ask again for the trust of the people of Israel," said Barak at a hastily convened news conference on Saturday evening at his Jerusalem office.

"Tomorrow morning I'll tell the president of my official decision to resign and lead the Labor Party to special elections for Israeli prime minister," Barak said in a televised address. "Afterwards I'll submit my letter of resignation to the government, as required by law."

His government had rejected another Israeli Prime Minister, who had been very active in the Middle East peace talks.

In one of the more remarkable comebacks in Israeli political history, former Gen. Ariel Sharon completed the long road back when the voters overwhelmingly chose him as prime minister of Israel on February 6, 2001.

Sharon's landslide victory was as much a product of disillusionment-with the peace process, with the ongoing Palestinian violence and with the personality of incumbent Prime Minister Ehud Barak-as it was an endorsement of Sharon himself.

The public's judgment was resounding, with 59.5 percent of the vote going to Likud leader Sharon and 40.5 percent to Barak, according to exit polls conducted by Israel Television.

By Israeli standards, it was a margin of historic proportions, and it came just 21 months after Barak swept into office with what seemed like a broad mandate.

Yet many Israelis, it appears, were disillusioned with both candidates.

Voter turnout was just 62 percent, the lowest in the nation's history. Israeli turnout generally is about 80 percent, among the highest rates in the democratic world.

Middle East Peace Efforts and a Month of Political Chaos

On November 7, 2000, President Bill Clinton appointed the Mitchell Committee to come up with a Middle East plan to help deal with the major violence in Israel and bring peace to the Middle East. On November 7, the Bush - Gore 2000 election turned into a five week political crisis. During the same period the Barak government in Israel was also in a political crisis and on the verge of collapse. Clinton met with PLO Chairman Yasser Arafat at the White House on November 9 to give his peace efforts one more try. Barak resigned as Israel's Prime Minister on December 9 and on December 13, the U.S. Presidential crisis was over with the acceptance speech of the new President, George W. Bush.

CHAPTER 2

Larry Downing - Reuters

U.S. CATASTROPHES AND EVENTS CONTINUED

The Major "Land for Peace" Efforts and the Corresponding Catastrophes or Events from March 31, 2001 to November 4, 2003

President Bush's Original Plan

President Bush originally wanted to be a facilitator and not an active participant in the ongoing Middle East talks. After violence worsened in Israel in early 2001 and at the urging of Egyptian President Hosni Mubarek, Jordan's King Abdullah II, President Bush agreed to become more involved.

Due to the stained relationship between Crown Prince Abdullah of Saudi Arabia; Secretary of State, Colin Powell, along with the U.S. Ambassador to Israel, Daniel Kurtzer, convinced President Bush to develop a comprehensive Middle East plan. The plan was to be given by Colin Powell to the UN General Assembly on September 24, 2001. However, the 9-11 terror events postponed the delivery of the speech. Powell eventually gave the message in November 2001, which was followed by months of horrific violence in Israel and failed peace efforts by retired Marine General Anthony Zinni.

President Bush, again frustrated with the terror and violence in Israel, brought Zinni home in late March and stopped actively working on the peace process. On April 3, 2002, the EU called on the United States to step down and let them take over the Middle East peace talks. President Bush hastily called a Rose Garden press conference the next day, April 4. He called on the Israelis and the Palestinians to get back to the peace table and said he was sending Colin Powell to the region the following week to discuss ways to jump-start the peace process again.

The violence continued and President Bush finally gave his long-awaited Middle East plan on June 24. The June 18 and 19 addresses were postponed due to two major suicide bombings in Jerusalem.

The Quartet (EU, UN, Russia and the U.S.) began to prepare their plan in late September, 2002, and after three months of work, the great world powers came together in agreement at the Oval Office on December 20 to formally affirm their plan on how to divide Israel's covenant land. However, there were still differences between the Quartet Plan and the Bush plan. Primarily, the Bush plan required the Palestinians to stop terror first and then the talks would continue. The World community wanted Israel to stop the settlement construction in conjunction with the cessation of terror. (*More on this later in the book.*)

Finally, a meeting was held in Jordan on June 3, 2003, between President Bush, Israeli Prime Minister Ariel Sharon and Palestinian Prime Minister Mahmoud Abbas.

Event #1
March 31- April 11, 2001: Bush's First International Crisis

On the day that Egyptian President Hosni Mubarek arrived in Washington to persuade President Bush to become more involved in the Middle East talks, a Chinese fighter jet "bumps" into an American EP-3 reconnaissance plane, forcing it, along with the 24-person crew, to make an emergency landing in China. The resulting crisis completely overshadowed the visits of both Mubarek and Jordan's King Abdullah II. After King Abdullah II spoke with Christian leaders, members of Congress and others to solicit support for the "land for peace" initiative, he visited the White House on April 10, and then returned home to Jordan. On the very next day China agreed to release the "detained" airmen from the downed plane.

Event #2
May 21-May 24, 2001: President George W. Bush and Secretary of State Colin Powell Endorse the Mitchell Plan; Republican's Lose Majority in the U.S. Senate

The Mitchell report was publicly released May 21. An international fact-finding committee, headed by former U.S. Senate Majority Leader George Mitchell, produced the plan over the previous six months. It recommended an immediate ceasefire, a halt to further settlement activity by the Israelis, and more effort by Palestinian leaders to suppress and denounce terrorism.

"The United States believes the [Mitchell] committee

has provided the parties with ideas that can help to find a solution to the terrible tragedy that has trapped the Israeli and Palestinian peoples in a continuing downward spiral of violence for the past eight months, a spiral that has gotten worse in the last few days," Powell said in Washington, May 21.

Powell called on Israelis and Palestinians to address the committee's primary recommendations by reaffirming their commitment to existing agreements and undertakings, immediately and unconditionally ceasing violence and resuming security cooperation. He also said that both sides "must avoid unilateral acts that prejudice the outcome of permanent status negotiations and that could be perceived by the other side as provocative during this very delicate time."

President Bush placed phone calls early May 22 to Egypt's President Hosni Mubarak and Jordan's King Abdullah II to discuss the escalating violence in the Middle East and the recommendations in the Mitchell committee report on ways to halt it and help return the Israelis and the Palestinians to the peace process, White House Press Secretary Ari Fleischer told reporters at the afternoon briefing.

"President Bush is committed to trying to facilitate peace in the region," Fleischer said. The President "is very concerned about the level of violence" and believes that "the best way to seize this moment, now that the Mitchell report is out, is for the parties involved to end the violence, so that the cycle of violence can be broken, and that the parties can indeed begin talking, with the United States playing a facilitative role."

Both Mubarak and King Abdullah "welcome the United States' endorsement of the Mitchell report, and they both told the President they are ready to work with the United States to encourage the parties to implement the report's recommendations," Fleischer said.

President Bush called Israeli Prime Minister Ariel Sharon and Palestinian leader Yasser Arafat May 23 and urged them to accept the Mitchell report as a framework to ending violence and resuming peace efforts, the White House and State Department said in Washington, May 23.

"The president urged both leaders to seize the opportunity offered by the Mitchell committee report to end the violence in the region, and the president urged both leaders to work with the plan.

Republican's Lose Majority in the U.S. Senate

As rumored on May 21-22, Vermont Senator James Jeffords left the Republican Party Thursday, May 24, becoming an Independent, which handed majority control of the Senate over to the Democratic Party for the first time since 1994.

Jeffords' decision created a crisis in the U.S. Senate for the Bush Administration and the Republican Party. The Republican's lost their majority and their very influential committee chairmanships. Jeffords' defection also had a very disruptive impact on Bush's judicial appointments and legislative agenda.

Catastrophe #3
June 5 – 13, 2001: Tropical Storm Allison – Estimated $5. 0 (5.1) billion damage/costs
CIA Director George Tenet Meets with Israelis and Palestinians over a Cease-Fire Agreement -- Tropical Storm Allison

CIA Director, George Tenet, who arrived in Israel from Egypt after meeting June 6 with President Hosni Mubarak, met Thursday, June 7, with Israeli Prime Minister Ariel Sharon and Israeli security chiefs, and later with Palestinian leader Yasser Arafat, in a bid to stem the violence that had claimed more than 600 lives since

September.

"The prime minister explained Israel's demand for a halting of the violence, terror and incitement, which have not ceased," a Sharon spokesman said after the meeting with Tenet.

Palestinian security sources said Tenet's meeting with Arafat was held in Ramallah, in the West Bank. Also attending were Palestinian negotiators, the Palestinian security chiefs in Gaza and the West Bank and U.S. Consul Roland Schliker.

Unrest continued in the West Bank and Gaza Strip June 8 despite Palestinian Authority leader Yasser Arafat's call for a cease-fire over that weekend and CIA Director George Tenet's meetings with Israeli and Palestinian officials. Tenet, Arafat and Sharon agreed to the Tenet Cease Fire agreement, but it was never officially signed.

Bush Hails Israeli-Palestinian Cease-fire Agreement

President Bush had welcomed an Israeli-Palestinian cease-fire plan that was brokered by the United States.

"I'm encouraged that both Israel and the Palestinian Authority have agreed to a cease-fire plan, and I'm proud of America's role in helping to achieve it," Bush said in a brief statement at the outset of a joint press conference in Brussels June 13 with NATO Secretary-General George Robertson.

Tropical Storm Allison Pummels Houston

Tropical Storm Allison, the first named storm of the 2001 Atlantic Hurricane Season, devastated portions of Southeast Texas, including the Houston Metro area and surrounding communities, with severe flooding. Allison spent five days over Southeast and East Texas and dumped record amounts of rainfall across the area. There were three distinct heavy rain events. The first event was associated with Allison's landfall on June 5 and affected northern Galveston and southern and eastern Harris counties. The second event on June 7 stretched from southern Liberty County southwestward into the Houston area and northern Fort Bend County. The third and most devastating event on June 8 and 9 stretched from Conroe to The Woodlands to Houston and on into northern Galveston County again. At least twenty-two fatalities associated with the flooding occurred with this third event. Nearly 37 inches of rain was recorded at the Port of Houston during Allison's five-day rampage!

On October 31, 2001, NOAA's National Weather Service released its Service Assessment for the Texas/Louisiana flood event associated with Tropical Storm Allison. The costliest tropical storm in the nation's history, Allison left 24 dead and caused more than $5 billion in damage in Texas and Louisiana before moving eastward to wreak havoc along the Gulf and East Coasts of the United States.

In Texas, 45,000 homes and businesses were flooded and 28 counties were declared federal disaster areas. In Louisiana more than 1,000 homes were flooded and a state of emergency was declared in 25 parishes.

"This devastating event reminds us once again that the current state of the science of forecasting and early warnings can only take us so far," said Larry Mooney, NWS service assessment team leader. "The National Weather Service and its emergency management.

The remnants of Tropical Storm Allison finally moved out to sea on Monday (June 18), after wreaking havoc from Texas to New England for 12 days.

Joe Allbaugh, director of the Federal Emergency Management Agency (FEMA), said on Tuesday, June 19, that the massive damage from the storm occurred in large part because people were taken by surprise.

It was "one of those freak accidents," Allbaugh told the media. "I don't think we can fault the forecasters. No one can predict 36 inches of rain." He added that flooding was to blame for many of the casualties. Although floods are one of the least-feared disasters among many Americans, they are a major hazard during almost any storm.

Catastrophe #4
September 11, 2001: World Trade Center and Pentagon terror events – Estimated cost $40 billion and higher

Total insurance claims — life insurance, workmen's compensation, property damage and business/rental interruption — was about $40 billion; the U.S. government committed an additional $20 billion for infrastructure structure repair in New York City and in Washington D.C. The U.S. government has also committed hundreds of billions of dollars to the war on terror.

On September 11, the greatest attack ever on American soil occurred. The hijacking of four airplanes and the attack on the World Trade Center (WTC) in New York City and the Pentagon left nearly 3,000 people dead. These suicide attacks by Muslim terrorists caused approximately $40 billion in damage and stunned the country. On this day, America came under the attack of terrorism on a scale not imagined. More Americans died on September 11, than in the attack on Pearl Harbor or the D-Day invasion. The attack was a complete surprise and came with no warning. The 9-11 events have cost the U.S. economy and nation hundreds of billions of dollars. There have been enormous costs associated with developing the office of Homeland Security, the wars in Afghanistan and Iraq have cost billions, President Bush received $67 billion for the war with Iraq and on September 8, 2003, requested an additional $87 billion. All of these costs have had a huge impact on the U.S. government's budget, which is projected to be $450 billion for 2003 and even higher in 2004.

The attack on the WTC was at the very heart of the U.S. financial center. The largest stock brokerage firms in the world were in the WTC, along with many of the international banks. The effect of this attack on the stock market was devastating. The attack on the Pentagon was at the very heart of the U.S. military. The plane intended for the political heart of America, the White House or the Capitol Building (depending on the accounts you read), crashed west of Pittsburgh when Todd Beamer and other passengers attempted to wrestle control from the highjackers, with the plane eventually crashing to the ground.

According to the *Washington Post*, seventeen days prior to the 9-11 terror events, President George W. Bush at the encouraging and involvement of Secretary of State Colin Powell and U.S. Ambassador to Israel Daniel Kurtzer, and in cooperation with the Saudis, were working on the most comprehensive plan and message ever to be offered on Israel's covenant land by an American President. President Bush and his top officials had completed a majority of their work on September 10. The plan was to be presented by Powell to the United Nations General Assembly on September 24, 2001. Saudi Arabia's Prince Bandar bin Sultan, who had been active in the negotiations, stated he went from being "the happiest man in the world" on Monday night, September 10, to experiencing the worst crisis of his career on September 11. Dreams of a new Middle East peace initiative evaporate. The realization that most of the hijackers were Saudis "fell on me ... like the whole house collapsed over my head," Bandar said later. He couldn't imagine a way to "do more damage or worse damage to Islam or to Saudi Arabia." The U.S. war on terror was birthed on 9-11-2001 at the very same time President Bush and his administration were completing a comprehensive plan on God's covenant land. What has happened since that time speaks volumes. The education president has now become the war president.

Catastrophe #5
October 2-October 31, 2001: Anthrax – Estimated cost to the U.S. Government was in the $3 billion range

Estimated cost to the U.S. Government was billions of dollars; by October 31, 2001, the U.S. Postal Service had purchased $2.5 billion in checking and sanitizing equipment, experienced an estimated $300 million in lost income, and had $60 million in damages from the attacks.

President Bush said on October 2 that a Palestinian state was always "part of a vision" if Israel's right to exist is respected. He said the two parties needed to get to work "on the Mitchell process" which he said provides a clear path to solving the crisis in the Middle East.

He refused, when asked, to say whether he had been prepared to announce his support for a Palestinian state prior to the Sept. 11 terrorist attacks on Washington and New York.

State Department and other senior administration officials told CNN on Monday, October 1, 2001, drafts of a major policy speech on the Middle East, to be delivered by U.S. Secretary of State Colin Powell, were circulating in the State Department for review.

Officials said the speech would "clarify its [U.S.] views on an end result" of the peace process, which would lead to the eventual "creation of a Palestinian state."

Capitol Hill Disrupted by Anthrax Attacks

The anthrax attacks cost the United States post office billions of dollars in lost trade and the implementation of a screening and sanitizing system, the postmaster general warned.

John Potter's statement came as the FBI announced it was preparing to sort through piles of congressional mail for possible cross-contamination from an anthrax-laced letter sent over two weeks ago to Senate Majority leader

Tom Daschle.

Traces of anthrax in several federal buildings interrupted the work of America's executive, legislative and judicial powers:

- White House mail was in quarantine
- Congressional offices had been sealed with staff having to work from temporary offices around the city
- Supreme Court judges were convening elsewhere for the first time in the court's 66-year history
- The State Department cut off mail to 240 embassies and consulates worldwide

Officials said the government had not been stopped from functioning, but James Thurber, a professor of government at American University said the terrorists seem to have succeeded "much beyond their own expectations."

"I can't think of anything that has disrupted government as much since the civil war," said Mr. Thurber.

Catastrophe #6
November 12, 2001: American Airlines Flight 587 Exploded over N.Y. City

President George W. Bush told the General Assembly of the United Nations in New York City on November 10, 2001:

> The American government also stands by its commitment to a just peace in the Middle East. We are working toward the day when two states–Israel and Palestine–live peacefully together within secure and recognized borders as called for by the Security Council resolutions.

At the same time that Bush and Powell were speaking about their positions, the U.S. received clear and ominous nuclear, chemical, and biological retribution warnings from both acknowledged terrorist leader Osama bin Laden and Iraqi dictator Saddam Hussein.

Putting this information into perspective, these statements and warnings were not days, weeks, or months apart. They happened almost simultaneously, and within a 48-hour period. As President Bush and Secretary of State Powell were speaking to the world of sacrificing God's covenant land for a Palestinian state, archenemies bin Laden and Hussein were threatening the U.S.

Sunday, May 11, Events

- On Sunday, Secretary Powell said that Bush's use of "Palestine" in his speech on Saturday was "deliberate and reflected administration policy." Speaking on NBC's "Meet the Press," Powell said, "If one is moving forward with a vision of two states side by side, it's appropriate ... to call those two states what they will be, Israel and Palestine." No United States president—Republican or Democrat—has ever made such a statement, according to Powell.
- On Sunday, the Middle East Newsline reported that United States intelligence agencies and the Pentagon agree that Saddam Hussein had made the most explicit threats since the 1991 Gulf war and that he was ready to use nuclear weapons. The assessment was that Iraq was threatening nuclear retaliation for any attack on the regime of President Saddam Hussein.
- On Sunday, in his address before the General Assembly, Arafat asked the UN to send international peacekeepers to Israel to protect his people from the "aggressors." Additionally he called for Israel to fulfill UN Resolutions 242 and 338, calling for "the evacuation of all settlers from the settlements on occupied land." Other Arafat demands included the establishment of a Palestinian state with "Holy Jerusalem" as its capital.

American Airlines Flight 587 Explodes over N.Y. City

The following day, on Monday, November 12, an American Airlines jetliner en-route to the Dominican Republic with 255 people aboard crashed moments after takeoff from Kennedy Airport, setting homes ablaze. The people that witnessed the plane's crash stated they saw an explosion in the plane's tail section. *USA Today* stated on the day of the accident, if the flight's crash was due to a terrorist incident that would have been the "last nail" in the coffin of the airline industry. Federal law enforcement and transportation officials stated a short time later that there was no evidence of terrorist involvement and that it was believed to be a mechanical failure in the tail of the plane.

Catastrophe #7
April 30, 2002. Maryland's F-5 Tornado

President George W. Bush and the State Department Negotiate Arafat's Release from Ramallah Compound

President Bush stated:

> Good afternoon. I am pleased by today's developments in the Middle East and believe they'll prove to be important steps along the path to peace in the Middle East.
>
> I commend the Israeli Cabinet for its decision this morning to allow Chairman Arafat to move freely, to accept international monitoring of six prisoners who are at Chairman Arafat's compound, and to withdraw its forces from Ramallah. The Palestinian Authority has agreed to accept this approach.
>
> This morning I called Crown Prince Abdullah to thank him for his visit to the United States. Our discussions forged a personal bond of friendship and strengthened the 60-year relationship between the United States and Saudi Arabia. The Crown

> Prince has offered a number of constructive ideas for making political progress between Israel and the Palestinians. We will continue to build on these ideas, as we move forward to fight terror and to promote peace in the Middle East.

Tornadoes Ravage Cities

Tornado-ravaged cities from Missouri to Maryland picked up the pieces Monday after an unusually wide and potent swath of thunderstorms weaved their way through the eastern half of the nation, killing at least six people.

Maryland was hit especially hard Sunday evening, with a tornado causing at least three deaths and 93 injuries in two counties south of the nation's capital. A twister caused serious damage to at least a 10-mile stretch of this town of about 6,500 -- even blowing windows out of the hospital.

A tornado in southern Maryland that killed three people and left a "war zone" of destruction in its wake was one of the strongest to ever hit the state, a National Weather Service spokeswoman said Monday.

A statement from the National Oceanic and Atmospheric Administration said its damage assessment team rated the tornado an F5 on the Fujita Tornado Damage Scale, "a monster of a tornado" with winds in the 261-318 mph range.

On Wednesday, May 1, White House Press Secretary Ari Fleischer released the following:

"The President today declared a major disaster exists in the State of Maryland and ordered Federal aid to supplement state and local recovery efforts in the area struck by a tornado on April 28, 2002."

Catastrophe #8
June 8, 2002: Colorado's Hayman Fire – 135,000 Acres Burned

President George W. Bush and Egyptian President Hosni

Mubarek Call on a Palestinian State and for Israel to Leave their Land – The Hayman Fire Begins in Colorado

President Bush, Camp David Address:

First, I want to thank the President of Egypt [Mubarek] for his country's strong support in our war against terror. I know there's been a lot of focus on obviously the Middle East, and I'll mention that in a second, but we're still in a war against people who want to harm America and people who want to harm Egypt. And we've had -- we've got a good friend, Americans have a good friend, when it comes to this war on terror, in Egypt.

The President understands that we've got a long way to go in order to be successful. He's now been told again by me that my most important job is to secure our homeland, and this country is plenty tough and plenty patient and plenty determined to achieve that objective.

Obviously, we spent time talking about the Middle East, and we share a common vision of two states living side by side in peace. And I appreciated so very much his -- listening to his ideas as to how to achieve that objective, that grand goal. The world -- the Palestinians hurt, and I know that. And my Concern is for the Palestinian people. And my view is, is that if the Palestinian people have a government that is transparent and open and willing to serve the people, Israel will be better off, Egypt will be better off, America will be better off, and we're more likely to achieve peace. And we discussed how to achieve those objectives.

Hayman Fire

Beginning in a campfire circle on the morning of June 8, 2002, the Hayman fire would quickly grow to become the largest recorded wildfire in Colorado's history. Spurred by record drought and extreme weather, the Hayman fire would burn nearly 138,000 acres over the course of three weeks. Two major fire activity periods, June 8-10 and June 17-18, marked by high winds and record-low relative humidity, would account for the majority of the total acreage burned as well as 93% of the 132 homes lost.

Catastrophe #9
June 18-26, 2002: Arizona's Rodeo and Chediski Fires – 550,000 Acres Burned

President George W. Bush planned to present his Middle East vision on June 18. However, his speech was postponed twice due to two major suicide bombings in Jerusalem.

On June 18, the Rodeo Fire began in Northeast Arizona. The next morning the Chediski Fire began in the same general area, these fast-moving fires merged quickly. On June 24, President Bush finally delivered his much-awaited Middle East vision. The next morning, rather than traveling directly to the G8 Summit in Canada as previously scheduled, he left Washington D.C. early in the morning for Arizona to survey the Rodeo – Chediski fires. On site, he called these combined wildfires one of the worst in Western U.S. history.

Later that day, after Wall Street had stopped trading, MCI declared that they had made a $3.6 billion accounting error, this news immediately sent shock-waves through U.S. and world financial markets. MCI soon became the largest bankruptcy filing in U.S. corporate history.

The Rodeo Fire: Arizona's "Perfect Fire," June 18

Mike Campbell, chief meteorologist at the National Weather Service office in Flagstaff, Arizona said the night of June 18 was made for the devil's ball that erupted.

Humidity was staggeringly low. Temperatures were

dangerously high. The air around Cibecue was poised to suck up flames and spew them hundreds of yards into lush undergrowth that experts say was thicker and drier than almost any time in the past century.

But nature wasn't alone in conjuring disaster that night. The crews called in to fight the fire made a major miscalculation.

Kent Butler, BIA fire management officer for the Fort Apache Reservation and his crews had decided to let the Rodeo fire burn Tuesday night, convinced it would run to waste when it reached a ridge that burned two years ago.

If the fire somehow leaped the ridge, Butler felt confident the flames would die at Carrizo Creek, a 20-foot wide swath of shallow, slow-moving waters.

Neither happened.

Chediskl Fire Begins on June 19

Mitch Jacob, news director of KPHO, said the Chediski fire - Chediski is the Apache word for White Rock - started some time shortly after 7 a.m. on Thursday, June 19.

The once-tiny signal fire was the fifth ingredient, converging with geography, weather, public policy and shear chance to create a fire like no other.

"It's like drawing a royal flush," said Stephen J. Pyne, an environmental historian at Arizona State University.

"Everything was in the cards, but it just doesn't happen. It all came together at maximum extenuating circumstances," he said.

Pyne said the worst time for fires in Arizona, historically, is around the summer solstice. Thursday was the day before the solstice.

The steep canyons of the Apache-Sitgreaves National Forests created what amounted to a chain of plumes and chimneys for fires that fed, in some cases, on a century's worth of untended, tinder-dry undergrowth.

And, finally, prevailing winds that day were from the southwest, pushing the fires northeast, into south-facing terrain that naturally attracts the highest temperatures and lowest humidity.

"You have everything that could possibly go wrong in the extreme," Pyne said. "Then you have the second fire set in a place where you can't control the perimeter of the first one. You can't put crews between them."

President Bush's Middle East Plan, June 24

Finally, after two previous delays, at 3:57 PM EDT, June 24, President Bush began delivering his Middle East vision for peace in the White House Rose Garden.

Here is an excerpt:

> In the situation the Palestinian people will grow more and more miserable. My vision is two states, living side by side in peace and security. There is simply no way to achieve that peace until all parties fight terror. Yet, at this critical moment, if all parties will break with the past and set out on a new path, we can overcome the darkness with the light of hope. Peace requires a new and different Palestinian leadership, so that a Palestinian state can be born.
>
> I call on the Palestinian people to elect new leaders, leaders not compromised by terror. I call upon them to build a practicing democracy, based on tolerance and liberty. If the Palestinian people actively pursue these goals, America and the world will actively support their efforts. If the Palestinian people meet these goals, they will be able to reach agreement with Israel and Egypt and Jordan on security and other arrangements for independence.
>
> And when the Palestinian people have new leaders, new institutions and new security

arrangements with their neighbors, the United States of America will support the creation of a Palestinian state whose borders and certain aspects of its sovereignty will be provisional until resolved as part of a final settlement in the Middle East.

In the work ahead, we all have responsibilities. The Palestinian people are gifted and capable, and I am confident they can achieve a new birth for their nation. A Palestinian state will never be created by terror -- it will be built through reform. And reform must be more than cosmetic change, or veiled attempt to preserve the status quo. True reform will require entirely new political and economic institutions, based on democracy, market economics and action against terrorism.

President Bush travels to Arizona, to visit displaced families and to review the fire damage, June 25

Here is an excerpt of his address given to displaced families at Eagar, Arizona, at 10:48 A.M. on June 25, 2002:

Thank you. It's nice to see you. I'm sorry we're doing so under these circumstances. But I want you to know that a lot of people in our country are pulling for you. They understand the suffering that families are going through because of worry about your most precious possession, your home. They understand that a lot of you are living in tents when you'd rather be in your own bed. They cry for you, and they hurt for you. And I'm here to say on behalf of the American people, God bless you.

Today, I signed a declaration declaring this an emergency, which then provides for federal help -- which means money to fight the fires. It means temporary housing money and long-term housing money. It means help for small business owners; I understand there's a lot of small business owners who are worried about your business, and I don't blame you. I'd be worried, too. So it provides help.

It helps provide counseling services, and a lot of folks here, I hope if you need counseling, you ask for it. A lot of people we want to help. So, this is the federal government's way of committing the resources allowed under the law, the full extent of the resources under the law.

You know, one of the great things about this country is that there's a lot of loving people here in this country. I always say. And not only is the Red Cross helping, but the Salvation Army is as well.

See, here's what I tell them. What the enemy didn't understand is when they attacked America; they didn't understand how kind and decent this country is. And so I'm here to say thanks on behalf of the volunteers, the people who are doing their best to spread compassion to people who need compassion, to spread love to people who need love, to spread guidance to people who seek guidance.

Bush Heads to Canada, June 25

President Bush then flew to Canada to discuss his Middle East peace plan (amongst other business) with G-8 leaders.

The U.S. markets were off on June 25, with the Nasdaq losing another 2.2% of its value. After the closing bell MSNBC broke a story that stated WorldCom (MCI) had engaged in what people close to the company described as a massive fraud that had only recently come to the attention of its board of directors. According to sources close to the company, WorldCom had inflated its EBITDA by some $3.6 billion over its last five quarters, by taking as capital expenditures costs that should have been treated as ordinary.

Putting this all into perspective

Arizona's Rodeo fire, began the very same day of a major suicide bombing in Jerusalem, which postponed President Bush's much-anticipated Middle East peace address. On June 19, the day the Chediski fire began, once again, his Middle East address was postponed by another major suicide bombing in Jerusalem.

Finally, on June 24 he delivered his Middle East vision. His next official speech was in Arizona at the site of a massive wildfire. Again, as President Bush was promoting the division of Israel's land, America's land was being devastated by massive record-setting wildfires.

Catastrophe #10
October 2- October 31, 2002:
Hurricane Lili - Estimated costs $750 million, and Washington D.C. area snipers

Congress Calls on President George W. Bush to Move the U.S. Embassy to Jerusalem; the President Refuses

As a candidate in 2000, President Bush backed Israel's claim on Jerusalem as its capital. But in office he turned aside a congressional demand for steps toward moving the U.S. Embassy from Tel Aviv to Jerusalem.

"U.S. policy regarding Jerusalem has not changed," Bush wrote in a statement as he signed an $8.6 billion spending bill for State Department programs around the world.

He criticized the provision that recommended recognizing Jerusalem as Israel's capital, saying it "impermissibly interferes with the president's constitutional authority to conduct the nation's foreign affairs."

Hurricane Lili and D.C. Sniper

Hurricane Lili was the first hurricane of the 21st

Century to strike the United States.

The Hurricane went from a Category 2 on Tuesday, to a Category 4 on Wednesday, miraculously back to a Category 2 on Thursday just before it hit land.

National Hurricane Center Director, Max Mayfield, was at a loss to explain the hurricane's fluctuations in the Gulf of Mexico. While colder water in the northern Gulf might explain why the hurricane weakened on Thursday, it did not account for why it had gained strength so dramatically the night before. "A lot of Ph.D.'s will be writing about this," he said.

Two snipers held Washington D.C. hostage for four weeks. The first shooting was within 24 hours of President Bush's decision not to move the U.S. Embassy to Jerusalem despite Congresses non-binding vote. The security checkpoints on the highways in Washington D.C. resembled the security checkpoints of Jerusalem; the D.C. area was paralyzed with fear over the snipers.

Catastrophe #11
November 6-13, 2002: 88 Tornadoes – Estimated $200 million in damage/costs

On Thursday night, November 7, 2002, President George W. Bush hosted a dinner and gave a speech to honor the beginning of Ramadan:

> Ramadan is a special time of prayer and fasting, contemplation of God's greatness, and service to those in need. According to Muslim teachings, this season commemorates the revelation of God's word in the holy Koran to the prophet Muhammad. Today this word inspires faithful Muslims to lead lives of honesty and integrity and compassion.
>
> In hosting tonight's Iftaar, I send a message to all the nations represented by their ambassadors here tonight: America treasures your friendship.

America honors your faith.

We see in Islam a religion that traces its origins back to God's call on Abraham. We share your belief in God's justice and your insistence on man's moral responsibility.

88 Tornadoes

An estimated 88 tornadoes slashed through Arkansas, Tennessee, Alabama, Mississippi, Georgia, Ohio, and Pennsylvania from late Saturday night, Nov. 9, through early Monday morning, according to the National Weather Service. Whole communities were reported demolished in Alabama, Tennessee, and Ohio.

The storm system that struck Tennessee and Ohio over the Veterans Day weekend was ranked as a category F4-storm, the second most severe on the Fujita scale. Winds, gusting to more than 200 miles per hour, cut a 100-mile swath across northwest Ohio, while two waves of tornadoes were generated in Tennessee, through western and middle Tennessee on late Saturday and early Sunday, and southeast of Nashville on Sunday night.

The occurrence of tornadoes in the South this time of year was unusual, according to the center. Peak tornado activity historically occurs from March through early July. This storm system, one of the worst November tornado outbreaks on record, was generated when a high-altitude cold front stretching from Texas to New York collided with a broad, warm and moist air mass drifting north from the Gulf of Mexico, according to the National Weather Service.

U.S. Official in Israel

On Sunday, November 10, U.S. Deputy Assistant Secretary of State David Satterfield was on his way to Israel to apply pressure on Israel to complete their work and comments on the Quartet's "road map" to peace. He had numerous meetings on Monday and Tuesday with Israeli officials. He also met with Palestinians officials.

Israel asked for an extension of the December 20 Quartet (EU, UN, Russia and the U.S.) deadline until after the elections. The Financial Times said no extension was approved. Then Ha'aretz, an Israeli news service, declared the White House had agreed to hold off until February or March—after a scheduled meeting between the head of the Prime Minister's Bureau, Dov Weisman, and National Security Advisor Dr. Condoleezza Rice at the White House.

Catastrophe #12
December 5, 2002: North Carolina Ice Storm - Estimated $133 million damages/cost

President Bush commemorated the end of Ramadan at The Islamic Center of Washington, D.C. on Thursday, December 5:

> Islam traces its origins back to God's call on Abraham. And Ramadan commemorates the revelation of God's word in the Holy Koran to the prophet Mohammad—a word that is read and recited with special attention and reverence by Muslims during this season.
>
> The spirit behind this holiday is a reminder that Islam brings hope and comfort to more than a billion people worldwide. Islam affirms God's justice and insists on man's moral responsibility. This holiday is also an occasion to remember that Islam gave birth to a rich civilization of learning that has benefited mankind.

The day before, Prime Minister Ariel Sharon had accepted in principle the U.S. roadmap for Israeli-Palestinian peace that envisages the creation of an independent Palestinian state within a few years.

An ice storm that officials declared the worst in Carolinas history cut power to nearly 2 million of the states' homes and businesses Thursday, December 5, and threatened to leave many without light and heat. Thousands of people sought warmth in shelters as utilities warned that power could be down for days—or even weeks to homes in isolated areas. Cities, counties and governors of both states issued emergency declarations that let officials restrict movement, raid budgets to pay overtime, regulate prices for key commodities and send out the National Guard, if needed. "This storm was obviously devastating," said Bryan Beatty, N.C., secretary of crime control and public safety, and emergency management.

Duke Power declared this storm worse than 1989's Hurricane Hugo, which knocked out power to 696,000 Carolinas customers—some for nearly 3 weeks—earning a dark spot in the memory of Charlotteans.

That Thursday afternoon, Duke had more than 1.2 million homes and businesses cut off from power in both states, with other utilities adding at least another 600,000.

Catastrophe #13
February 1, 2003: Space Shuttle Columbia Disaster

President George W. Bush Signaled He Would Become Much More Involved in the Israeli Palestinian Talks – Space Shuttle Columbia Broke Up Over Palestine, Texas

The United States shuddered again under the burden of a terrible tragedy, as the news spread about the breakup and loss of the Columbia Space Shuttle 39 miles above Texas, as it was descending from its mission and just 16 minutes from landing at Cape Canaveral.

The first report from *MSNBC* declared that the initial search area was around Palestine, Texas. Maps from *MSNBC* and *USA Today* had Palestine, Texas, in the center of the breakup area. People from around the world saw the same maps centering on Palestine.

The *Houston Chronicle* provided a National Weather radar image of Columbia that showed the majority of the debris falling just east of Palestine between Nacogdoches and Lufkin.

The "pride of America" (our nation's space program) and the "pride of Israel" (Colonel Illan Ramon) tragically broke up over Palestine, Texas. Is it symbolic that the "pride of America and of Israel" broke up over Palestine [Texas]? Is this a warning sign to Israelis and Americans alike that Palestine could break up our nations, too?

All seven astronauts on board, including the first Israeli ever to be on a space mission and at least three Christian believers, were pronounced dead. In a short speech to the nation several hours later, President George W. Bush said:

> In the skies today, we saw destruction and tragedy. Yet farther than we can see, there is comfort and hope. In the words of the prophet Isaiah, (Lift you eyes and look to the heavens. Who created all these? He who brings out the starry hosts one by one and calls them each by name. Because of His great power and mighty strength, not one of them is missing.
>
> The same Creator who names the stars also knows the names of the seven souls we mourn today. The crew of the shuttle Columbia did not return safely to Earth; yet we can pray that all are safely home.

We can rejoice in having a President who draws upon God's Word for comfort and solace for the families left behind and for all who grieve for the loss of these seven astronauts. But in our role as watchmen, we would be remiss if we did not call attention to the apparent significance of the sequence of events and seeming coincidences, which surrounded and infused this tragedy.

On Friday afternoon, less than 24 hours before this tragedy, U.S. Secretary of State Colin Powell said in a speech that President Bush would become more involved in the Israel-Palestinian conflict and that the administration "would resume its pursuit of a settlement."

He went on to declare that the Bush Administration would use the "roadmap" devised in partnership with the European Union, Russia, and the United Nations. This roadmap, he said, aims "to create a Palestinian state by the year 2005, carved out of land that Israel has held for more than 35 years."

Also, on the same day, President Bush and Britain's Prime Minister Tony Blair met at the White House over the pending Iraq war. They agreed to give Iraq six more weeks to comply. Ironically, this is the same amount of time President Bush has just agreed to give Israeli Prime Minister Ariel Sharon to form his coalition government and for his formal response to the Quartet's Road Map.

Catastrophe #14
May 1-10, 2003: 412 Midwest Tornadoes – Estimated $2.2 billion damage/costs

International mediators presented a long-awaited Mideast peace plan on Wednesday, April 30, 2003, just hours after Palestinian Prime Minister Mahmoud Abbas was sworn in.

U.S. Ambassador Daniel Kurtzer presented the plan to Israeli Prime Minister Ariel Sharon at the prime minister's Jerusalem home, and representatives of the four parties in the "Quartet" of Mideast mediators delivered it to Palestinian Prime Minister Mahmoud Abbas in the West Bank town of Ramallah.

The so-called "road map" to peace was drafted by the Quartet, made up of the United States, European Union, United Nations and Russia.

On Saturday, May 3, Secretary Powell headed to the Mideast for talks about implementing the Road Map peace plan.

On Sunday, May 4, Secretary of State Colin Powell, committed to Syria, a Middle East peace that "would include Syria and Lebanon, and would include the Golan Heights." Within 24 hours there were 83 Tornadoes in America's heartland.

Also, on Sunday, a deadly swarm of 83 tornadoes ripped through eastern Kansas, Missouri, Arkansas and Tennessee, killing at least 38 people and doing extensive damage to homes and buildings. It was "the most devastating series of tornadoes we've ever had in the state of Missouri," Gov. Bob Holden said after walking the rubble-strewn streets of Pierce City, where eight of the missing were from.

On Monday, May 5, less than 24-hours after the 83 tornadoes and the Powell news, U.S. Middle East envoy William Burns met with Palestinian Authority Prime Minister Mahmoud Abbas (Mahmoud Abbas) in the West Bank city of Ramallah. He stated that the Palestinians must carry out a decisive fight against terrorism and Israelis must halt settlement activity.

On Saturday May 10 and Sunday May 11 Colin Powell had meetings with Israeli Prime Minister Ariel Sharon and Palestinian Prime Minister Mahmoud Abbas in Israel.

During the first ten days of May there had been 412 tornadoes; the most observed since the National Oceanic and Atmospheric Administration began record keeping in 1950. The previous record for the first 10 days of May was 177 tornadoes set in 1999.

The tornadoes, which swept across parts of the U.S., have the potential to be the costliest in U.S. history, according to the Insurance Information Institute (I.I.I.). Boston-based AIR Worldwide, which uses a computer-modeling program to estimate insured losses from catastrophes, put the damages at $2.2 billion.

Along with the tornadoes there were 535 windstorms, and 1385 hailstorms in America's heartland. More than 300 counties affecting 19 states suffered losses and more than 40 deaths were blamed on the storms.

The final tornado occurred as Powell was leaving Israel for Jordan and a meeting with King Abdullah II.

Catastrophe #15

May 1 – August 17, 2003: The nations represented in the Quartet experience record-setting heat, drought, rains, floods, blackouts and related deaths. Estimated damage into the billions of dollars and billions of euros.

The European Union stated on Thursday, May 1, that the United States was not the sole author or owner of the "Road Map" for Israeli-Palestinian peace.

"This is not a problem to be solved by only one country, it is a problem to be solved by the cooperation of....members of the international community that have been engaged in this peace process for a long time," said EU foreign policy chief Javier Solana.

"The Road Map is not the property of one country, it is the property of the Quartet," he told reporters. The Quartet partners include many nations of the world through its 4 bodies - the European Union, the United Nations, the United States and Russia.

A spokeswoman for European External Affairs Commissioner Chris Patten also wanted to speak out against the comments that the Road Map was an American proposal. "I would like to remind you all that although I hear and read quite frequently that this is America's Road Map, it is not America's Road Map," Emma Udwin told a news briefing. "It is the Road Map of the Quartet."

The White House has said it is "a set document." Udwin stated, "The Road Map remains what the international community sees as the best option for peace in the foreseeable future."

When the Quartet's Road Map was delivered to the Israelis and Palestinians weather related havoc and chaos began, it intensified throughout the summer as meetings continued.

It started with the United States experiencing the most traumatic tornado outbreak in history. In the first ten days of May there were 412 tornadoes in the Midwest. This was also the beginning of horrible weather related events in Europe. Below are highlights of the events.

Heat Records

Climatologists who have seen or studied a lot, haven't seen the world patterns in such a strong and persistent form.

Clearly, they said, irregular bends in the jet stream were involved. But no clear-cut reason for that pattern had emerged. In their hunt for answers, some scientists were looking as far away as the monsoons of South Asia for clues to Miami's unseasonable rains and Madrid's outdoor oven.

"The inherent instability of the atmosphere by itself can produce a persistent pattern, such as the one that has dominated over North America and Europe this summer," said Angie Seth, an associate research scientist at the International Institute for Climate Prediction at Columbia University's Earth Institute.

Between June and August of 2003, Europe experienced its hottest summer for at least 500 years, according to Swiss university reasearchers. This heat wave triggered several thousand more deaths than usual, average temperatures eclipsed the previous record set in 1757, according to a study by the University of Bern's geography department.

"While the heat wave gripping Europe in the summer of 2003 was making headlines around the world, the United States was setting its own records for scorching heat in the West and torrential rains in the East," wrote Joan Lowy for Scripps Howard News Service.

Lowy continued, "Every Western state except California suffered temperatures much warmer than normal last month. Numerous daily and monthly records were shattered, according to the National Oceanic and Atmospheric Administration's National Climatic Data Center in Asheville, N.C. Idaho and the cities of Phoenix, Las Vegas, Cheyenne, Wyoming, and Grand Junction, Colorado, all experienced their warmest July on record," the center said.

Conditions were similar to the weather that caused the catastrophic 'dust-bowl' of the 1930's depression years.

Nobody seemed to know why this was happening or what, if anything, it means. It may or may not have been related to the record-breaking heat waves that year in Europe and parts of the American west, said Jim Laver, director of the NOAA Climate Prediction Center in Camp Springs, Md. Typically, he and Barnston said, prolonged climatic anomalies of this scale would be associated with unusual ocean warming or cooling in the tropical Pacific and Indian oceans, the sort of atmospheric domino effect associated with the ocean current known as El Nino.

"But this year nothing appears to be going on in the Pacific that would trigger anything," they said.

Record setting European and world weather begins the first week of May 2003

Earthweek reported that one of the causes of the great European heat epidemic was a shift northward of the "meteorological equator" over Africa. This directly caused the killer heat wave as the hot air mass that usually sits over the Sahara Desert shifted to Europe. This represented a major new climatic shift in world weather patterns.

One thing was nevertheless certain, global weather patterns are changing. The increasing heat, which most radically affects the equatorial regions over the planet's oceans, was spawning storms of ever-increasing magnitude.

The Geneva-based World Meteorological Organization (WMO), to which the weather services of 185 countries contribute, took the view that events in Europe, America and Asia were so remarkable that the world needed to be made aware of it immediately. They pointed to global warming, however, we point to the repercussions of dividing God's covenant land. To this point, most of the chaotic events that had happened in the United States occurred because the U.S. had become the sole sponsor of record. But this changed when the Quartet came forward with their "land for peace" plan and the EU, the UN, and Russia began experiencing the repercussions of attempting to divide God's covenant land.

The WMO normally confines itself to issuing scientific reports and statistics compiled from climate data. However, the weather events of 2003 had proved so remarkable, officials say that the organization felt compelled to issue a generalized warning of the emerging pattern.

World and European Heat Records 2003

- Average temperatures over world land areas climbed to the highest levels ever recorded in May, according to the World Meteorological Organization.
- The combined global land and sea average for May was the 2nd highest on record since observations began in 1880, WMO said.
- A study released by the WMO, explained that the world is experiencing record numbers of extreme weather events, such as droughts and tornadoes. They laid the blame firmly at the feet of global warming, ironically

they also stated this period of extreme weather occurred quickly and caught many experts by surprise.

- Beginning in May 2003 there was an all-time record heat wave across parts of Western Europe and the Indian subcontinent, which caused outbreaks of heat stroke and widespread power disruptions.
- Britain experienced the highest temperatures in 350 years of record keeping on Sunday, August 10, 2003. Britain also surpassed 100 degrees for the first time ever and was coupled with high humidity. The previous national record in Britain was 98.8 degrees, which was set August 3, 1990.
- France was the worst hit. In some French areas, the thermometers reached an incredible 105 degrees, while in the south of France average temperatures were between 5 and 7 degrees Celsius (9 to 13 degrees Fahrenheit) warmer than the long term average.
- Germans, too, had record heat. In the Bavarian city of Roth, the temperature hit nearly 105 degrees. The previous record of 104 was also in Bavaria, set in 1983. Temperatures in Bavaria hit 105 degrees, setting a new German record.
- Spain and Portugal have suffered the worst of it. In some areas of the Iberian Peninsula, temperatures surpassed 43 degrees Celsius, or 110 degrees Fahrenheit.
- Several visitors to the Vatican fainted in St. Peters Square as the temperature soared to 98 degrees Fahrenheit - the hottest June reading in Rome since record keeping began in 1782.
- The heat and drought-driven fires across the continent prompted Pope John Paul II to urge people to pray for rain.
- Switzerland experienced its hottest June in at least 250 years. Some of the lower Glaciers melted, sending mudslides down on villages below.

- Records continued to fall across Europe as temperatures hit 98 in Prague, 100 in Vienna and 105 in parts of northern Italy.
- In Afghanistan, major sandstorms affected more than 12,000 people, and were described as the "worst sandstorms in living memory." Sandstorms began in the region during early June and continued during July. Up to 20 villages had to be evacuated because they were completely covered in sand, and many irrigation canals and waterways had also been filled.
- A pre-monsoon heat wave, which hit India caused peak temperatures of between 45 and 49 degrees Celsius (113 to 120 degrees Fahrenheit), killing more than 1400 people.
- Cold and snowy weather characterized conditions across much of New Zealand during the first week of July, where locally 30 cm (12 inches) of snow fell in parts of the country. The snowstorm was described by local media as the worst in 50 years, causing thousands of power outages to homes and businesses and stranding hundreds of motorists (*New Zealand Herald*).

Crop Loss

The affect of the heat wave on European agriculture has also been catastrophic. This will have a domino affect on other factors of European health and economy.

- European Union agricultural experts said that adverse weather conditions since winter (2002) were likely to cause crop losses totaling several billion Euros.
- The summer's European drought and record heat wave crippled agriculture and triggered a public health crisis.
- Unusually high temperatures and a summer-long dearth of rain wrought serious damage to crops and weather-related deaths throughout Europe, a continent of increasingly scorched earth.

- France's oyster supplies were submerged under the flood of toxic black sludge that poured from the hull of the Prestige oil tanker. Then the Bollinger harvest was ravaged by a freak storm of golf ball-sized hailstones. After further gloomy news about the premature heat-related deaths of millions of prize chickens, the death by suffocation of much of the country's trout stocks, the shriveling of the honey crop, and the withering of thousands of hectares of fruit trees, the latest cause of the French gourmet's annus horribilis looks certain to be the truffle. Exceptionally dry weather in May and June meant that few truffle spores germinated; the unprecedented temperatures in July and August meant that those few truffles which had begun to develop were unable to mature - diminishing further France's already tiny supply.
- In Italy, the harvests of grapes, olives, peaches and apricots turned out to be 50 percent below usual. Agricultural groups estimated the financial toll on Italian farmers was about $6 billion.
- The German Association of Farmers reported that more than 1/2 of the year's grain crop in the east of the country was threatened from drought. The halt of fresh water into Germany's river Spree had even caused the waterway to begin flowing upstream in some of its lower reaches.
- The worst drought in Croatia's history had devastated the country's spring crops and brought about an acute water shortage. Croatia's farmers' union reported that the drought had affected the livelihoods of a million people.

Drought

- In July 2003 rivers reached their lowest levels in 100 years across parts of Italy, where officials imposed a 100-Euro fine for watering plants.

- Ships plying the Danube River in Eastern Europe were carrying restricted loads so that they did not scrape bottom. Water levels in the river had declined so much that in Romania, dredgers deepened some channels so that ships could pass.
- Croatia's major rivers, including the Sava, Drava, Kupa and Danube, were reported at their lowest levels ever. In neighboring Serbia, the ecology minister reported that the country's rivers were at their lowest levels in 100 years
- A swarm of locusts forced residents of an Inner Mongolia town into taking drastic measures to stop the insects from settling on surrounding pastures and grasslands. Residents of the Chinese border town of Erenhot were maintaining a blackout at night, as electric lighting tended to attract the insects.
- The *Yangcheng Evening News* reported that the locusts -- which arrived in the region in June -- were "like snow falling from the sky." Crushed insects blanketed the roads of the remote town and the swarm had engulfed more than 11 million hectares of Inner Mongolia's grasslands. "The affected area was almost all grassland."

Fires

The early summertime warmth caused a devastating wildfire season across Europe and Russia.

- July's fires in France, thought to have been started deliberately, were the worst in the region for decades. Fires ravaged the French Riviera, killing 4. There were scenes of panic as the flames engulfed caravans, cars and electricity poles, forcing people to ditch their vehicles by the side of the road. Some tourists were stranded wearing nothing but their swimming suits. "There has rarely been such a powerful blaze in the region," said a spokesman for the regional emergency center.

French Interior Minister Nicolas Sarkozy flew to the scene of what he described as an "ecological disaster."

- The fires in Portugal, the worst in a generation, had come amidst a heat wave stretching from Russia to the Iberian Peninsula.
- Some 431 fires burned across Russia in July, 2003.
- The summer drought contributed to 300 forest fires in Germany in summer 2003.

Power Grid

- Britain canceled some trains on busy routes and imposed reduced, temporary speed limits on others to make sure that rails did not buckle in atypically intense temperatures.
- Power grids in many countries were under significant strain, as people in countries normally suspicious of air conditioning suddenly jettisoned their reservations and embraced - or longed for - even a manufactured breeze.
- France called emergency talks on August 11 due to overheating at nuclear power plants.
- Paris sweltered through its hottest night on August 10, 2003, since records began. Temps hit around 104 degrees Fahrenheit, spelling trouble for France's nuclear reactors, many of which are cooled by river water. With river levels falling and the mercury rising, authorities face the choice of spewing out hotter water, risking ecological damage, or cutting output, potentially leading to electricity blackouts.
- Record heat across France and Italy caused widespread power failures as residents strained power grids by firing up air conditioners to escape the scorching conditions.
- Some areas along the Mediterranean saw the highest use of air conditioning on record due to the heat, threatening power blackouts.

Heat Related Deaths

The heat wave, which saw temperatures consistently above 100 degrees in some parts of Europe, brought a sharp increase in death rates in several countries.

- While the death toll from weeks of unrelenting heat may never be determined, wire service reported estimates that well over 22,000 had died in 14 countries.
- More than 4,200 elderly Italians died in the summer's heat wave.
- France's Health Minister Jean-Francois Mattei, said that 11,435 more deaths than normal were registered August 1-15, when daily temperatures of 40°C and above roasted the country. The French government eventually estimated that more than 15,000 people died as a result of the unusual weather, and the inability of the health system to cope.
- The Netherlands estimated 1,400 died of heat-related issues. Portugal announced 1,300 deaths and British officials estimated 900 weather-related deaths.

Record setting U.S. weather begins May 1, 2003

Violent Weather

- There were 562 tornadoes, which hit the United States in May 2003, a record, far higher than the previous record monthly peak of 399 set in June 1992.
- In June alone, twisters tore up fields in South Dakota and Iowa.
- Residents of one town in Nebraska reported hail on June 24 that look "like someone dropping volleyballs down." One resident of Aurora said hail punched a hole in his roof that was large enough for him to crawl through, said Dale Obermeier, a weather service spotter in Aurora, who said the hail also dug holes in his yard.

Heat

- With an average temperature of nearly 98 degrees, July

2003 branded the record books as the hottest month in Phoenix since the National Weather Service started keeping track in 1896. In Phoenix, where 100 degrees in summer is almost balmy, the highs were breathtaking: 15 days over 110 degrees and, on July 15, the warmest overnight low ever -- 96 degrees. The days were so hot, windshields were shattering or falling out, dogs were burning their paws on the pavement, and candles were melting indoors.

- July's punishing heat: Almost everywhere in the region, it cooked the record books. Six Western cities registered their hottest month ever. Six others charted their warmest July ever.
- Others tallied record strings of 100-degree days, historic highs for numerous July dates, even record-high marks for the overnight low temperature. "There were records on so many levels," said Mark Ressler, a meteorologist for The Weather Channel.
- Places unaccustomed to triple digits suffered multi-day runs at 100 degrees or higher. Salt Lake City had 10 in a row and Boise had 9 straight and 12 for the month. Others accumulated 100's like never before. Pueblo, Colorado, which had its hottest day ever (109 on July 13), reached 100 or more on 23 days in July. Grand Junction reached 100 or more 17 times. Greeley, which set or tied all-time highs on 10 dates, hit 100 on 18 days. Redding, California, north of Sacramento, hit 100 on 20 days.
- Temperatures soared to 109 degrees Wednesday afternoon August 7, at Dallas-Fort Worth International Airport, surpassing the old record of 108 set in 1952.
- It wasn't just north Texas that was sweltering. In the west, Lubbock tied its record high for the date of 102, and to the south, Rio Grande City was near 104.
- Texans cranked up their air conditioners to cope. The Electric Reliability Council of Texas, which manages

the power grid for 85% of the state, broke its usage record, said spokeswoman Dottie Roark. Most residents appeared to be handling the heat in stride.

Heavy Rains

- Between May 1 and Sunday, August 17, Washington's weather station at Reagan National Airport recorded 69 overcast days (63 percent, about double the usual) and nearly twice the usual amount of rain.
- Far colder and wetter conditions than normal also prevailed in the eastern and southeastern part of the U.S. for much of May and June.
- Wilmington, Delaware and New York City recorded their wettest Junes in more than a century.
- Between May 1 and July 31, nearly 40 inches fell on Mobile, Alabama, the most in 123 years.
- During the May 1-July 31 period, Alabama's largest city, Birmingham, recorded a total of 29.59 inches of rain making it the wettest since record keeping began there in 1890. With 39.65 inches, Mobile also set a new record for the period. Again, the total was more than twice the average (17.65 inches), since record keeping began there 123 years ago.
- Atlanta experienced its 3rd wettest May-July since record keeping started in 1878 with a total of 22.62 inches of rain.
- During that three month period, NOAA National Weather Service Forecast Offices in Mississippi, Alabama and Georgia issued nearly 350 flash flood warnings.
- At the same time, 421 separate flood events were forecast by the NOAA Southeast River Forecast Center, which serves portions of Mississippi, Alabama, Georgia, Florida, North and South Carolina, Virginia and Tennessee.

Drought

- The combination of generally warmer and drier -than-average conditions during the June –September led to an increase in the drought coverage area to about 41 percent of the United States by October.
- Spring was very dry in the southern Plains, with Texas experiencing the driest March-May in the 109-year record during 2003.
- Much of the West was in the sixth consecutive year of drought. Snow pack and stream runoff in the red areas were 30-70 percent below normal. The drought contributed to devastating forest fires, increased ground water consumption, and agricultural failure. Water levels in large storage reservoirs along the Colorado River, Lake Powell, and Lake Mead were record low levels.

Eastern U.S. Blackout, August 14-15, 2003.

- The latest great Northeast Blackout left millions stranded. More than 5,000 people had to be evacuated from New York subway trains that were stranded deep inside tunnels--some underneath the Hudson River. Hotels with rooms could not rent them to desperate people because their computers were down and they didn't know which rooms were occupied or empty. Grand Central station was shut down. All the major airports had to shut down because of unreliable power supplies to run the computers for traffic control and the navigational systems.
- More than fifty million people in the Northeast of the United States and the Province of Ontario, Canada, lost electricity when the system suddenly broke down--causing the greatest "black-out" in history,
- All the facts as to what caused the catastrophic electrical break down are not in. But the heat wave that had lingered for days over the region certainly played a part,

since air conditioners were running at record levels. This placed a great strain on the entire electrical system. When the electrical system was running at near maximum capacity, the margin for error became extremely small. The problem is that the entire infrastructure of modern cities is built around the assumption of an uninterrupted electrical power supply. Most of the transportation system is dependent upon either electrically powered engines or upon equipment that is necessary for their safe operation. I refer to such things as subways, trains, automobiles, airports, aircraft and ships. Most multi-story buildings do not even have windows and are totally dependent on air-condition systems. Elevators are an absolute necessity for many people who cannot walk up and down enormous numbers of flights of stairs. And buildings with upward of fifty stories are rendered virtually useless.

Catastrophe #16
May 12, 2003: Riyadh Terror Bombing

Colin Powell met King Abdullah II in Amman, Jordan on Middle East peace. Within 8 hours of Powell's scheduled arrival in Riyadh, Saudi Arabia to visit with Crown Prince Abdullah to discuss the Middle East peace process Tuesday morning, American interests were bombed late Monday evening May 12. Al Qaeda claimed responsibility for the largest terror event targeting Americans since 9-11.

At least 29 people, including 10 U.S. nationals, were killed and about 200 injured when suicide car bombings devastated three housing compounds for foreigners.

Washington blamed the Al Qaeda network for the bombings, with President George Bush vowing to be relentless in the "war on terrorism" and to hunt down those responsible for the attacks.

The attacks were "suicide bombings using booby-trapped cars filled with explosives," the Saudi interior ministry said.

Catastrophe #17
July 15, 2003: Hurricane Claudette – Estimated $100 million in damage/costs

While Palestinian officials were on Capitol Hill meeting with members of Congress on the Bush Administration's "road map," Hurricane Claudette was clobbering President Bush's home state.

According to the Associated Press, Ministers in Palestinian Prime Minister Mahmoud Abbas' Cabinet met with members of Congress to discuss the Bush administration's "road map" plan to end Israeli-Palestinian violence.

The meetings, which ended Wednesday, July 15, came just more than a week ahead of Abbas' arrival in Washington to meet President Bush.

Claudette

Hurricane Claudette the first Atlantic hurricane of 2003, made landfall on the middle of the Texas coast midday Tuesday, July 15 according to the National Hurricane Center (NHC). It was a Category 1 storm, classified as the least destructive on a scale of 1-5. Claudette's winds reached a maximum of 80 mph, and five to eight inches of rain fell as a direct result.

Catastrophe #18
July 17 and July 24, 2003: Two-high profile suicides

The Strange Timing Of Two High-Profile Suicides, Are The Tragedies Symbolic?

Thursday, July 17, British Prime Minister Tony Blair addressed the U.S. Congress. Blair stated that terrorism would not be defeated without peace in the Middle East between Israel and Palestine.

At a joint press conference with U.S. President George

W. Bush in Washington on Thursday night, Blair noted "the first steps, albeit tentative," have now been taken toward achieving a two-state solution.

On the next day, Blair began to face the biggest political crisis in his six years as Britain's Prime Minister, when the body of Dr. David Kelly, Britain's chief bio-warfare expert, was found dead. The government's chief expert and former weapons inspector in Iraq took his own life.

On July 24, 2003, Palestinian Prime Minister Mahmoud Abbas visited Capitol Hill in Washington to meet with Senators and Congressmen. Later in the day he gave a speech to members of the Council on Foreign Relations (CFR).

On Friday, July 25, Abbas and members of his Cabinet were guests of President Bush at the White House. Following an oval office meeting which included President Bush, Vice President Dick Cheney, Secretary of State Colin Powell, National Security Advisor Dr. Condoleezza Rice and other staff, Bush and Abbas held a Rose Garden press briefing.

On Thursday, July 24, 2003, President Bush's friend Oilman Colin McMillan, who was awaiting Senate confirmation as Navy secretary, was found dead from a single gunshot wound, and investigators said Friday it was self-inflicted. According to Fox News, he died around lunchtime Thursday.

Two employees found his body at his southern New Mexico ranch, said Roswell Mayor Bill Owen, a family spokesman and longtime McMillan employee. The 55,000-acre Three Rivers Ranch is on the edge of the White Sands Missile Range.

McMillan had run Permian Exploration Corp. in Roswell, chaired Bush's New Mexico presidential campaign in 2000 and served as an assistant defense secretary under the first President Bush.

Political Suicide

Are these tragic events, symbolic of the political suicide Bush and Blair are bringing on themselves if they continue to involve themselves with the dividing of God's covenant land?

Catastrophe #19: September 6-19, 2003: Hurricane Isabel – Estimated $4.0 billion in damages

During the week of September 15 the United States told Israel any money spent on settlements would be subtracted from their $9 billion in loan guarantees; the security fence was under discussion too. On Thursday, September 18, King Abdullah arrived at Camp David to discuss with President Bush the Road Map, Iraq and bilateral relations. At the time of their meeting Hurricane Isabel came ashore and devastated North Carolina, Virginia and Maryland.

Hurricane Isabel became a tropical storm on Saturday, September 6, on the very same day Palestinian Prime Minister, Mahmoud Abbas, resigned from office.

From its beginning as a tropical storm Isabel's path took her straight westward towards the U.S. Her intensity increased from a Category 4 to Category 5 on the afternoon of September 11, the same afternoon that the U.S. told Israel not to expel Yasser Arafat. Isabel's intensity on Friday and Saturday stayed in the Category 5 range (excluding a few hours as a Category 4). Sunday afternoon it dropped 1 MPH below 156 MPH (the beginning of Category 5) making it a Category 4, and was at 140 MPH and fluctuating Sunday evening.

According to early computer models, the storm was expected to come ashore between South Carolina and New Jersey, with most models having it heading directly towards the Washington D.C. area once it came ashore.

On Tuesday, September 16, the U.S. vetoed a UN

Security Council bill that called on Israel to guarantee Yasser Arafat's security. The United States' UN Ambassador John Negroponte stated that the United States does not support the elimination or forced exile of Arafat and believes that his diplomatic isolation is the best course. However, he said the United States was forced to use its veto because the resolution failed to name groups such as Hamas and the Al-Aqsa Martyrs Brigade, which have claimed credit for numerous suicide bombings and other attacks against Israelis.

Also on Tuesday, the U.S. told Israel they would deduct money spent on settlements from their $9 billion loan guarantee. The U.S. also stated they were considering whether to reduce money spent on the security fence from the loan guarantees. U.S. Treasury Secretary Jack Snow reminded Israeli Finance Minister Benjamin Netanyahu that Israel is required to reduce its debt as another contingency of their loan guarantees. Due to Bush Administration pressure, Israeli Prime Minister Ariel Sharon delayed his cabinet meeting on Wednesday to discuss the course of the security fence.

Isabel and Abdullah

On Wednesday, September 17, President Bush was briefed at the White House on Hurricane Isabel. The Federal Government called for all offices to be closed on Thursday and Friday. President Bush's next official public meeting was to take place at Camp David with King Abdullah II of Jordan in which they are to discuss how to proceed with the Road Map effort, Iraq and bilateral relations. Hurricane Isabel caused President Bush to rearrange his schedule. He flew to Camp David Wednesday night instead of Thursday. His joint press availability with Jordan's King Abdullah II was moved up to Thursday morning from Friday due to Isabel.

President Bush Welcomed King Abdullah II at Camp

David:

First, I'm so pleased to welcome my friend, King Abdullah and Queen Rania to Camp David. I want to thank them so very much for rearranging their schedules to get up here ahead of Hurricane Isabel. Laura and I look forward to spending some quality time with two really fine people.

We're going to have some serious discussions today, then we'll have a nice lunch and then we'll batten down the hatches and spend a good evening with our friend.

Hurricane Isabel

North Carolina, Virginia and Maryland took the brunt of Hurricane Isabel's intensity.

The storm was still an enormous event, a tragedy for those losing family members, but fortunately it didn't hit Washington D.C, Baltimore, Philadelphia or New York City straight on which would have killed many people and caused billions of dollars in property damage. Initial NOAA estimates have the damage at $4 billion (that figure does not include flood-related damage covered by federal flood insurance), which will place Isabel as the third most costly U.S. Hurricane according to the Insurance Information Institute.

Federal offices in Washington D.C. were closed as well as the schools in the D.C. and Baltimore area. The Metro trains and buses were not running, the airports were closed, over one million people were without power (eight million total), and there were major concerns about flooding due to very saturated ground from the last 10 months of rain, but the cities were mercifully spared.

Within 72-hours of Isabel over one million people were still without power in the Washington D.C. metro area. Moreover, over one million homes were told to boil their water due to contamination. The long and arduous cleanup process began.

On Monday, September 22, President Bush's next official day at work, he flew to Richmond, Virginia to visit the Virginia State Police Academy to participate in a briefing on Hurricane Isabel's damage. He also toured the temporary Virginia Emergency Operations Center.

Surrounded by photographs of Hurricane Isabel slamming into the Atlantic coast, President Bush offered federal help to states that took the worst hits from the storm.

"The true character of this country comes out in times of stress and emergency. This country has responded once again," Bush said at the Virginia State Police Academy to a room filled with more than 250 emergency relief workers from 12 federal agencies who coordinated recovery efforts in the state.

"On behalf of a grateful nation I want to thank people at all levels of our government for working extra hard to help our country when it needed help," Bush said.

In Washington, Senate Appropriations Committee Chairman Ted Stevens, R-Alaska, said he expected the storm to eventually cost the federal government billions of dollars. Stevens said Isabel was "the most major storm we've seen in recent history in terms of damage."

This powerful and costly storm with its intricate tie-in to Israel is another warning judgment to those involved in the dividing of God's covenant land.

Catastrophe and Events #20
October 24-November 4, 2003: Record solar flares and California wildfires - wildfires left an estimated $3 billion in damage

Bush Says Fence Will Impede Emergence of a Palestinian State, Hosts White House Ramadan Dinner – The Sun's Produces Record Setting Explosions, and Southern California

Has Record Wildfires

"The fence is an opportunity to make it difficult for a Palestinian state to emerge," U.S. President George Bush said in a news conference on October 28, after being asked about the security fence Israel is constructing with the stated goal of keeping out terrorists.

"There is a difference between security and land acquisition," Bush said, "and we have made our views clear on that issue."

Bush said his problem with the fence, as with Jewish settlements on the West Bank and in Gaza, was whether it would interfere with conditions for setting up a Palestinian state.

President Bush, for the third year in a row, sponsored a Ramadan dinner at the White House on October 28, 2003, to celebrate the beginning of the Muslims thirty-day fast.

Bush hosted Ambassadors and Muslim leaders. The following is an excerpt from his address:

> According to the teachings of Islam, Ramadan commemorates the revelation of God's word in the Holy Koran to the prophet Mohammed. In this season, Muslims come together to remember their dependence on God, and to show charity to their neighbors. Fasting during Ramadan helps Muslims focus on God's greatness, to grow in virtue, and cultivate compassion toward those who live in poverty and hunger.

The White House also developed a Ramadan 2003 section for their web site.

http://www.whitehouse.gov/infocus/ramadan/index.html

Record Solar Flares

On Wednesday, October 29, scientists warned that

communications on Earth could be disrupted by another spectacular eruption on the surface of the Sun and that it might even hamper firefighting efforts in California.

"It's headed straight for us like a freight train," said John Kohl, a solar astrophysicist at the Harvard-Smithsonian Centre for Astrophysics in Cambridge, Massachusetts. "This is the real thing."

A second huge magnetic solar storm hit Earth on Friday, October 31, just a day after an earlier one hurtled into the planet in what one astronomer called an unprecedented one-two punch.

"It's like the Earth is looking right down the barrel of a giant gun pointed at us by the sun ... and it's taken two big shots at us," said John Kohl of the Harvard-Smithsonian Centre for Astrophysics in Massachusetts.

On Tuesday, November 4, the Sun cut loose with three severe flares and unleashed its largest recorded solar flare, capping 10 days of unprecedented activity.

Paal Brekke, deputy project manager of the SOHO spacecraft, was digesting the significance of the three additional outbursts on top of two back-to-back monster flares October 28 and 29.

"I think the last week will go into the history books as one of the most dramatic periods of solar activity we have seen in modern time," Brekke told SPACE.com.

"As far as I know there has been nothing like this before."

None of the latest eruptions were aimed directly at Earth, but glancing blows did occur.

The "perfect non storm" – October 27 – November 5

Everything that could go wrong in Southern California did – everything except rain to help put out the fires. "It's the perfect non-storm," said Greg Forbes, a meteorologist with the Weather Channel. Regardless how the fires start, what keeps them growing and devastating such huge areas, instead of being able to be stopped right away...is the perfect weather conditions all brought together at the same time. Meteorologist Forbes ran down the list: Temperatures in the Los Angeles Basin topped 90 degrees. Humidity has been as low as 10%. Swirling winds gust at speeds that frequently top 40 mph. "So those 3 factors – very warm, very low humidity, and windy conditions – that's perfect for rapid development and spread of fires," he said. And they have come together in an area filled with dry brush – and houses – almost waiting to burn.

On November 4, firefighters got a morale boost from a visit by President Bush, who surveyed some of the damage done by the blazes that have killed at least 22 people, destroyed about 3,600 homes and burned more than 740,000 acres of brush and timber.

"This will be the most expensive fire in California history, both in loss of property and the cost of fighting it," Dallas Jones, director of the state Office of Emergency Services, said.

***Important Note from Insurance Institute of America:**

Since 1990, insurers paid out $107.3 billion for natural disasters -- about $700 million per month many times more than in previous decades. This includes well-known events such as Hurricane Andrew and the Northridge earthquake, but also hundreds of smaller disasters associated with tropical storms, wildfires, hail, and snow. The extraordinary costs associated with these disasters is one of the primary reasons for the rising cost of homeowners insurance which is estimated to go up 9 percent in 2003, according to research conducted by the Institute.

Hurricane Isabel, together with the major tornadoes that hit the Midwest earlier in the year, makes 2003 a relatively bad year for catastrophe-related losses. According to the Insurance Services Office, insured catastrophe losses through August 2003 totaled $7.6 billion.

CHAPTER 3

THE MAJOR U.S. CATASTROPHES AND EVENTS IN PERSPECTIVE

The following information summarizes the record setting catastrophes or events that occurred in the 1990's and into the year 2003 when President George Herbert Walker Bush, President Bill Clinton or President George W. Bush or one of their top staff were applying pressure on Israel to give up her covenant land.

The major catastrophes or events begin with the Madrid Peace Conference of October 30, 1991 to November 4, 2003:

- The Three Largest Insurance Events in U.S. History
- Seven of the Ten Natural Disasters Ranked By FEMA Relief Costs
- Four of the Seven Costliest Hurricanes in U.S. History
- Three of the Four Largest Tornado Swarms in U.S. History

The odds against these catastrophes or events happening at the same time are astronomical. These are not mere coincidences. When the land of Israel is at risk so is the land of the nation promoting the "land for peace" talks.

The Major Catastrophes or Events During Bush, Sr., Clinton and George W. Bush Administrations

President George H.W. Bush's Presidential Term 1989 - 1993 (also shown in 2004 Dollars)

- Catastrophe #1: October 20, 1991: Oakland Firestorm – Estimated $2.5 (3.5) billion damage/costs
- Catastrophe #2: October 30-November 1, 1991: Perfect Storm
- Catastrophe #3: August 23-24, 1992: Hurricane Andrew - Estimated $27. 0 (35.6) billion damage/costs
- Event #4: October 1 to November 3, 1992: Perot Candidacy Helps Cost Bush Reelection

President Bill Clinton's Two Presidential Terms 1993-2001 (also shown in 2004 Dollars)

- Catastrophe #5: February 26, 1993: World Trade Center Bombing – Estimated Damage $750 million
- Catastrophe #6: March 12-15, 1993: Storm of the Century - Estimated $3.0–6.0 (3.8– 7.6) billion damage/costs
- Catastrophe #7: May–September 1993: Midwest Flooding - Estimated $21.0 (26.7) billion damage/costs
- Catastrophe #8: January 16, 1994: Northridge Earthquake - Estimated $15.3 (18.9) billion damage/costs
- Catastrophe #9: October 17-21, 1994: Texas Flooding - Estimated $1.0 (1.2) billion damage/costs
- Catastrophe #10: September 27 – October 5, 1995: Hurricane Opal - Estimated $3.0 (3.6) billion damage/costs
- Catastrophe #11: March 1-2, 1997: Mississippi and Ohio Valley Flooding and Tornadoes – Estimated $1.0 (1.1) billion damage/costs
- Catastrophe #12: April 1- May 14, 1997: Northern

Plains Flooding - Estimated $3.7 (4.1) billion damage/costs

- Event #13: July 1997 - October 1998. Foreign Financial Contagion - Loss of hundreds of billions of dollars and other currencies worldwide
- Catastrophe #14: January 4-9, 1998: Northeast Ice Storm - Estimated $1.4 (1.5) billion damage/costs
- Event #15: January 20-22, 1998: Lewinsky Scandal
- Catastrophe #16: January - February 1998: Southeast Severe Weather - Estimated $1.0 (1.1) billion damage/costs
- Event #17: May 1 - June 5, 1998: U.S. - China Technology Scandal
- Catastrophe #18: September 24–28, 1998: Hurricane Georges - Estimated $5.9 (6.5) billion damage/costs
- Catastrophe #19: October 17-22, 1998: Texas Flooding – Estimated $1. 0 (1.1) billion damage/costs
- Event #20: November 30, 1998: Mideast Donors Conference
- Event #21: December 11-19, 1998: Clinton Impeachment
- Event #22: March 24- June 10, 1999. Kosovo War Begins – War cost estimated at $3 billion
- Catastrophe #23: May 3-4, 1999. Oklahoma – Kansas Tornadoes – Estimated $1.6. (1.7) billion damage/costs
- Catastrophe #24: August 24- September 7, 1999: Hurricane Dennis – Estimated $1. 0 (1.1) billion damage/costs
- Catastrophe #25: September 7-17, 1999: Hurricane Floyd – Estimated $6. 0 (6.5) billion damage/costs
- Catastrophe and Events #26: October 14-15, 1999: Hurricane Irene, Hector Mine Earthquake, and a Major Stock market sell off costing billions of dollars
- Catastrophes and Events #27: January 1- July 1, 2000: Trillion dollar Nasdaq Losses and Billion Dollar Fires

and Drought
- Event #28: July-August, 2000: Drought/Heat Wave - Estimated $4. 0 (4.2) billion damage/costs
- Event #29: October 30 – December 13, 2000: U.S. and Israel Political Crisis

George W. Bush's Presidential Term 2001 to present (also shown in 2004 Dollars)
- Event #1: March 31- April 11, 2001: Bush's First International Crisis
- Event #2: May 21-24, 2001: Bush / Republican Party Loses Senate Majority
- Catastrophe #3: June 5 – 13, 2001: Tropical Storm Allison – Estimated $5. 0 (5.1) billion damage/costs
- Catastrophe #4: September 11, 2001: World Trade Center and Pentagon terror events - Total insurance claims – life insurance, workmen's compensation, property damage and business/rental interruption – was about $40 billion; the U.S. government committed an additional $20 billion for infrastructure structure repair in New York City and in Washington D.C.
- Catastrophe #5: October 2-31, 2001: Anthrax – Estimated cost to the U.S. Government was billions of dollars; by October 31, 2001, the U.S. Postal Service had purchased $2.5 billion in checking and sanitizing equipment, experienced an estimated $300 million in lost income, and had $60 million in damages
- Catastrophe #6: November 12, 2001: American Airlines Flight 587 Exploded over N.Y. City
- Catastrophe #7: April 30, 2002. Maryland's F-5 Tornado
- Catastrophe #8: June 8, 2002: Colorado's Hayman Fire – 135,000 Acres Burned
- Catastrophe #9: June 18-26, 2002: Arizona's Rodeo and Chediski Fires – 550,000 Acres Burned
- Catastrophe #10: October 2-31, 2002: Hurricane Lili -

Estimated costs $750 million, and Washington D.C. area snipers -

- Catastrophe #11: November 6-13, 2002: 88 Tornadoes - Estimated $200 million in damage/costs
- Catastrophe #12: December 5, 2002: North Carolina Ice Storm - Estimated $133 million damages/cost
- Catastrophe #13: February 1, 2003: Space Shuttle Columbia Disaster
- Catastrophe #14: May 1-10, 2003: 412 Midwest Tornadoes - Estimated $2.2 billion damage/costs
- Catastrophe #15: May 1 - August 17, 2003: The Nations Represented in the Quartet Experience record-setting heat, drought, rains, floods, blackouts and related deaths.
- Catastrophe #16: May 12, 2003: Riyadh Terror Bombing
- Catastrophe #17: July 15, 2003: Hurricane Claudette - Estimated $100 million in damage/costs
- Catastrophe #18: July 17 and July 24, 2003: Two-high profile suicides
- Catastrophe #19: September 6-19, 2003: Hurricane Isabel - Estimated $4.0 billion in damages
- Catastrophe and Events #20: October 24-November 4, 2003: Record solar flares and California wildfires - wildfires left an estimated $3 billion in damages

Top Ten Natural Disasters Ranked By FEMA

The following chart lists seven of the ten largest FEMA (Federal Emergency Management Agency) events occurred when President George Herbert Walker Bush, President Bill Clinton or President George W. Bush or one of their top staff were applying pressure on Israel to give up her covenant land.

The other three Top Ten events were also included with their corresponding event.

Event / FEMA Funding*	Date	Corresponding Event
Northridge 6.9 Earthquake Funding: $6.99 billion (CA)	Jan. 16, 1994	On January 15 in Geneva, Switzerland, Bill Clinton and Syria's Haffez Assad call on Israel to give up the Golan Heights (Northridge occurred within 24-hrs)
Hurricane Georges Funding: $2.333 billion (AL, FL, LA, MS, PR, VI)	Sept. 27-28, 1998	Sept. 28: Arafat and Netanyahu meet with Clinton at the White House. They agree to an Oct. 13 land-giveaway meeting. That afternoon Arafat addresses U.N. calling for a Palestinian state by May 1999, as Hurricane Georges was slamming into the Gulf Coast.
Hurricane Andrew Funding: $1.849 billion (FL, LA)	Aug. 23, 1992	The Madrid "land for peace" Conference convenes in Washington as Hurricane Andrew clobbers Florida and eventually Louisiana.
Hurricane Hugo Funding: $1.308 billion (NC, SC, PR, VI)	Sept. 22, 1989	On September 22, Hugo Slams into South Carolina as the U.S. Supreme Court was hearing the "Hodgson vs. Minnesota" abortion case. Bush Administration didn't make oral statements by the Friday, Sept 22, deadline that could have led to the overturning of Roe vs. Wade case.
Midwest Floods Funding: $1.141 billion (IL, IA, KS, MN, MO, NE, ND, SD, WI)	June 27, 1993	USA Today reported the skies opened up from June 19-21, filling the tributaries in the Mid Western U.S. The Missouri and Mississippi overflow their banks on national Gay Pride

		Day, June 27. This is the largest flood in U.S. history.
Hurricane Floyd Funding: $1.085 billion (CT, DE, FL, ME, MD, NH, NJ, NY, NC, PA, SC, VT, VA)	Sept. 13-16, 1999	On September 13, U.S. Secretary of State Madeleine Albright meets in Israel with Israeli and Palestinian foreign ministers to work on the final status of Israel's land giveaway; pertaining to the borders of a Palestinian state, the status of Jerusalem and the Jewish settlements.
Tropical Storm Allison $879.5 million (FL, LA, MS, PA, TX)	June 8-9, 2001	CIA Director George Tenet meets with Israeli and Palestinian leaders in Ramallah to forge a security agreement. As they sit down Allison hits Houston and stays in place for 24 hrs, 28 inches of rain falling. George Bush Intercontinental Airport was closed. Allison continues along southern U.S. Coast and works its way up the East coast, hitting Pennsylvania before heading east towards the ocean.
Loma Prieta 7.1 Earthquake Funding: $865.5 million (CA)	October, 17, 1989	On October 15, 50,000 people attended a San Francisco "Abortion Rights Rally." Senators Diane Feinstein and Barbara Boxer are in attendance. The October 17 earthquake occurs during a nationally televised World Series game at San Francisco's Candlestick Park.

Red River Valley Floods Funding: $734.0 million (MN, ND, SD)	April 5 to May 7, 1997	The freak blizzard that hit the valley April 5 altered all the equations. Forecasters depend on a network of river gauges, but ice jams and unprecedented flows upstream forced huge volumes of water out of normal channels and around the gauges. At the same time Netanyahu is under pressure by Clinton to stop construction in Jerusalem. They meet on April 7 at the White House to discuss the Jerusalem apartment construction and the peace process. Pressure on Israel subsides after the meeting. The flood crest from the Red River empties into Lake Winnipeg May 8. The United Nations General Assembly resumes on May 7, its tenth emergency special session to consider an agenda item on "illegal Israeli actions in Occupied East Jerusalem and the rest of the Occupied Palestinian Territory," a spokesman for the President of the 189-member body announced.
Hurricane Fran Funding: $621.2 million (MD, NC, PA, VA, WV)	Sept. 5, 1996	On September 5 the U.S. Senate debates the Defense of Marriage Act. The act is to disallow same-sex marriages. It eventually passes. Fran hits North Carolina at the very same day of the debate in the Senate.

*Amount obligated from the President's Disaster Relief Fund for FEMA's assistance programs, hazard mitigation grants, federal mission assignments, contractual services and administrative costs as of February 28, 2002. Figures do not include funding provided by other participating federal agencies, such as the disaster loan programs of the Small Business Administration and the Agriculture Department's Farm Service Agency. Note: Funding amounts are stated in current dollars.

Three Largest Insurance Events in U.S. History

The three largest insurance claims in U.S. history all have direct connection to American involvement in the Middle East peace talks when Israel was being pressured to give up God's covenant land in exchange for peace.

On the front page of its Business Section on October 21, 2001, the *Washington Post* was "Putting a Price on 'What Ifs'." A story, which contained the dollar amounts, along with accompanying photos, of these three insurance events.

These three claims are listed below followed by the connection to the ongoing Middle East "peace process," in which the issue of "land for peace" was a key factor.

- Terrorist Attacks at the World Trade Center and Pentagon: $30-$50 billion. These September 11 events happened at the same time that the Bush Administration was putting the final touches on its Middle East initiative, which included recognition of a Palestinian state, endorsement of the Mitchell Plan, and position statements about Palestinian refugees and the status of Jerusalem. This initiative was to be shared with the Saudi Ambassador to the United Nations on Sept. 13, followed by a formal presentation to the UN General Assembly by Secretary of State Colin Powell on September 24.
- Hurricane Andrew: $19.6 billion. This event

happened on August 23, 1992, the same day that the Madrid Peace Conference re-convened in Washington to discuss the Israeli-Palestinian crisis and "land for peace" issues.

- Northridge Earthquake: $16.2 billion. This event happened on January 16, 1994, within 24 hours of President Bill Clinton and Syria's President Haffez el-Assad's call for Israel to give up the Golan Heights to Syria at a public meeting in Geneva.

Billion Dollar Hurricanes

Four of the seven costliest hurricanes in U.S. history all have a direct tie-in to U.S. - Israeli peace efforts. The costs were all calculated using 2002 dollars.

Hurricane # 1
Andrew, 1992, $26.5 billion - The sixth round of Madrid conference talks begin in Washington D.C.

Hurricane Andrew was the most destructive United States hurricane of record. It blasted its way across south Florida on August 24, 1992. NOAA's National Hurricane Center had a peak gust of 164 mph--measured 130 feet above the ground--while a 177 mph gust was measured at a private home.

Andrew caused 23 deaths in the United States and three more in the Bahamas. The hurricane caused $26.5 billion in damage in the United States, of which $1 billion occurred in Louisiana and the rest in south Florida. The vast majority of the damage in Florida was due to the winds. (NOAA)

Hurricane #2
Isabel, 2003, $4 billion - President George W. Bush welcomes King Abdullah II of Jordan to Camp David. They meet to strategize on how to restart the stalled Road Map.

The Category 2 hurricane made landfall in eastern

North Carolina, causing considerable storm surge damage along the coasts of NC, VA, and MD, with wind damage and some flooding due to 4-12 inch rains in NC, VA, MD, DE, WV, NJ, NY, and PA. North Carolina, Virginia and Maryland took the brunt of Hurricane Isabel's intensity.

Within 72-hours of Isabel over one million people were still without power in the Washington D.C. metro area. Moreover, over one million homes were told to boil their water due to contamination.

Hurricane # 3
Georges, 1998, $3.2 billion - Israeli Foreign Minister and Arafat's Deputy work out a final-status deal on Israel's land

From September 21-30, 1998, Hurricane Georges left a trail of destruction in the Caribbean region and across the southern U.S. Gulf coast. More than 600 people were killed as the storm pushed its way across the islands of the Caribbean.

Georges made landfall during mid-morning of the 25th in Key West, Florida. After moving away from Key West, Georges turned more to the northwest, then north-northwest, and gradually slowed down on the 26th and 27th. The hurricane made landfall near Biloxi, Mississippi on the morning of the 28th with estimated maximum sustained one-minute winds of 90 knots. After landfall, the system meandered around southern Mississippi and was downgraded to a tropical storm on the afternoon of the 28th.

Extreme flooding was reported with rainfall amounts in excess of 20 to possibly 30 inches along portions of the southern U.S. Gulf coast. Mobile, Alabama received 13.0 inches of rain from the storm, which boosted the monthly total to 23.0 inches, breaking the September record of 16 inches set 100 years ago. The highest individual storm total reported was in Munson, Florida, which reported 25.0 inches of rain from Georges. (NOAA)

Hurricane # 4
Floyd, 1999, $2.5 billion - Israelis and Palestinians finalizing final status language

Floyd brought flooding rains, high winds and rough seas along a good portion of the Atlantic seaboard from the 14th through the 18th of September 1999. The greatest damages were along the eastern Carolinas northeast into New Jersey, and adjacent areas northeastward along the east coast into Maine. Several states had numerous counties declared disaster areas. Flooding caused major problems across the region, and at least 77 deaths have been reported.

Floyd's large size was a greater problem than its winds, as the heavy rainfall covered a larger area and lasted longer than with a typical category 2 hurricane. Approximately 2.6 million people evacuated their homes in Florida, Georgia, and the Carolinas--the largest peacetime evacuation in U.S. history. Ten states were declared major disaster areas as a result of Floyd, including Connecticut, Delaware, Florida, Maryland, New Jersey, New York, North Carolina, Pennsylvania, South Carolina and Virginia. (NOAA) (Source: Insurance Information Institute -- http://www.iii.org)

Billion Dollar U.S. Weather Disasters 1980 - 2003
http://www1.ncdc.noaa.gov/pub/data/special/billionz-2003.pdf
The Deadliest, Costliest, And Most Intense United States Hurricanes From 1900 To 2000 (Not adjusted for inflation)
http://www.nhc.noaa.gov/pastcost.shtml

Largest Tornado Outbreaks in U.S. History

Three out of the four largest tornado outbreaks (swarms) in U.S. history coincided with President Bill Clinton or President George W. Bush or one of their top officials meetings on Israel's covenant land.

Super cells with enormous size and power spawned the following major record-breaking tornadoes.

Tornado Outbreak # 1
May 3, 1999 - Major Tornado Swarm and 316 MPH Record Wind Speed - 85 Tornadoes

The Powerful Super Tornado occurred on the day that Yasser Arafat was scheduled to declare a Palestinian state with Jerusalem as the capital. This was the most powerful tornado storm system ever to hit the United States. It swept across Oklahoma and Kansas and the winds were clocked at 316 mph -- the fastest wind speed ever recorded. Over 70 tornadoes touched down in north Texas, central Oklahoma and southern Kansas producing $1.2 billion in damage.

Arafat's declaration was postponed from May 3 until December 1999, at the request of President Clinton. The Clinton letter to Arafat encouraged him in his "aspirations for his own land." Clinton also wrote that the Palestinians have a right to "determine their own future on their own land" and that they deserve to "live free, today, tomorrow and forever."

Tornado Outbreak # 2
November 10-11, 2002 - 88 Tornadoes

The weekend of November 10-11, 2002 we heard about and observed enormous storms and tornadoes that hit thirteen U.S. states. MSNBC reported that 35 people in five states were killed and 200 others injured. In Tennessee alone, 100 homes were destroyed and 1,000 damaged. AP reported there were 88 tornadoes. There were also major thunderstorms reported from the Gulf Coast to the Great Lakes.

On Sunday, November 10, 2002, U.S. Deputy Assistant Secretary of State David Satterfield was on his way to Israel to apply pressure on Israel to complete their work and comments on the Quartet's "Road Map" to peace. He had numerous meetings on Monday and Tuesday with Israeli officials. He also met Sunday with Palestinians officials.

Tornado Outbreak # 3
May 1-10, 2003 - 412 Tornadoes

The 412 tornadoes during the first 10 days of May were the most since the National Oceanic and Atmospheric Administration began record keeping in 1950. The previous record for the first 10 days of May was 177 tornadoes set in 1999. More than 300 counties affecting 19 states suffered losses and more than 40 deaths were blamed on the storms. Boston based AIR Worldwide, which uses a computer modeling program to estimate insured losses from catastrophes, has put the damages at $2.2 billion.

The Quartet's Road Map was delivered to Israeli and Palestinian officials on April 30, 2003.

On Saturday, May 3, U.S. Secretary of State Colin told Syrian President Bashar Assad that the U.S. commitment to Middle East peace "would include Syria and Lebanon and would include the Golan Heights," a particularly sensitive issue for Syria.

On Sunday, May 4, Secretary Powell announced he would visit Israel on Saturday, May 10, for talks about implementing the Road Map peace plan.

On Monday, May 5, U.S. Middle East envoy William Burns met with Palestinian Authority Prime Minister Mahmoud Abbas in the West Bank city of Ramallah. He stated that the Palestinians must carry out a decisive fight against terrorism and that the Israelis must halt settlement activity. Burns also bashed Fundamental Christians and Orthodox Jews for opposing the Road Map in a meeting with Peace Now activists in Jerusalem.

Powell was in Israel May 10-11, 2003, to meet with Israeli and Palestinian officials, Ariel Sharon and Mahmoud Abbas to push the Road Map ahead.

CHAPTER 4

The Washington Post

HOME EDITION

Wednesday, July 30, 2003

Bush Urges Israelis to Help Revitalize Peace Process

President Bush and Israeli Prime Minister Ariel Sharon meet at the White House, the eighth visit there by Sharon in the Bush presidency. In Oval Office session, Bush pressed Sharon to support Palestinian counterpart Mahmoud Abbas. Story, Page A12.

Bush Won't Release Classified 9/11 Report

Saudi Foreign Minister Calls Accusations an 'Outrage'

Memo Warns Of New Plots To Hijack Jets

EIGHT DISRUPTIVE PERIODS

In late August and early September 2001, President George W. Bush made a conscientious attempt to appease an angry Crown Prince Abdullah of Saudi Arabia, who felt he [Bush] was favoring Israel. President Bush worked with Prince Bandar the Saudi Ambassador to the U.S., U.S. Secretary State Colin Powell and U.S. Ambassador to Israel Daniel Kurtzer to develop a comprehensive Bush Middle East peace plan that was to be approved by Crown Prince Abdullah. Powell was to deliver the Bush plan to the UN General Assembly on September 24, 2001. The plan was a way to divide Israel in return for "peace and security" guarantees for Israel and to provide for a Palestinian state. The plan's completion and presentation were disrupted by the 9-11-2001 terror events, which occurred at the World Trade Center and at the Pentagon. For a brief moment the God of Israel had lifted his restraining hand of protection over America as evil people attacked America. That moment was also the beginning of the very costly and complex war on terror. Furthermore, life in America had been forever changed.

In this book, we are not in any way condemning President Bush for his peace efforts, but only emphasizing the dire consequences for those who have and will continue to attempt to divide Israel and touch the "apple of God's eye." We have already provided 48 major catastrophes and events that have taken place when Israel's land is at risk, in this chapter you will read about the periods of disruption that occur when President Bush called for a Palestinian state or applied pressure on Israel to comply with his peace vision. Unbeknown to President Bush and the leaders of the Quartet (the UN, the EU and Russia) who are now actively involved in the Middle East peace process, they are on a direct collision course with God over the covenant land of Israel.

In this chapter and next you will read about the "eight periods of disruption"that immediately followed President Bush major statements about his favoring a Palestinian state and/or increasing his efforts in the dividing of the nation of Israel.

Below, Bob Kaiser Associate Editor of the *Washington Post* wrote an extremely insightful article to what was transpiring with President Bush and his administration the seventeen days prior to the 9-11 terror events. He co-authored his work with David Ottoway in a three-part article that was published in the *Washington Post* on February 10,11, and 12, 2002.

Bob Kaieser and David Ottoway *Washington Post*

On August 24, 2001, Crown Prince Abdullah ibn Abdulaziz, the leader of Saudi Arabia, was in his palace in Riyadh watching President Bush's televised news conference in Texas when Bush was asked about the Israeli-Palestinian "peace process," which had again been undermined by a new round of violence.

"The Israelis will not negotiate under terrorist threat, simple as that," Bush said. "And if the Palestinians are interested in a dialogue, then I strongly urge Mr. Arafat to put 100 percent effort into . . . stopping the terrorist activity. And I believe he can do a better job of doing that."

Abdullah interpreted the president's remarks as absolving Israel and blaming Yasser Arafat, the Palestinian leader, for worsening conditions, according to a senior Saudi official. An impulsive, emotional man, Abdullah "just went bananas," the same official said. The crown prince picked up the telephone and called his ambassador to the United States, Prince Bandar bin Sultan, who was watching the same news conference at his palatial residence in Aspen, Colorado.

Abdullah said he wanted Bandar to see Bush at once and deliver a harsh message, the culmination of months of tension between Saudi Arabia and the new Bush administration. The message delivered by Bandar to national security adviser Condoleezza Rice and Secretary of State Colin L. Powell was summarized by a senior Saudi official in these terms:

"We believe there has been a strategic decision by the United States that its national interest in the Middle East is 100-percent based on [Israeli Prime Minister Ariel] Sharon." This was America's right, the message continued, but Saudi Arabia could not accept the decision. "Starting from today, you're from Uruguay, as they say. You [Americans] go your way, I [Saudi Arabia] go my way. From now on, we will protect our national interests, regardless of where America's interests lie in the region."

Bandar was instructed to cut off further discussion between the two countries. The time had come to "get busy rearranging our lives in the Middle East."

Bandar's message was a shock to the Bush administration. As had often happened in the past, these two countries – intimate strangers in many respects – had not really been hearing each other. But over the next two days, the United States went to extraordinary lengths to try to repair the relationship, its closest with any Arab country, finally satisfying the Saudis with a personal letter to Abdullah from the president himself.

Two Disparate Nations

Not really hearing each other has long helped both countries sustain the idea that they are close allies, and not an odd couple. In fact, they could hardly be more different. Saudi Arabia is an Islamic monarchy ruled secretively by one family, the huge Saud clan, in collaboration with Islamic fundamentalists; it has neither free media nor transparent legal institutions, nor any guarantees of human or civil rights.

By not acknowledging their fundamental differences, neither country has had to confront them. Their relations have been a diplomatic version of "don't ask, don't tell," a phrase Bandar said might have been inspired by a verse from the Koran: "Ask not about things which, if made plain to you, may cause you trouble."

What has been plain to officials of both countries is their self-interest. Saudi Arabia wants, and has always received, American protection. The United States needs, and has nearly always received, Saudi oil. What can cause trouble is the realization that these two allies have very little in common beyond security and oil.

"Have we [the United States and Saudi Arabia] understood each other particularly well?" asked Brent Scowcroft, national security adviser to the first President Bush. "Probably not. And I think, in a sense, we probably avoid talking about the things that are the real problems between us because it's a very polite relationship. We don't get all that much below the surface."

Oil and security did provide the basis for a fruitful relationship from the mid-1970s through the Persian Gulf War in 1991. With U.S. backing, Saudi Arabia transformed itself from a medieval desert kingdom to a modern and wealthy state. Saudi money greased the relationship and supported U.S. policy goals from Afghanistan to Nicaragua, while Saudi leaders often defended U.S. interests in the councils of Arab states.

September 11 and its aftermath confronted Americans with the impolite fact that their principal Arab ally is a theocratic monarchy that has supported Islamic fundamentalism throughout the Muslim world. Even more upsetting, Osama bin Laden and 15 of the terrorists who crashed planes into the Pentagon and the World Trade Center were Saudis. These discoveries prompted an angry American reaction that alarmed the Saudis and shook their confidence in their most important diplomatic relationship.

But as Abdullah's own anger in August demonstrated, the relationship was coming under serious strain even before September 11. After the Cold War and the Gulf War, "a lot of common interest disappeared," said Chas. W. Freeman Jr., a former

U.S. ambassador to Saudi Arabia.

Sharp differences had already emerged about how to deal with Iraq and Iran – two of the three countries in Bush's "axis of evil" and both neighbors of Saudi Arabia. Potentially more threatening have been starkly differing views over how to deal with Israel and Arafat, which caused the previously unreported incident in August. Saudis have begun to question the continued efficacy of the U.S. military presence in their country. Altogether, points of disagreement now threaten to overwhelm the two countries' shared interests.

These articles will explore the evolution of this "special relationship" and examine its uncertain future as Bush presses the U.S. war on terrorism beyond Afghanistan. They are based on official documents and more than 60 interviews with U.S. officials and senior Saudi analysts and officials, many of whom insisted on anonymity. Senior U.S. officials refused to discuss the August episode or the future of Saudi-U.S. relations, apparently because of the extreme sensitivity of the relationship. "We've decided we won't be participating in these articles," said Sean McCormack, spokesman for the National Security Council.

High Expectations

The year 2001 began with a sense of hope for the Saudis. The new U.S. president was the son of the most popular American in Saudi Arabia, George H. W. Bush, a national hero for his role in protecting the kingdom from Iraq's Saddam Hussein in 1990-91. Saudis, who know about dynasties, had high expectations for the son.

Those expectations turned into bitter disappointment as the year progressed and Israeli-

Palestinian relations continued to deteriorate. Throughout the Arab world, frustration grew with the United States for standing silently on the sidelines as the violence intensified. Abdullah, Saudi Arabia's de facto ruler because of the prolonged incapacitation of King Fahd, his half-brother, became increasingly angry, according to Saudi sources.

The Americans realized that Abdullah was upset and tried repeatedly to calm him, U.S. officials said. Bush invited him to visit Washington, Camp David, his ranch in Crawford, even the Franklin D. Roosevelt Library in Hyde Park, N.Y. – a venue proposed because Roosevelt and Abdullah's father, King Abdulaziz, known also as ibn Saud, established the modern Saudi-American relationship in a meeting onboard a ship on the Great Bitter Lake in the Suez Canal in 1945. The president's father telephoned Abdullah to try to assure the crown prince that the new president's "heart was in the right place." But Abdullah rebuffed all of these advances.

Making Frustrations Clear

Palestine, and then Israel, had been a sensitive subject in Saudi-U.S. relations since Roosevelt's first contacts with ibn Saud. Israel's battlefield successes provoked a Saudi-led oil embargo against the United States in 1973. After Ariel Sharon was elected Israel's prime minister in February 2001, the Saudis pressed the United States repeatedly to restrain Sharon and bring him back to the negotiating table.

In a series of letters to Bush and in other messages to Washington, Abdullah made his frustrations clear. "Don't they see what is happening to

Palestinian children, women and the elderly?" Abdullah asked in an interview with the Financial Times in June. He was seeing this himself, his associates said, on television almost every night. Official Saudi television showed extensive film clips of the fighting and of Israel's forceful military actions in nearly every news broadcast.

But the Bush administration did not respond, and did not take action to stop the violence. The new administration sought to distance itself from the policy of Bush's predecessor, Bill Clinton, who made the last serious effort to negotiate an Israeli-Palestinian peace agreement in his final weeks in office. The Bush administration told the Israelis and the Palestinians that if they wanted to resume the peace talks, they should do so themselves.

In July, the Saudis issued a statement in the name of King Fahd, warning that Israel's "systematic actions" against the Palestinians risked plunging the Middle East "into a dangerous phase." Two weeks later, Vice President Cheney gave an interview that appeared to endorse Israel's preemptive attacks against Palestinians whom Israel suspected of terrorism, further upsetting the Saudis.

On August 9, the Saudi ambassador to Britain, Ghazi Qussaibi, published an article in Al Hayat, a London-based Arabic newspaper, that ridiculed Bush as a know-nothing governed by "complexes" – first of all, a desire to avoid looking like his father or his predecessor. "In a few months, this man created enemies for America to an extent making him worthy of a new prize, to be called the prize for transforming friends into adversaries, effortlessly," wrote Qussaibi. Saudi diplomats learned that Bush saw an account of this article and that he was not amused.

On the night of August 23, Israeli tanks made their deepest incursion yet into the West Bank, into the town of Hebron, marking a new escalation of the fighting. On the same day, according to two Saudi officials, Abdullah saw news footage from the West Bank of an Israeli soldier holding a Palestinian woman to the ground by putting his boot on her head. "Abdullah saw that and he went berserk," one senior Saudi recounted. "A woman being beaten by a man – he just felt this is the ultimate insult."

Abdullah responded by calling Bandar, his unusual ambassador in Washington. Bandar is the son of Prince Sultan, the Saudi defense minister and Abdullah's half-brother. Bandar's mother was a servant, and Sultan did not recognize him as a legitimate son until he was a teenager. After training as a pilot, Bandar became the Saudi Air Force's one-man acrobatic team – its version of the Blue Angels. He was then assigned to Washington as a military attaché, lobbying Congress to approve the sale of F-5 fighter jets to Saudi Arabia and learning about U.S. politics. He was just 34 when King Fahd, his uncle and mentor, named him ambassador to the United States in 1983.

Over the years, Bandar came to personally embody the Saudi-American relationship. His gregarious charm and gift for the big gesture won him easy access to high-level officials, and he became a close personal friend of the first President Bush, invited to family events at the Bush compound in Kennebunkport, Maine. The dean of the diplomatic corps by virtue of his long assignment in Washington, Bandar is the only ambassador who has his own State Department security detail – granted to him because of "threats" and his status as a prince, according to a State Department spokesman. But in the 1990s, held at arm's length by the Clinton administration, he seemed to lose his fire for the job. "I was getting completely bored," Bandar acknowledged.

When Abdullah telephoned that day in August, Bandar was in Aspen at the vast compound he built there, appraised at $55 million by the local tax collector. The 70,000-square-foot main house has 15 bedrooms and 16 baths. Bandar also has a house overlooking the Potomac in McLean, a palace in Saudi Arabia and a country estate in the English countryside.

Bandar was out when the crown prince called, and by the time he got home, according to a Saudi official, it was the middle of the night in Riyadh, the Saudi capital – too late to talk with Abdullah. The next morning, after the Bush news conference, Abdullah called again to dispatch him with his message.

The Saudi embassy thought there might be a U.S. answer within four or five days, but it came in only 36 hours. "We were told there was an answer ready to go back [to Abdullah] that answers every point," one senior official said. Bandar picked up the letter and took it personally to the crown prince in Riyadh.

For the Saudis, Bush's letter was "groundbreaking ... Things in it had never been put in writing," one Saudi official said. According to Saudi accounts, Bush outlined an even-handed approach to settling the Arab-Israeli dispute that differed considerably from Sharon's positions on the peace process. One Saudi official said this was a key element: a U.S. vision of a peace settlement that was acceptable to the Saudis, and that differed from any Israeli plan.

Bush's letter, according to Saudi officials, endorsed the idea of a viable Palestinian state on the West Bank and Gaza Strip. He expressed a willingness to begin participating more actively in the peace process. Altogether, said Adel Jubeir, a foreign policy adviser to Abdullah, "where he stood was not that much different from where Clinton stood when he left office."

A particularly important passage in Bush's businesslike, two-page letter, Saudi officials said, was his response to Abdullah's complaints about the ways Israelis were treating Palestinians in the occupied territories. In the message to Bush that was conveyed by Bandar, the crown prince said, according to a Saudi official's account: "I reject this extraordinary, un-American bias whereby the blood of an Israeli child is more expensive and holy than the blood of a Palestinian child. I reject people who say when you kill a Palestinian, it is defense; when a Palestinian kills an Israeli, it's a terrorist act." He also referred to the scene he saw on television of the Israeli soldier putting his boot on the head of a Palestinian woman.

In reply, a Saudi official recounted, Bush said he believes the blood of innocent people is the same – Palestinian, Israeli, Jewish, Christian or Muslim. He rejected the humiliation of individuals, which Abdullah took as a response to his comment about the Israeli soldier's boot. "Suddenly, what came through in that letter was the humane part of George W.," said a senior Saudi official.

It is impossible to say what might have happened if Bush had not so quickly mollified the crown prince at the end of August. According to well-placed sources, the Saudis had conveyed to the United States their intention to convene an emergency summit meeting of Arab leaders to offer full support to the Palestinians. They alluded to the possibility of ending all law enforcement and intelligence cooperation with the United States – of which there had been a great deal. And they signaled their intention to reconsider the Saudi-U.S. military relationship.

Abdullah made this last threat virtually explicit. On August 24, the Saudi chief of staff, Gen. Salih Ali bin Muhayya, arrived in Washington for a high-level review of Saudi-U.S. military collaboration. On the 25th, when he spoke to Bandar by telephone, Abdullah ordered that Salih return immediately to Riyadh, without meeting any Americans. He also ordered a delegation of about 40 senior Saudi officers who were about to leave for Washington to get off their plane. The annual review of military relations was canceled.

"You don't cancel visits like this on the day before," said a senior adviser to the crown prince. "It was a big, big event, and we downplayed it completely." In fact, the cancellation received no public attention at all. But it shocked the Pentagon, according to a senior Defense Department official who had expected to join the meetings with the Saudis.

Bush's letter transformed his reputation in the small circle of Saudis who run their country. Before the letter, these people had come to the conclusion that Bush was a lightweight – "goofy," as one of them put it. After the letter, "he was strong, judicious, deliberate. . . . His reputation went from rock bottom to sky high."

Abdullah decided to share his correspondence with Bush – his message delivered by Bandar, which filled 25 pages, and Bush's two-page reply – with other Arab leaders, including the presidents of Egypt and Syria and the king of Jordan. He summoned Arafat, who was in South Africa, to Riyadh to read it.

According to Saudi officials, they extracted from Arafat a written pledge to satisfy Bush's demands for what Arafat had to do to revive the peace talks, and they sent it back to Washington with their own enthusiastic reply to Bush's letter. The crown prince sent Bandar back to Washington to try to convert the letter into policy and action, first by urging the president to say in public what he had told the Saudis in his letter.

Bandar was convinced that Bush could not have adopted the positions outlined in his letter in just 36 hours. "This must have been something . . . that the administration was thinking about, that they just didn't share with everybody [but] were waiting for the right time," he said. But before he could pursue the matter, he needed to patch things up with U.S. officials. A knowledgeable source quoted American officials as telling Bandar when he returned to Washington, "Hey, you guys scared us." And Bandar reportedly replied: "The hell with you – we scared ourselves."

On Friday, September 7, Bandar told U.S. officials that Saudi Arabia was "pleased and grateful," as one official put it, to discover that it had misread the Bush administration's attitude toward the Middle East. Saudi Arabia would continue to try to protect U.S. interests, he promised. The Americans indicated a willingness to pursue a new Mideast initiative immediately, Saudi officials said – a sharp departure from the administration's policy for seven months.

Over the weekend of September 8 and 9, officials of the two countries discussed what should happen next: a speech by Bush, or by Powell, or perhaps both? There was also discussion of a Bush-Arafat meeting at the United Nations later in September, an important point for the Saudis, who were pleased that Bush seemed willing to have the meeting. Powell left for a previously scheduled trip to Latin America on Monday, September 10, with these decisions still pending.

Even without the final decisions, Bandar was euphoric. After months in what he called "a yellow mood" over the deteriorating situation in the Middle East, "suddenly I felt the same feeling I had as we were going to Madrid [to the peace conference that followed the Gulf War in 1991], that we really were going to have a major initiative here that could save all of us from ourselves – mostly – and from each other."

So "the happiest man in the world that night, on Monday night, was Bandar bin Sultan. I was in the [indoor] swimming pool [of the McLean residence], smoking a cigar. I gave myself a day off because I worked the whole weekend. I had been to Saudi Arabia . . . out with the [Bush] response, back with our response. I worked on the weekend up to 3 o'clock, 4 o'clock in the morning. . . . I worked all Monday. And I said to my office, Tuesday I'm taking the day off."

Tuesday was September 11. Instead of a day off, Bandar got the worst crisis of his career. Dreams of a new Mideast peace initiative evaporated. The realization that most of the hijackers were Saudis "fell on me ... like the whole house collapsed over my head," Bandar said later. He couldn't imagine a way to "do more damage or worse damage to Islam or to Saudi Arabia."[1]

A Day Which Will Live In Infamy - September 11, 2001

It was a date which will live in infamy – Sept. 11, 2001, the day terrorist hijackers sent four airliners to devastating crashes into New York's World Trade Center, the Pentagon and the woods of rural Pennsylvania. It was a day of terror and fear, courage and heroism.

On 9-10-2001, President George W. Bush was completing the most comprehensive Middle East peace plan ever to be drafted, which was to call for a Palestinian state. No other American President had ever publicly stated their approval of a Palestinian state. President Bush was attempting to appease Crown Prince Abdullah of Saudi Arabia who believed Bush was favoring Israel in the Middle East peace process. On 9-11-2001, instead of finishing the work on his Middle East plan, he was confronted with the largest terror event in American history. Furthermore, he began his new role as a comforter to America and the War President.

One of Merriam- Webster's definition for appease is: to buy off (an aggressor) by concessions usually at the sacrifice of principles.

The God of Israel will not allow His covenant land and His nation to be divided with the enemies of Israel. The people who continue to appease the enemies of Israel will continue to pay a very dear price. No one is excluded.

America Under Attack the 9-11-2001 Timeline

8:45 a.m. (all times are EDT): A hijacked passenger jet, American Airlines Flight 11 out of Boston, Massachusetts, crashes into the north tower of the World Trade Center, tearing a gaping hole in the building and setting it afire.

9:03 a.m.: A second hijacked airliner, United Airlines

Flight 175 from Boston, crashes into the south tower of the World Trade Center and explodes. Both buildings are burning.

9:17 a.m.: The Federal Aviation Administration shuts down all New York City area airports.

9:21 a.m.: The Port Authority of New York and New Jersey orders all bridges and tunnels in the New York area closed.

9:30 a.m.: President Bush, speaking in Sarasota, Florida, says the country has suffered an "apparent terrorist attack."

9:40 a.m.: The FAA halts all flight operations at U.S. airports, the first time in U.S. history that air traffic nationwide has been halted.

9:43 a.m.: American Airlines Flight 77 crashes into the Pentagon, sending up a huge plume of smoke. Evacuation begins immediately.

9:45 a.m.: The White House evacuates.

9:57 a.m.: Bush departs from Florida.

10:05 a.m.: The south tower of the World Trade Center collapses, plummeting into the streets below. A massive cloud of dust and debris forms and slowly drifts away from the building.

10:08 a.m.: Secret Service agents armed with automatic rifles are deployed into Lafayette Park across from the White House.

10:10 a.m.: A portion of the Pentagon collapses.

10:10 a.m.: United Airlines Flight 93, also hijacked, crashes in Somerset County, Pennsylvania, southeast of Pittsburgh.

10:13 a.m.: The United Nations building evacuates, including 4,700 people from the headquarters building and 7,000 total from UNICEF and UN development programs.

10:22 a.m.: In Washington, the State and Justice departments are evacuated, along with the World Bank.

10:24 a.m.: The FAA reports that all inbound transatlantic aircraft flying into the United States are being diverted to Canada.

10:28 a.m.: The World Trade Center's north tower collapses from the top down as if it were being peeled apart, releasing a tremendous cloud of debris and smoke.

10:45 a.m.: All federal office buildings in Washington are evacuated.

Remarks by the President After Two Planes Crash Into World Trade Center Emma Booker Elementary School - Sarasota, Florida

THE PRESIDENT: Ladies and gentlemen, this is a difficult moment for America. I, unfortunately, will be going back to Washington after my remarks. Secretary Rod Paige and the Lt. Governor will take the podium and discuss education. I do want to thank the folks here at Booker Elementary School for their hospitality.

Today we've had a national tragedy. Two airplanes have crashed into the World Trade Center in an apparent terrorist attack on our country. I have spoken to the Vice President, to the Governor of New York, to the Director of the FBI, and have ordered that the full resources of the federal government go to help the victims and their families, and to conduct a full-scale investigation to hunt down and to find those folks who committed this act.

Terrorism against our nation will not stand.

And now if you would join me in a moment of silence. May God bless the victims, their families, and America. Thank you very much.

Statement by the President in His Address to the Nation – September 11, 2001

THE PRESIDENT: Good evening. Today, our fellow citizens, our way of life, our very freedom came under attack in a series of deliberate and deadly terrorist acts. The victims were in airplanes, or in their offices; secretaries, businessmen and women, military and federal workers; moms and dads, friends and neighbors. Thousands of lives were suddenly ended by evil, despicable acts of terror.

The pictures of airplanes flying into buildings, fires burning, huge structures collapsing, have filled us with disbelief, terrible sadness, and a quiet, unyielding anger. These acts of mass murder were intended to frighten our nation into chaos and retreat. But they have failed; our country is strong.

A great people has been moved to defend a great nation. Terrorist attacks can shake the foundations of our biggest buildings, but they cannot touch the foundation of America. These acts shattered steel, but they cannot dent the steel of American resolve.

America was targeted for attack because we're the brightest beacon for freedom and opportunity in the world. And no one will keep that light from shining.

Today, our nation saw evil, the very worst of human nature. And we responded with the best of America – with the daring of our rescue workers, with the caring for strangers and neighbors who came to give blood and help in any way they could.

Immediately following the first attack, I implemented our government's emergency response plans. Our military is powerful, and it's prepared. Our emergency teams are working in New York City and Washington, D.C. to help with local rescue efforts.

Our first priority is to get help to those who

have been injured, and to take every precaution to protect our citizens at home and around the world from further attacks.

The functions of our government continue without interruption. Federal agencies in Washington which had to be evacuated today are reopening for essential personnel tonight, and will be open for business tomorrow. Our financial institutions remain strong, and the American economy will be open for business, as well.

The search is underway for those who are behind these evil acts. I've directed the full resources of our intelligence and law enforcement communities to find those responsible and to bring them to justice. We will make no distinction between the terrorists who committed these acts and those who harbor them.

I appreciate so very much the members of Congress who have joined me in strongly condemning these attacks. And on behalf of the American people, I thank the many world leaders who have called to offer their condolences and assistance.

America and our friends and allies join with all those who want peace and security in the world, and we stand together to win the war against terrorism. Tonight, I ask for your prayers for all those who grieve, for the children whose worlds have been shattered, for all whose sense of safety and security has been threatened. And I pray they will be comforted by a power greater than any of us, spoken through the ages in Psalm 23: "Even though I walk through the valley of the shadow of death, I fear no evil, for You are with me."

This is a day when all Americans from every walk of life unite in our resolve for justice and peace. America has stood down enemies before, and we will do so this time. None of us will ever forget this day. Yet, we go forward to defend freedom and all that is good and just in our world.

Thank you. Good night, and God bless America.

How much did the September 11 terrorist attacks cost America?

Institute for the Analysis of Global Security - http://www.iags.org/costof911.html

Counting the value of lives lost as well as property damage and lost production of goods and services, including the loss in stock market wealth – the market's own estimate arising from expectations of lower corporate profits and higher discount rates for economic volatility – the price tag approaches $2 trillion.

Among the big-ticket items:

- The loss of four civilian aircraft valued at $385 million.
- The destruction of major buildings in the World Trade Center with a replacement cost of from $3 billion to $4.5 billion.
- Damage to a portion of the Pentagon: up to $1 billion.
- Cleanup costs: $1.3 billion.
- Property and infrastructure damage: $10 billion to $13 billion.
- Federal emergency funds (heightened airport security, sky marshals, government takeover of airport security, retrofitting aircraft with anti-terrorist devices, cost of operations in Afghanistan): $40 billion.
- The amount of damaged or unrecoverable property hit $21.8 billion.
- Losses to the city of New York (lost jobs, lost taxes, damage to infrastructure, cleaning): $95 billion.

- Losses to the insurance industry: $40 billion.
- Loss of air traffic revenue: $10 billion.

Additional Loss Breakdown

The Milken Institute estimated 1,300,000 jobs were lost across the country as a result of 9/11 by the end of 2002 and a concomitant decrease of $150 billion in annual income or Gross Domestic Product (GDP).

As a consequence of 9/11, the federal government and the states budgeted for nearly $40 billion in 2003 for anti-terror and security related items. U.S. non-governmental agencies and businesses spent about $33 billion in 2002 for added security measures.

In spite of a $15 billion government bailout, a couple of U.S. airlines filed for bankruptcy and all of the carriers combined lost about $11 billion in large part due to a passenger fear of flying following 9/11.

Social Impact of events subsequent to September 11, 2001 to October 25-26, 2001

(http://www.ilo.org/public/english/dialogue/sector/techmeet/imhct01/index.htm).

According to estimates by the *World Travel and Tourism Council* (WTTC), the events of September 11th and subsequent developments caused more than six and a half million jobs to be lost in the travel and tourism industry over the years 2001 and 2002 - some 6.9% of the total employed, as compared to a normal growth that could have been expected in normal times without the impact of a crisis. This estimate does not include those related sectors providing inputs to travel and tourism, where employment may have suffered in similar proportions.

Throughout the following discussion, metropolitan areas are based upon Census Bureau definitions of metropolitan statistical areas. Standard tools of regional economic analysis were used to estimate the impact.

- Of the total direct estimated metropolitan job loss of 760,000 relative to the baseline scenario (no terrorist attack) in 2002, two-thirds are in travel and tourism and related sectors. Overall, roughly 1.64 million jobs were lost in America's metropolitan economies as a result of September 11.
- The largest percentage declines were in air transportation (roughly 20 percent), followed by amusement and recreational services, and hotels and motels. The most exposed metros were destinations with high concentrations of foreign tourists as well as domestic tourists who generally arrived by air. New York was the (unfortunate) exception because many tourists who would have come by car or train stayed away anyways.
- Early data released in the aftermath of September 11 gegan to shed some light on the probable severity of the impact on the travel and tourism industry. In September 2001, consumption expenditures on airline travel plunged by 38.2 percent, a decline of $12.5 billion. There was a recovery of $3.7 billion in October 2001 as some airline-travel resumed. Nevertheless, relative to 2000, October's 2001 expenditures were down by $13.2 billion or 35.6 percent. During October and November 2001, the airline industry cut employment by a combined 81,000, a 6.2 percent decline from September. Many more layoffs occurred. Transportation services, which included travel agencies, cut 12,000 positions in November, 2001 alone.
- Foreign travel to the U.S. witnessed the largest decline since the terrorist attacks. Foreign tourists cut U.S. travel expenditures by $25.9 billion (26.5 percent) in September 2001. October 2001 witnessed an additional decline of $5.6 billion (7.8

percent), and spending was down by 31.3 percent from the same period one year ago. The loss of foreign travel to the U.S. explains much of September's $11.1 billion drop in spending at restaurants and bars.

Thompson Releases Report on Fiscal Impact Of 9/11 on New York City, 2/9/2002

Attacks May Cost New York Up to $95 Billion.

City Down 146,000 Jobs Because Of World Trade Center.
Among the report's findings:

- The economic cost to the city from the attacks on 9/11 will total between $83 billion and $95 billion. The final figure will depend, in part, on the number of jobs that are eventually relocated out of the city.
- It will cost $21.8 billion to replace the buildings, infrastructure and tenant assets lost as a result of September 11. In all, the attacks destroyed 13 million square feet of prime office space - equal to the entire office space inventory in the central business districts of Atlanta or Miami.
- Job losses attributable to 9/11 have already cost the city more than $17 billion in lost wages. New York City is down a total of 146,000 jobs as result of the attacks. There are 83,000 fewer jobs here now than there were before 9/11, and the city has not gained a projected 63,000 jobs that would have resulted from its recovery from recession.
- The attacks have cost the City nearly $3 billion in lost taxes and nearly $500 million in unreimbursed expenses. Roughly half of the $6 billion budget gap that had to be closed to balance fiscal year 2003, was attributable to 9/11.
- Federal officials have pledged $21.4 billion in total federal assistance to the City. But only $2.7

billion has been released to date.

Homeland Security Appropriations
October 1, 2002

President George W. Bush signed the Homeland Security Appropriations Act of 2004 at the Department of Homeland Security in Washington, D.C., Wednesday, Oct. 1, 2003.

> "The Homeland Security bill I will sign today commits $31 billion to securing our nation, over $14 billion more than pre-September 11th levels. The bill increases funding for the key responsibilities at the Department of Homeland Security and supports important new initiatives across the Department," said the President in his remarks.

A Costly Day

September 11, 2001, was an extremely tragic day for those who lost their lives, for those who lost members of their families, or for those who lost a friend. It was also a very trying day for America. In the few months following 9-11 polls stated seven out of ten Americans had experienced or were experiencing depression. Furthermore, the enemy Israel faced at home had now become an enemy America had to face at home. Moreover, life as we know it in America had forever changed.

Eight Disruptive Periods When President Bush is Involved With Israel's Land

After the 9-11 terror events, when President George W. Bush or high-level members of his administration began applying pressure on Israel to give up her land or made major statements about her land, the Bush Administration and/or America would experience intense disruptive periods.

We have recorded that when President George W.

Bush or one of his top officials applied pressure on Israel to give up her covenant land, one or more of the following would occur.

- National terror alerts and warnings would immediately follow and increase in frequency as the pressure continued to be applied on Israel.
- The Bush Administration would be required to defend their actions over 9-11, the war on terror, the economy, Iraq, etc.
- Top-level administration officials would resign (White House Counselor Karen Hughes, Secretary of Treasury Paul O'Neil, White House economic adviser Larry Lindsey, White House Press Secretary Ari Fleischer and EPA Director Christine Todd Whitman.)
- The nation would experience violent record-setting weather consisting of tornadoes, hurricanes, rain and flooding, ice storms, and major forest fires.
- National anthrax events, and heightened concerns over bio-terrorism attack, nuclear attacks, and small-pox.
- Major economic concerns: bad economic news, corporate bankruptcies and accounting scandals.
- Political, judicial and or legislative chaos would occur.

Following are the eight periods of disruption that immediately followed President George W. Bush's declarations concerning his commitment to a Palestinian state and/or efforts on the Middle East peace process:

The First Disruptive Period: October 1-31, 2001: President Bush confirmed his interest in a Palestinian state: Anthrax crisis and major terror warnings increased substantially in the U.S. during this period.

The Second Disruptive Period: November 2-17, 2001: President Bush prepared and then delivered a major address to the UN General Assembly. In his speech he stated, "We are working toward the day when two states--Israel and Palestine--live peacefully together within secure and recognized borders as called for by the Security Council resolutions." Major terror warnings increased substantially in the U.S. during this period.

The Third Disruptive Period: April 20 to May 2, 2002: President Bush delivered his Middle East vision in a national radio address. He again mentioned a Palestinian state and the U.S. war on terror. Major terror warnings increased substantially in the U.S. during this period.

The Fourth Disruptive Period: May 12 - 20, 2002: President Bush held fast on a Palestinian state after Israel's Likud Party voted against a Palestinian state. Major terror warnings increased substantially in the U.S. during this period.

The Fifth Disruptive Period: June 13 - 29, 2002: President Bush prepared, and then delivered, his Middle East vision which included a Palestinian state. Major terror warnings increased substantially. Major fires and financial fires occurred in the U.S. during this period.

The Sixth Disruptive Period: October 1 to December 22, 2002: The Quartet met in NYC to begin preparing the Road Map to peace. They coordinated their activity with the Bush Administration. Major terror warnings increased substantially during this period.

The Seventh Disruptive Period: April 30 to November 16, 2003: The Quartet, with President Bush's blessing, delivered the Road Map. Powell was in Syria to start talks on the Road Map, then headed to Israel for talks. President Bush and Powell put pressure on Israel to accept the Road Map and President Bush decided to sponsor a three-way summit between Bush, Sharon and Abbas in Jordan. Post-war Iraq caused enormous pressure for President Bush. Major terror warnings increased in the U.S. during this period.

The Eighth Disruptive Period: December 18, 2003 to January 9, 2004: Secretary of State Colin Powell told the Palestinians on December 17 that a cease-fire deal would seal statehood. Israeli Prime Minister Ariel Sharon the next day presented a major address (that received a positive response from the Bush White House) on the future of Israel's disputed land. Within 24-hours of Sharon's address there was a significant increase in major terror warnings in the U.S., the first mad-cow case in U.S. history was reported, there was a major 6.5 earthquake in Central California, there was a significant increase in insurgent chaos in Iraq and there was a major suicide bombing in Tel Aviv, Israel.

The First Disruptive Period: October 1 - 31, 2001

Bush: Palestinian State 'Part of a Vision' if Israel Respected

According to CNN, President Bush stated on Tuesday October 2, 2001 that a Palestinian state was always "part of a vision" if Israel's right to exist is respected. He said the two parties needed to get to work "on the Mitchell process" which he said provides a clear path to solving the crisis in the Middle East.

He refused, when asked, to say whether he had been prepared to announce his support for a Palestinian state prior to the September 11 terrorist attacks on Washington and New York.

The President's statement at a meeting with congressional leaders follows news that the administration is considering a series of high-profile steps related to the

Israeli-Palestinian conflict to secure much needed Arab support for the international coalition against terrorism.

State Department and other senior administration officials told CNN the day before that draft of a major policy speech on the Middle East, to be delivered by U.S. Secretary of State Colin Powell, are circulating in the State Department for review.

Officials said the speech will "clarify its [U.S.] views on an end result" of the peace process, which would lead to the eventual "creation of a Palestinian state."

Powell had expected to deliver the speech September 24, 2001 to the UN General Assembly, but that plan was put on hold after the September 11 terrorist attacks on the World Trade Center and Pentagon.

Following the attacks, Powell's aides believed the speech needed some major revisions to reflect the current situation.

"It will go farther than we have ever gone," one official said. "There is an awful lot more that we view as being the end result than what we have said so far."

One point being hotly debated is whether to "call for ending all settlement activity," including so-called natural growth of existing settlements - something previous U.S. administrations have come close to doing, but never done.

The official said such a speech would be a "powerful palliative" to the Arab world.

"It eases the pain," the official said. "It would end the perception we only move against Islam."

"We are getting hammered in the Arab world," this official said. "And it is not a mystery that one of the ways to diffuse this is to see some movement on the Israeli-Palestinian conflict."

Administration sources acknowledged that Arab support on the international coalition is crucial to winning the U.S.-led war against terrorism to send a signal the war is not against Islam, but against Osama bin Laden and his terrorist network.

The Bush administration also wanted Arab states to cut the flow of money from wealthy Islamic supporters in their countries to bin Laden.

Officials were also debating whether the administration should invite Palestinian leader Yasser Arafat to Washington to meet with Bush or Powell. Although Arafat had met Powell outside of Washington, he had yet to meet Bush.

Some in the administration believed inviting the Palestinian leader to Washington could give Arafat the "empowerment" he needed to deal with extremist factions of his Palestinian forces.

"Arafat needs a visit," one official said, noting that Arafat has publicly condemned terrorism and called for a cease-fire.

Headlines tell the Story

Following Bush's Palestinian state statements, October 2001 was dominated by anthrax and terrorism headlines as follows:

- Before Attacks, U.S. Was Ready to Say It Backed Palestinian State -- October 1
- Bush: Palestinian State 'Part of a Vision' If Israel Respected -- October 2
- Arab Leaders Warn No End To Terrorism Without Mideast Solution -- October 3
- Greyhound Suspends U.S. Services After Crash -- October 3
- U.S. Confirms Isolated Case Of Anthrax In Florida -- October 4
- U.S. Government Officials Believe Terrorism Plot Against U.S. Far From Over -- October 5
- Government Stockpiles Supplies For Bioterrorism -- October 5
- First Wave Of U.S. Strikes Against Taliban Begins --

October 6

- Officials: Anthrax Shown In Co-Worker And Work Place Of Florida Man Who Died Of Anthrax -- October 8
- U.S. Government Officials Believe Terrorism Plot Against U.S. Far From Over -- October 8
- Foul Play Likely In Anthrax Cases -- October 9
- Third Person Tests Positive For Anthrax In Florida -- October 10
- FBI: More Terrorist Attacks Expected Within Days -- October 11
- Anthrax Case Reported In NBC News, New York -- October 12
- Ashcroft Issues New Mail Warning -- October 12
- Cheney Suspects Bin Laden Could Be Behind Anthrax Cases -- October 12
- Three Exposed To Anthrax In New York Amid Fears Of Bioterrorism -- October 14
- Bush: Anthrax Letter Sent To Daschle -- October 15
- Anthrax, Smallpox, Plague: Reborn As Bioweapons? -- October 16
- Survey: Hospitals Not Ready For Large Bio Attack -- October 16
- Florida And New York Anthrax Strains The Same -- October 17
- State Sponsor? Anthrax Suggests Government Expertise -- October 17
- Anthrax Found In New York Governor Pataki's Office -- October 17
- U.S. House Of Representatives To Adjourn Following More Anthrax Cases -- October 17
- 31 Daschle Staffers Tested Positive For Anthrax -- October 17
- CDC Warns Docs To Be On Lookout For Bioterror Outbreak -- October 19
- Anthrax Scare Hits World's Mailrooms (But, Don't

Live In Fear) -- October 19

- Anthrax Spores Found In House Building At U.S. Capitol Complex -- October 20
- Anthrax Strains Not 'Weaponized', Could Be From Same Batch -- October 21
- U.S. Postal Worker Diagnosed With Respiratory Anthrax -- October 21
- Postal Worker Very Ill With Inhalation Anthrax; 5 Others May Have It Also -- October 22
- Anthrax Found At White House Annex -- October 23
- Potent Inhalation Anthrax Not Stuff Of Amateurs -- October 23
- Two Postal Workers Die Of Anthrax -- October 23
- State Dept Mailman Tests Positive For Anthrax -- October 25
- Anthrax Found In Fifth Capitol Location -- October 25
- Three Nations Known Capable Of Making Anthrax Additive -- October 25
- U.S. Anti-Terror Law Widens Police, Federal Powers -- October 25
- Anthrax Scare Hits CIA -- October 26
- Bin Laden Acquires Nuclear Materials -- October 26
- Anthrax Spreads To CIA, Supreme Court, 3 House Offices On Capitol Hill, & An Army Institute -- October 26
- D.C. Anthrax Probe Broadens -- October 27
- Confusing Symptoms Of Flu And Anthrax This Winter: The Differences -- October 29
- FBI Renews High Alert Warning For Terrorism Against U.S. This Week -- October 29
- U.S. Readies For Feared Attacks -- October 30
- Anthrax Found In Four More Buildings -- October 30
- FBI Furious Over Nuclear Plant Suspects -- October 31
- U.S. Sees Increased Possibility Of Nuclear Attack -- October 31

The Second Disruptive Period: November 2 - 17, 2001

Bush Calls for Palestinian State

According to the Financial Times, in a Friday, Nov 2, 2001 article, the Bush administration was preparing to make a fresh policy statement on the Middle East that was expected to underline U.S. commitment to the creation of a viable Palestinian state. Details of the U.S. blueprint, which will build on President George W. Bush's backing of the concept of a Palestinian state, were still being debated within the administration. Both Arab states and Israel were trying hard to influence the outcome.

In the context of the Middle East negotiations, the word "viable" is generally understood to mean that the Palestinian state would have sufficient geographical, economic and political integrity to stand on its own. The statement, was made by Colin Powell, U.S. Secretary of State, did not include prescriptions on the final status of Jerusalem and Palestinian refugees. The planned U.S. move would make it easier for Arab allies, all of who are contending with public disenchantment with U.S. policy, to continue to support the war against terror.

In President George W. Bush's first address to the General Assembly of the United Nations in New York City on November 10, 2001, he spoke briefly about his vision for Middle East peace. The following is an excerpt:

> The American government also stands by its commitment to a just peace in the Middle East.
>
> We are working toward the day when two states--Israel and Palestine--live peacefully together within secure and recognized borders as called for by the Security Council resolutions.
>
> We will do all in our power to bring both parties back into negotiations. But peace will only come when all have sworn off forever incitement, violence and terror.

Headlines tell the Story

The following are seventeen days of headlines that began with President Bush's plan to call for a Palestinian state. They consisted of terror warnings and the tragic explosion of an American Airlines Flight within miles of the UN meetings in New York City:

- Bush To Call For Palestinian State -- November 2
- U.S. Officials Rushing To Prepare For Smallpox -- November 2
- Californians Cringe As Anxiety About More Attacks Moves West -- November 3
- Bush Urged To Restructure FBI, CIA -- November 4
- PA: Powell To Present Peace Plan At UN -- November 5
- Bush Says Terrorists Seeking Nuclear Weapons; Warns Of Global Instability -- November 6
- U.S. Remains On Alert For Attacks -- November 7
- President Bush To Address Nation On Safety Fears Tonight -- November 8
- Powell May Meet Arafat At UN -- November 8
- Iraq Issues Nuclear Threat To West -- November 10
- Bush Calls For Israel And Palestine Living Side By Side In Peace At UN -- November 10
- Bin Laden May Have Shipped Nuclear Bomb To U.S. -- November 10
- Bush At UN Warns Terrorists Seeking Nuclear Weapons -- November 10
- Bin Laden: Yes, I Did It -- November 11
- Hizbullah Calls On Arab States To Oppose American Request -- November 11
- Powell: 'Palestine' Is Part Of Administration Language -- November 12
- Powell Meets Arafat, Peres, Annan And Russian, EU Officials On Mideast -- November 12
- American Airlines Flight 578 Explodes Near Kennedy Airport -- November 12
- Arafat Denounces Israel At UN -- November 12

- Plane Crash Prompts UN Lockdown -- November 12
- More Anthrax Found In U.S. Senate Building As Authorities Trace Letters -- November 12
- Saudi Says Al Qaeda Planning More Attacks -- November 12
- Cheney: U.S. Fears Massive Attack -- November 15
- U.S. Prepares 'For Mass Casualties' -- November 15
- Supreme Leader Calls For 'Extinction Of America' -- November 15
- Rumsfeld: We'll Find Bin Laden -- November 15
- Ridge: Nuclear Weapons Documents Found In Al Qaeda Safehouse -- November 15
- Christian Leader, Franklin Graham, Condemns Islam As Wicked, Violent -- November 17
- U.S. Says Won't Introduce New Mideast Plan -- November 18

The Third Disruptive Period: April 20 to May 2, 2002

The Fallout from Bush's Palestinian State Declaration

The following events happened in a nine-day period as President Bush intensified his efforts in the Middle East talks:

On Saturday, April 20, 2002, a 5.1 Earthquake in New York was felt from Buffalo, New York, to Boston, Massachusetts, and Baltimore, Maryland. The epicenter was 50 miles from Saranac Lake, where President Bush would be delivering his Earth day address 48 hours later.

Within a few hours of the quake, as a part of his address concerning terrorism and the Middle East, the President gave a national radio address acknowledging the need for a Palestinian state and overview of his vision for peace between the Israelis and the Palestinians.

The following Tuesday, White House Counselor, Karen Hughes, a top advisor, director of communications, and a close confidant of the President Bush, resigned.

On Wednesday President Bush's father, George H. W. Bush, met with Crown Prince of Abdullah of Saudi Arabia in Washington. The next day President Bush met Crown Prince Abdullah in Crawford, Texas, while massive rains fell on part of Texas with subsequent flooding.

On Friday, April 26th, President Bush's father met again with Crown Prince Abdullah in Houston and took a train ride with him to College Station for a speech at Texas A&M University.

Also on Friday, Wall Street closed down after experiencing the largest one-week capitalization loss since 9-11.

On Sunday, April 28th, the United States brokered a deal with Israel arranging for Arafat to be released from captivity in Ramallah.

Early that Sunday, a series of tornadoes swept through southeastern Missouri, Illinois and western Kentucky, killing three people, and damaging homes and buildings. The tornado that hit Maryland was part of a storm system with heavy rain, high winds and hail that rumbled east from the Ohio Valley.

The Maryland storm was a F5 tornado on the Fujita Tornado Damage Scale, "a monster of a tornado." With winds in the 261-318 mph range, it was the strongest ever to hit Maryland.

President Bush's April 20, 2002, Middle East Address and Subsequent News

- President Bush's National Radio Address On Middle East Peace, A Palestinian State And War On Terrorism -- April 20
- Earthquake Rattles Northeast, Felt From Maine To Pennsylvania -- April 20
- U.S. Quakes And More -- April 22
- Al Qaeda Brags It Can Build And Smuggle Dirty Bombs Into U.S. -- April 23
- FBI Warns Agents Of Terrorist Attacks On

Supermarkets And Shopping Centers -- April 24

- CIA Warns Of Chinese Plans For Cyber-Attacks On U.S. -- April 24
- Bush Getting Impatient, Tells Israel To Withdraw "Now," Meets With Saudi's Abdullah -- April 24
- President Bush Meets With Crown Prince Of Saudi Arabia -- April 25
- U.S. Mountain West In Serious Drought With Wildfires -- April 26
- Northwest Texas County Deluged By Floods, Eleven Inches Of Rain In A Few Hours -- April 26
- Bush Administration Opposes Urgent Aid To Israel -- April 26
- The Panel Consists Of The United States, The European Union, The United Nations And Russia -- April 28
- Killer F-5 Tornado Becomes One For The Books In Maryland -- April 29
- Wild Weekend Weather Leaves Devastating Mark & Record Tornado -- April 29
- U.S. Brokers End To Arafat Siege; UN Mission Delayed -- April 29
- U.S. Promise On Jenin Won Arafat's Freedom -- April 30
- Blair's Dinner Diplomacy Was Vital To Arafat Release And Deal -- April 30

The Fourth Disruptive Period: May 12 - 20, 2002

Bush holds fast on a Palestinian State

According to an article in the Guardian (UK) from Monday May 13, 2002, President Bush held fast to his support of a Palestinian state. This may possibly foreshadow a sharp dispute with Israel and its dominant Likud party who had voted against a Palestinian state in a Sunday May 12, 2002 meeting in Israel.

"The President continues to believe that the best route to peace is through the creation of the state of Palestine and side-by-side security with Israel," White House spokesman Ari Fleischer said in response to Likud's decision.

Headlines tell the Story

As the President held fast on a Palestinian state the following headlines and subsequent terror warnings occurred. The Bush administration was defending their pre-9/11 actions and high-level admission of the risk of bio-terrorism events:

- Likud Votes To Reject Palestinian State --May 12
- Bush Holds Fast On Palestinian State -- May 13
- 25 Islamic Extremists Have Entered The U.S. -- May 13
- U.S. Prepares For Terror Attack In Food -- May 13
- Bush Administration Was Warned Of Potential Terror
  Event Prior To 9-11 -- May 15
- Dr. Condoleezza Rice Defends Bush Administration's Handling Of Pre-9-11 Terror Warning (White House Press Briefing) -- May 16
- Democrats End United Support Of Bush On War; Democrats Say Bush Must Give Full Disclosure -- May 16
- Defense Secretary Says Another Terrorist Attack On U.S. Is Likely -- May 17
- Lay Off U.S. Powell Tells Europeans -- May 17
- Bush Defends Pre-9/11 Actions -- May 17
- U.S. Intercepting Messages Hinting At A New Attack -- May 18
- U.S. Bioterrorism Plan Inadequate -- May 19
- Cheney Predicts More Attacks -- May 19
- FBI's Director Mueller: Suicide Bombers Likely In U.S. -- May 20
- Strife, Dissent Beset Hill's September 11 Panel: Bipartisan Group Disagrees On Mission -- May 20

The Fifth Disruptive Period: June 13 - 29, 2002

President Bush Prepares Middle East Peace Plan

President Bush in cooperation with Secretary of State Colin Powell were completing the final touches to the Presidents much awaited Middle East plan to be presented from the White House Rose Garden on June 18. The following few days composed of high-level terror warnings and two major suicide bombings in Israel:

- Bush Polishing Palestinian State Proposal And Powell Suggests Interim Palestinian State -- June 13
- Nation's Mayors Not Ready For Attacks -- June 13
- Arab Leader Warns U.S. On Terror War -- June 14
- Talk That Powell Could Quit -- June 15
- Bush Gives CIA Power To Get Rid Of Saddam -- June 16
- Al Qaeda Plans Attacks On U.S. Targets -- June 17
- Bush To Postpone Policy Speech Due To Terror Attack -- June 18
- U.S. Expresses Reservations About Fence In Israel -- June 18
- 19 Dead, 52 Wounded In Suicide Bus Bombing In Jerusalem -- June 18
- FBI Searches Los Angeles Coast For Al Qaeda -- June 18
- Suicide Bombing In Jerusalem -- June 19
- Bush To Propose Provisional Palestinian Statehood As Soon As September -- June 19
- President Bush Postpones His Middle East Message For The Second Time In Two Days Due To Jerusalem Bombings -- June 19
- Lightning Disables Two Of Four Fire And Medical Emergency Radio Antennas In Washington D.C. -- June 19
- Package Scare At Federal Reserve, Building Evacuated -- June 19
- Plane Prompts White House Evacuation -- June 19

President Bush finally gave his Middle East speech the afternoon of June 24 from the White House Rose Garden. His next official business was the following morning in Arizona where he declared Arizona a major natural disaster and the 500,000 acre fire one of the worst in Western U.S. history. Later in the day WorldCom admitted to massive bookkeeping fraud.

- Stocks Trade Near Post-September 11 Lows -- June 24
- Dollar Slides To Brink Of Free Fall -- June 24
- Bank Of Japan Moves To Stop Dollar Plunge -- June 24
- Worldwide Web Of Debt Unravels -- June 24
- United Seeks $1.8B Federal Loan -- June 24
- Arizona Firefighters Scramble To Save Town -- June 24
- Bush Travels To Arizona Fire; Declares The "Rodeo/Chediski" Arizona Fire As One Of The West's All Time Worst And A Natural Disaster -- June 25
- Massive Fraud Alleged At WorldCom -- June 25
- Bush Urges Congress To Extend Debt Limit -- June 25
- Bush Calls WorldCom Scandal Outrageous -- June 25
- World Leaders Stand With Arafat -- June 25
- Stocks Plunge Amid Huge WorldCom Scandal News -- June 25
- Bush Urges Congress On Debt Limit -- June 25
- Bush Signs A Law Extending Benefits To Same-Sex Couples -- June 25
- Worst Wildfire In Arizona's History -- June 25
- 1st Time Ever: Pledge Of Allegiance Ruled 'Unconstitutional' In 9 States -- June 25
- President And The Senate Call Pledge Decision Outrageous -- June 25
- Judge Stays Decision On Pledge Of Allegiance -- June 27
- U.S. Senate Unanimously Condemns Pledge Ruling & Joins In Public Pledge -- June 27
- Angered Bush Gives Speech On Corporate Reforms --June 27
- Suspicion: Terror Web Attack On Our Nation's Power

Grid And More -- June 27
- 20,000 Gas Masks Have Arrived On Capitol Hill -- June 27
- WorldCom Profits Scandal Shakes Stock Markets -- June 27
- Xerox Restates $6.4 Billion In Latest Mess -- June 28
- Bush To Be Sedated For Colon Test Saturday -- June 28
- Pres. Bush Returns To Power: Colonoscopy Shows No Abnormalities -- June 29
- Amid Controversy, FBI Chief Expresses Support For Muslim Group -- June 29

The Sixth Disruptive Period: October 1 to December 23, 2002

The Quartet Meets in NY for Final Touch to Middle East Peace Plan

The Quartet met in New York in late September to formulate the Middle East Road Map. The Quartet consists of the UN, the EU, Russia and the U.S. The U.S. stock market had its worst September since the Great Depression and was at the lowest level since the 9-11 terror attacks. Moreover, Washington D.C. was paralyzed by a sniper that was holding the metro area hostage for three weeks, there was a near miss of a major hurricane in the Gulf of Mexico, a California earthquake, a major dock strike on the West Coast that forced President Bush to intervene, a major terror warning by Al Qaeda's Osama bin Laden, and weekly terror warnings across America. November consisted of major terror warnings and massive record tornadoes.

Also, in early December there was a major political crisis for President Bush when Senate Majority Leader Trent Lott made a statement December 5 at Senator Strom Thurmonds 100th birthday party. There were major terror warnings too. There was the talk of a national smallpox vaccine effort and the debate over when to release the Quartet Road Map.

The Headlines from October 1 to December 23, 2002:

- U.S. Stock Market's Have Worst September Since Great Depression -- October 1
- Hurricane Lili Could Be Major When Hitting U.S. -- October 1
- Wall Street Stocks Hammered -- October 2
- Bush And Congress Differ Over Jerusalem Bill Passed -- October 2
- Hurricane Lili's Power Grows, Now Powerful Category 4 -- October 2
- Shooting Spree In D.C. Suburbs; 5 Killed In Area; Schools In Lockdown -- October 3
- Strong Quake Hits In Gulf Of California -- October 3
- Sniper Shootings Linked -- October 5
- Intelligence Reports: Islamic Terrorists Targeting American Schools For Attack -- October 4
- Doctors Warn Of Bioterrorism Risks; Health Officials Need To Be On Alert -- October 4
- Hurricane Lili Fizzled, But Why? Rapid Reversal Unexplained -- October 4
- U.S. Stocks Fall, Pushing S&P 500 To Lowest Level Since April, 1997 -- October 7
- Bush To Intervene In The Major West Coast Port Lockout -- October 7
- Bin Laden Tape Warns U.S. -- October 7
- Arafat Signs Law On Jerusalem As Future Capital -- October 7
- Terror Threat For U.S. Ships In Yemen -- October 8
- Bush Seeks To Answer Iraq Questions - Speech Tonight -- October 7
- Whole Pacific Rim Is Suffering From Closure Of All U.S. West Coast Ports -- October 8
- D.C. Area On Edge As Sniper Eludes Cops -- October 8
- Hurricane Lili Damage Set At $170 Million -- October 8

- Terror Threat For U.S. Ships In Yemen -- October 8
- Court Orders West Coast Ports To Reopen On Bush's Request -- October 9
- Tape Of Al-Qaeda Deputy Warning Of More Attacks On U.S. Appears To Be Genuine -- October 9
- 'This Is Like A War Zone': Recurring Terror In D.C. -- October 9
- FBI Warns Of Possible Attack On U.S. Due To Al Qaeda Tapes -- October 10
- House Passes Iraq Resolution -- October 10
- Sharon Warns: Dark 'War Clouds' Are Hovering Over The Region -- October 10
- Signs Of A Revived Al Qaeda; New Wave of Attacks -- October 13
- State Department Issues Warning To Americans Abroad -- October 13
- Largest Meat Recall In USDA History - 27.4 Million Pounds -- October 14
- Expect More Terrorist Attacks, Senator Says; Beginning Of New Wave -- October 15
- FBI Analyst Is Beltway Sniper's Latest Victim -- October 15
- Terrorism A Possibility Behind Shootings -- October 15
- Bush, Sharon Discuss Protection Of Israel -- October 16
- D.C. Sniper Terror: Shootings To Spread To Other Cities? -- October 17
- U.S.: North Korea Admits Nuke Program -- October 17
- Sniper Hunt: Al Qaeda Detainees To Be Questioned About Attacks -- October 17
- Al-Qaeda Globalizes Its Jihad; Mobilizing Whole Islamic World Against America -- October 21
- Are Terrorists Behind The D.C. Sniper Attacks? -- October 21
- Burns Reports Progress On Plan For Palestinian State -- October 21
- At Least 16 Killed In Homicide Attack In Israel --

October 21

- Peres: Bus Bombing Aimed At Undermining Burns Visit To Israel -- October 21
- U.S. Envoy: Israel Bomb Hinders Palestinian State -- October 22
- Burns Reports Progress On Plan For Palestinian State -- October 22
- Sniper Could Damage D.C. Economy -- October 22
- New York Will Face Bus Bombs, MTA Security Czar Is Warning -- October 22
- John Muhammad & Stepson Arrested In Sniper Case; More Warrants Out -- October 24
- Attack On Heart Of Internet Fails To Bring It Down -- October 24
- FBI Warns Of Possible Terrorist Attack Against Transportation Systems -- October 24
- Report: U.S. In 'Grave Danger' -- October 25
- FBI Seeks To Trace Massive Net Attack -- October 25
- White House Says It Can Build Anti-Iraq Coalition Without UN -- October 26
- Sharon Tells Burns Of Reservations With Road Map -- October 25
- Al-Qaeda Changes, As Does Its Threat -- October 26
- U.S. Diplomat Shot And Killed In Jordan -- October 28
- Israel Coalition Gov't Falls Apart -- October 30
- Iraq VP Sends U.S. Harsh Warning -- November 1
- FBI Warns Of Hizbullah Terrorism In America; Now Seeking Their Targets -- November 1
- Saudi Bases Out For Attack On Iraq -- November 4
- U.S. Warns Of New Terror Plots, Including Suicide Attacks -- November 7
- Jets Strike Iraqi Site Second Day In A Row -- November 7
- President George W. Bush Hosts Ramadan Dinner At The White House -- November 7
- Iraqi Preachers Call For Jihad Against U.S., Britain --

November 8

- Al Qaeda Seen Planning Major Strikes - Interpol -- November 8
- Geologists Dissect Massive Alaskan Quake; The Biggest Earthquake In The World This Year -- November 8
- 88 Tornadoes And Major Thunderstorms From The Gulf Coast To The Great Lakes, Affecting Thirteen States -- November 9-10
- Five People Were Killed At Kibbutz Metzer In Israel -- November 10
- U.S. Deputy Assistant Secretary Of State David Satterfield Flies To Israel To Push The Quartet's December Deadline -- November 10
- Satterfield Meets With Israeli Officials -- November 11-12
- It's Like A War Zone Or Worse; Storms Leave Destruction And Death Across Eastern U.S. -- November 11
- 4.2 Earthquake -- 30 miles (45 km) SSW From Charleston, South Carolina -- November 11
- Bush States U.S. Ready For War At Veteran's Event -- November 11
- Israeli Helicopters Fire Missiles At Gaza City Weapons Factories -- November 12
- Troops Enter Nablus; Israeli Helicopters Fire Missiles Into Downtown Gaza City -- November 12
- Peace Quartet Refuses To Bow To Israeli Agenda Timing -- November 12
- U.S. Agrees To Put 'Road Map' On Hold Until After Elections -- November 12
- David Satterfield Meets With Minister Of Planning And International Cooperation Nabil Shaath And Minister Of Local Government Saeb Erekat In Jericho -- November 13
- U.S. Official: Voice Sounds Like Bin Laden --

November 12

- Peter Bergen: Tape Is Bin Laden's Voice -- November 13
- Terrorist Chatter Increasing -- November 13
- Man Taken Into Custody In D.C. After Threats On President -- November 13
- Bush Takes On Christian Right Over Anti-Islam Words -- November 13
- Official: Voice On Tape Is Bin Laden's -- November 13
- Voice Warns U.S. Allies: 'Just Like You Kill Us, We Will Kill You' -- November 13
- U.S. To Suspend Oil To North Korea -- November 14
- As New Tape Is Evaluated, Bush Calls Al Qaeda Threat Real -- November 14
- You Are A Suspect; "Total Information Awares About Every Citizen" -- November 14
- FBI: Hospitals In Four Cities Possible Targets Of Terror Attacks -- November 14
- Annan: Israel Must Relinquish Land Won In 1967 War -- November 14
- FBI: Hospitals Possible Targets Of Terror Threats -- November 14
- Sharon Says A Palestinian State Is All But A Given -- November 14
- Hebron Shootings Kill 12 Israelis, Wound 15 -- November 15
- Military Smallpox Vaccinations Planned -- November 15
- Bush Closer To Smallpox Vaccine OK -- November 15
- North Korea Steps Up Threats Of Missile Tests -- November 16
- Alleged Al Qaeda Statement Warns Of More Attacks On New York, D.C. -- November 17
- New York City On Guard For Car Bombs -- November 17
- New Draft Of U.S.-EU Mideast Plan Addresses Palestinian Concerns -- November 18
- U.S. And British Jets Bomb Northern Iraq's "No-Fly"

Zone -- November 18
- U.S. Asks Syria To Close Islamic Jihad Office -- November 18
- Terror War Hits Home -- Detroiters Caught In Widening Investigation -- November 18
- U.S. Concludes It Is Bin Laden On Tape -- November 18
- Israel Preparing For Mega-Terror Attack -- November 20
- Netanyahu Attacks Sharon Over Palestinian State -- November 20
- Revised 'Road Map' Asks For Immediate Israeli Acceptance Of Palestinian State -- November 21
- New Road Map: Israel Forfeits Physical And Diplomatic Right To Self Defense -- November 21
- New 'Road Map' Draft Is Tougher On Both Israel And PA -- November 21
- Muslim-Americans Asked Bush To Defend Islam -- November 20
- In North Korea And Pakistan, Deep Roots Of Nuclear Barter -- November 21
- New U.S. Road Map Termed 'Anti-Israeli' -- November 22
- 9-11 Hijackers: A Saudi Money Trail? -- November 24
- Full Text: Bin Laden's 'Letter To America' -- November 24
- Senators Question U.S.-Saudi Ties -- November 24
- PA Legislator Threatens U.S. With Suicide Bombings -- November 25
- Bush Okays Covert Ops Against Terror -- November 25
- Bush Signs Terrorism Insurance Bill -- November 26
- Pat Robertson Pleads For Scrutiny Of Koran -- November 26
- U.S.-Saudi Ties Face More Turbulence -- November 26
- Bush Readies Plan For Smallpox Vaccine -- November 27
- Troubles Deepen For The Secret Service -- November 29
- Terrorist Striking 'Soft' Targets Complicates Security

-- November 30

- Conservatives Dispute Bush Portrayal of Islam As Peaceful. -- November 30
- Critics, Including Some Policy Advisers, Call Stance Political -- November 30
- Cruise Ship Woes Not Terrorism, Feds Say -- December 2
- U.S. Establishing New Gulf Command Center For War December 2
- U.S. Bombs Northern Iraqi Air Defense Site December 2
- Conservatives Dispute Bush On Islam; Critics Say Its Political, Not Intellectual -- December 2
- U.S. Establishing New Gulf Command Center For War -- December 2
- Pentagon To Call Thousands Of Reservists -- December 5
- Al Qaeda Says 'Gift' Of Terror On Its Way -- December 5
- Iranian Spiritual Leader Fires Off Against U.S. And Israel At End Of Ramadan Holiday Celebration -- December 6
- White House: Believe Us Or Saddam -- December 6
- Iraq Is Hiding Arms, Bush Says; Claims Of Proof Raise Specter Of War -- December 6
- Treasury's O'Neill Announces Surprise Resignation - December 6
- O'Neil, Lindsey Resign: Treasury Secretary, Top Adviser Leaving In Major Shakeup Of Bush's Economic Team -- December 6
- Ice Storm Worst In Carolinas History - Nearly 2 Million Without Power -- December 6
- Small Plane Hits Federal Reserve Building; Accident Or Deliberate? -- December 6
- Political Chaos Over Senate Majority Leader Trent Lott's Statement -- December 6

- Al Qaeda Vows Faster Strikes Against U.S. & Israel -- December 9
- FBI Tracking Saddam Sympathizers In U.S. -- December 11
- U.S. Warns Potential Enemies: Retaliation Could Include Nukes -- December 11
- Bush To Offer Smallpox Vaccine To All -- December 12
- U.S. Has Photos Of Iran's Secret Large Nuclear Sites -- December 13
- FBI Director: 100 Terror Attacks Thwarted -- December 16
- Al Qaeda Could Avoid Mideast & Strike U.S. -- December 16
- Film To Fight Fear Of Islam - (Islam media campaign in U.S. has begun) -- December 16
- President Bush: U.S. To Deploy Missile Defense By '04 -- December 16
- Al Qaeda Could Avoid Mideast & Strike U.S. -- December 17
- President's National Security Team Recommends U.S. Declare Iraq In Violation -- December 18
- Trent Lott Resigns As Senate Republican Leader -- December 20
- The Quartet Mediators Discuss Mid-East Peace Plan At White House -- December 20
- U.S. Urges UN To Authorize War In Iraq -- December 20
- President Bush Receives Smallpox Vaccination -- December 21
- North Korea Disabling Monitoring Equipment At Nuclear Facility -- December 22
- Republican Senators Prepare To Elect New Leader -- December 23

CHAPTER 5

EIGHT DISRUPTIVE PERIODS

PERIOD 7 & 8

The Seventh Disruptive Period:
April 30 to June 14, 2003

The Quartet Road Map is Presented

President George W. Bush and the Quartet Call on Israel to Give up Her Covenant Land

After much delay, the Quartet delivered the Road Map on April 30 to the Israelis and the Palestinians. It was the world's plan on how Israel was to divide her covenant land.

Secretary of State Colin Powell headed to the Middle

East for meetings. In a meeting with Syrian President Bashar Assad on May 4, he stated his approval of Syria receiving the Golan Heights. Powell's associate William Burns met with Israeli peace advocates on May 5, where he stated Christian fundamentalists where an obstruction to peace in the Middle East.

The following weekend Powell met with Israeli Prime Minister Ariel Sharon and Palestinian Prime Minister Mahmoud Abbas in Israel on May 11.

From May 1, to May 10, 412 tornadoes slammed the Midwest. More than 300 counties affecting 19 states suffered losses and more than 40 deaths were blamed on the storms.

Powell met with Middle East leaders on the Road Map

- Powell had meetings with King Abdullah II in Jordan -- May 12
- U.S. offered to finance PA security forces -- May 12
- U.S. insisted on immediate implementation of Road Map -- May 12
- Major terror bombing in Riyadh hours before Powell meets with Crown Prince Abdullah - May 12
- Powell held Sharon accountable for the impasse -- May 15
- Sharon met with Mahmoud Abbas -- May 17
- Sharon postpones trip to the White House after Jerusalem bombing -- May 18

The following week U.S. Ambassador Daniel Kurtzer and President Bush called on Sharon to approve the Road Map. Here is what transpired.

- The U.S. decided to press Israel to approve the Road Map quickly. U.S. Ambassador to Israel Dan Kurtzer delivered this message to Sharon on May 20, and Bush reiterated it in a telephone conversation with the Prime Minister on Wednesday. Bush also talked with Mahmoud Abbas on May 21

- Bush said terrorism will not stop the Middle East peace process -- May 22
- Discussions began on a Bush-Sharon-Abbas meeting in Egypt after the G-8 meetings -- May 22
- President Bush planned a three-way summit with Sharon and Abbas in Jordan -- May 27
- Colin Powell met Pope John Paul II at the Vatican to discuss Iraq and the Israeli-Palestinian conflict -- June 2
- Bush met with Arab leaders in Egypt to discuss the Road Map -- June 3
- President Bush met with Jordanian President King Abdullah II, Israeli Prime Minister Ariel Sharon, and Palestinian Prime Minister Mahmoud Abbas for Aqaba Summit in Jordan -- June 4
- Bush demands a halt to Jewish settlements -- June 4
- Bush says two states must share the Holy Land -- June 4

Five -Week Summary

The following will provide a perspective on what happened five weeks after the United States became actively involved with the Quartet's Road Map. The greater the U.S. pressure, the greater the intensity of events.

Week One May 4-11: Powell represented the U.S. in Syria and Israel while record setting tornadoes and major storms devastated the Midwestern United States.

Week Two May 12-18: Powell continued his travels to Middle East countries and Russia to promote the Road Map, while Al-Qaeda terror bombings were aimed against Americans in Riyadh and Jews in Casablanca. The turning point for Ariel Sharon began when Secretary of State Colin Powell blamed Sharon for the impasse (May 15) over his refusal to freeze and dismantle settlement issue.

Then, following the Ariel Sharon and Mahmoud Abbas meeting, five suicide bombings in 48-hours broke the silence in Israel once again.

Week Three May 19-25: The Bush Administration called on Sharon to approve the Road Map. On the same day the Homeland Security Office raised the terror alert status to Orange (high) and the Defense Department increased its terrorism threat to its top level. Fighter jets began patrolling the skies over Washington D.C. Also, Iran was being pressured over their alleged nuclear program and the civil chaos began increasing in Iraq.

Week Four May 26-June 1: President Bush traveled to Poland, Russia, and France for the G-8 meetings. He then traveled to Egypt and Jordan to push the Road Map. While he was on his trip his administration was put on the defense for embellishing the intelligence information that he used to justify Iraqi Freedom.

Week Five: June 2-7: Palestinian Prime Minister Mahmoud Abbas's cease-fire talks with Hamas failed. Hamas, Islamic Jihad and Al-Aqsa Intifada attacked and killed four Israelis at a Gaza Checkpoint. Israel attempted to assassinate the head of Hamas. Hamas blew up a bus in Jerusalem killing 16 Israelis and injuring 100. Israel struck back with missile attacks on militant leaders in Gaza. President Bush called for calm and condemned the killings, while his credibility is on the line over his personal commitment to a solution.

The top news headlines from May 4 to May 29, 2003:

- EU Says Mideast Peace 'Road Map' Does Not Belong To U.S. -- May 4
- Burns Criticizes Israel Supporters In U.S. -- May 4
- 28 Dead In Midwest Tornadoes -- May 5

- Powell Offers CIA Help For Palestinian Government To Crack Down On Terrorism -- May 5
- Vicious Twister Destroys Small Town - Pierce City, MO -- May 6
- New Twisters Has Midwest On Edge -- May 7
- EU Gets the Go-Ahead To Slap Record Sanctions On U.S. -- May 9
- Rights Group: Hatred Of Jews At Highest Level Since WWII -- May 10
- Powell Has Meetings With King Abdullah II In Jordan -- May 12
- U.S. Offers To Finance PA Security Forces -- May 12
- U.S. Insists On Immediate Implementation Of Road Map -- May 12
- Riyadh Shaken, Bloodied By A 'Saudi September 11' -- May 12
- Powell Meets With Crown Prince Abdullah In Riyadh -- May 12
- Iran Pledges To Maintain Support For Hizbullah -- May 13
- Powell Holds Sharon Accountable For The Impasse -- May 15
- Powell Looks To Bush On Mideast Stalemate -- May 16
- Intercepted Terrorist 'Chatter' Indicates New Attacks -- May 16
- Airlines: SARS Worse Than 9/11 On Industry -- May 16
- Iraqis Says Anarchy Could Lead To Anti-U.S. Violence -- May 16
- At Least 20 Die In Casablanca Blasts -- May 17
- Crisis In Abbas Government -- May 17

The following news headlines emphasis the disruption

- Saturday: Sharon Meets With Mahmoud Abbas -- May 17
- Israel Has Five Suicide Bombings In Two Days -- May

17-19

- Sharon Postpones Trip To The White House After Jerusalem Bombing -- May 18
- Ari Fleischer Resigns As White House Press Secretary -- May 19
- Thousands Of Al-Qaeda Suspects Ready To Attack, Warns U.S. Official -- May 19
- Homeland Security Increases Terror Alert To High -- May 20

The Following News Headlines is What is being discussed in Israel and the United States.

- U.S. Presses Israel To Approve The Road Map Quickly: Kurtzer Delivers This Message To Sharon – May 20
- Homeland Security Increase Terror Alert To High - May 20
- Bush Reiterates To Sharon By Phone The Importance Of Approving The Road Map – May 21
- Bush Said Terrorism Will Not Stop The Middle East Peace Process — May 22
- Cabinet Member Christine Todd Whitman Head Of EPA Resigns -- May 20
- Officials: 'Chatter' Hints At Major Attack -- May 20
- Terror Threat Shuts U.S. Saudi Embassies -- May 20
- Bush Calls Abbas, Reiterates Plea For Peace -- May 20
- Bush and Kurtzer call on Sharon to Accept Roadmap -- May 20,21
- Alleged Al-Qaeda Tape Urges More Attacks -- May 21
- Military On Highest Domestic Terror Threat Alert -- May 21
- U.S.: Al-Qaeda Plotting From Iran -- May 22
- Bin Laden At large As Al-Qaeda Stages Comeback: Raids Along Afghan-Pakistani Border Fails To Capture Terror Chief -- May 22
- Fighter Jets Deployed Over D.C. -- May 23

- Bush, Sharon And Abbas Plan Three Way Summit -- May 27
- U.S. Rejects Iran's Nuclear Denials -- May 27
- U.S. And Russia Press Iran On Al Qaeda & Nuke Weapons -- May 28
- China & Russia Call For Multipolar World To Counter U.S. Dominance -- May 28
- Iran's Leader: U.S. Building Tension & Trying To Force Renouncing Of Islamic Values -- May 29
- U.S. Considers More Deployments Around Baghdad After Wave Of Violence -- May 29
- Pat Robertson: 'Road Map' Is Beginning Of End For Israel -- May 29
- Rumsfeld Pushes For Regime Change In Iran -- May 29
- North Korea Warns U.S. Of Nuclear Retaliation -- May 29

Bush Heads to Russia, Europe and the Middle East

After President Bush met in Aqaba, Jordan a major political crisis in Israel developed over the Road Map and the settlements. At the same time two of the most active proponents of the Road Map, U.S. and Britain, were experiencing a political crisis over intelligence reports that stated Iraq had weapons of mass destruction (WMD).

The Iraq crisis began to surface in the U.S. on May 30 the same day President Bush left for his trip to Poland, Russia, France, Egypt, Jordan and Qatar.

After his meetings in Europe and Russia, President Bush met in Egypt with Arab leaders on the Road Map. He then went to Jordan to meet with Israeli Prime Minister Ariel Sharon and Palestinian Prime Minister Mahmoud Abbas.

Bush was focused on Israel's covenant land, while at the same time he was facing a crisis at home, over alleged faulty intelligence information pertaining to Iraq's weapons of mass destruction.

The U.S. headlines during President Bush's trip to Europe, Russia and the Middle East:

- President Bush Leaves For Trip To Poland, Russia, France, Egypt, Jordan And Qatar -- May 30
- President Bush And First Lady Tour Auschwitz -- May 31
- President Bush Meets With Russian President Vladimer Putin -- June 1
- President Bush Arrives At Evian, France For G-8 Meetings -- June 1
- President Bush Meets With French President Chirac On Middle East And Other Matters -- June 2
- Colin Powell Meets Pope John Paul II At The Vatican To Discuss Iraq And The Israeli-Palestinian Conflict -- June 2
- Bush Greeted At Airport By Egyptian President Hosni Mubarek -- June 2
- Bush Meets With Arab Leaders In Egypt -- June 3
- Bush Has Three-way Summit With Sharon And Abbas -- June 4
- Bush Demands A Halt To Jewish Settlements -- June 4
- Bush: Two States Must Share The Holy Land -- June 4
- President Bush Tells Powell & Rice: Make Mid-East Peace Plan Top Priority -- June 4
- Bush Greets U.S. Soldiers In Qatar -- June 5

The following headlines coincided with President Bush's commitment to a greater involvement in the Middle East:

- Rumsfeld Denies 'False Pretext' For Iraq War -- May 30
- Iraq War 'Not Over,' U.S. General Warns -- May 30
- U.S. Intel 'Simply Wrong' On Chemical Attack-General -- May 30
- Wolfowitz Comments Revive Doubts Over Iraq's Mass Destruction Weapons -- May 30
- Tenet Defends Iraq Intelligence: CIA Chief Disputes Allegations Of Administration Pressure On Iraq -- May 31

- Straw, Powell Had Serious Doubts Over Their Iraqi Weapons Claims -- May 31
- Powell Defends Information He Used To Justify Iraq War -- May 31
- Pressure Mounting On Bush And Blair As Weapons Hunters Find No Unconventional Arms -- May 31
- Bush And Blair Under Heat Over Iraq -- June 1
- Iraqi Troops, Tribes To U.S.: Leave Or Face War -- June 2
- Weapons Of Mass Disappearance -- June 2
- Ex-Army Boss: Pentagon Won't Admit Reality In Iraq -- June 3
- Lawmakers Seek Answers On Iraq's WMD Intelligence -- June 4
- Ratchet Up The Urgency On Iraq Weapons Search -- June 4
- Blix Challenges War Leaders On WMDs -- June 5
- CIA To Give Congress Thousands Of Documents On Iraq Intelligence -- June 5
- Bush Defends Iraq War In Qatar In Meeting With U.S. Troops -- June 5
- Some Iraq Analysts Felt Pressure From Cheney Visits -- June 5
- Bush Pledges To 'Reveal The Truth' On WMD -- June 5

U.S. News Headlines Following President Bush's Return From The Middle East:

- Blix Decries Coalition's Intelligence On Iraq Arms -- June 6
- UN Presses Bush On Iraq: Return Of Weapons Inspectors Urged -- June 6
- Pentagon's Intelligence Service Reported No Reliable Evidence Of Iraqi Weapons Last September -- June 6
- Ex-Official: Evidence Distorted For War -- June 7
- White House Says Bush Fully Supports New Palestinian Leader -- June 8
- Palestinians Attack Israeli Army Post, Kill Four -- June 8

- Three States Battling Monkeypox Outbreak -- June 9
- Israelis Attempt To Assassinate Hamas Leader -- June 10
- Bush 'Deeply Troubled' By Israel Attack -- June 10
- 'High Probability' Al Qaeda Will Use WMD Within Next 2 Years -- June 10

The news headlines following the June 11, 2003, Jerusalem suicide bombing:

- FBI: Cell Phones Found In Saudi Probe Rigged To Trigger Bombs -- June 11
- U.S. Can't Rule Out North Korea Strike, Perle Says -- June 11
- Senate Intelligence Panel To Hold Iraq WMD Assessment -- June 11
- Israel Retaliates After Homicide Bus Bomber Kills 16 In Jerusalem -- June 11
- U.S. Will Monitor Foreign Seaports -- June 11
- Bush Under Fire In Congress For Criticizing Israel -- June 12
- Mideast Peace Effort Shaken After Attacks -- June 12
- Powell To Meet Quartet Leaders In Aqaba -- June 12
- Hamas Vows To Murder Sharon -- June 12
- Israel, Hamas Vow Fight To The Finish -- June 12
- Hamas Warns Foreigners To Leave Israel -- June 12

News Headlines June 13 - June 28, 2003

- Saudis Admit Funding Hamas -- June 13
- The White House Is Blaming George Tenet For Faulty WMD Intelligence -- June 15
- Bush Blasts 'Revisionist Historians' On Iraq -- June 16
- The War Built On A Lie -- June 16
- Israel's Weisglass Meets With Powell, Rice -- June 16
- Powell Heading To Jerusalem For Peace Talks -- June 17
- Israel Seeks Pause On Road Map -- June 17
- Hamas Chief Calls For Full Withdrawal -- June 17
- Kerry Says Bush Misled Americans On War -- June 18

- Ex-CIA Director: Bush Stretched Facts On Iraq -- June 19
- Sen. Carl Levin: CIA Deliberately Misled UN Arms Inspectors -- June 19
- Kerry Says He'll Filibuster Supreme Court Nominees Who Do Not Support Abortion Rights -- June 20
- U.S. Troops Frustrated With Role In Iraq: Soldiers Say They Are Ill-Equipped For Peacekeeping -- June 20
- Rising U.S. Death Toll In Iraq Spurs Concern: 9 Soldiers Killed In Attacks This Month -- June 20
- Powell With Sharon: Israel 'Quite Faithful' To Aqaba Commitments -- June 20
- U.S. Closes Embassy In Kenya After Serious Terror Threat -- June 20
- Powell Says Cease-Fire Not Enough -- June 20
- Kids And Parents In Stores Awaiting Harry Potter Midnight Sale -- June 20
- Arizona Wildfire Burns Out Of Control -- June 20
- Iran Defies International Pressure On Nuclear Aims -- June 20
- U.S. Told Japan North Korea Has Nuclear Warheads -- June 20
- East Is East, And Wet Is Wet: Spring Rains Of Biblical Proportions -- June 20
- Iraq Weapons Rattle The Hill -- June 21
- PM: Killing Of Hamas Militant 'Successful' Operation -- June 21
- Powell: Israeli Attack On Hamas Leader Could Set Back Peace Process -- June 22
- Sharon: Israel Can Continue Expanding Settlements -- June 22
- Terror Expert Warns Of Al-Qaeda's Third Wave -- June 25
- Pres. Bush Demands Europe Stop Funding Hamas -- June 25
- U.S. Troops Targeted In Flurry Of Attacks In Iraq -- June 26

- New Explosion Hits Key Iraqi Oil Pipeline -- June 26
- Supreme Court Overturns Texas Sodomy Law -- June 26
- Supreme Court's Gay Sex Ruling Will Strike Down Anti-Sodomy Laws In Other States -- June 28

Rice Raised Objections with Sharon on the Security Fence

While meeting with Palestinian leaders on June 29, Dr. Condoleezza Rice, the national security adviser, listened intently to complaints about the Israeli fence walling off Palestinians in the West Bank. The next day, she raised objections to the fence with Prime Minister Ariel Sharon. American and Israeli officials say P.M. Sharon politely rebuffed Dr. Rice, at least for that moment.

The exchange, administration officials said, illustrates their new willingness to prod Israel and to get involved in the minutiae of the negotiations.

A senior official said that at that time it is a certainty that more pressure will be applied on Israel to cease construction of the fence in coming weeks. "The very fact that Condi Rice raised the issue of the fence with Sharon is significant," said an administration official. "We will be back on this issue if things don't improve."

The exchange between Dr. Rice and Mr. Sharon also showed, administration officials said, a decision to direct pressure from both the White House and the State Department, which had long been warring over Middle East policy.

The week before Dr. Rice's visit, for example, Secretary of State Colin L. Powell was in Israel pressing for an Israeli withdrawal from the Gaza Strip, even to the point of discussing individual checkpoints on maps of the area.

News Headlines from June 29 to July 24

- As The Weapons Hunt Intensifies, So Does The Finger Pointing. A Preview Of The Coming battle --

June 29

- Condoleezza Rice Meets Sharon In Israel -- June 29
- Tropical Storm Bill Forms In Gulf Of Mexico - Heads Towards The U.S. -- June 29
- Gays & Lesbians Parade With A New Sense Of Pride -- June 30
- Wildfire Season Heating Up -- June 30
- Hurricane Watch In Louisiana - Tropical Storm Bill Approaches -- June 30
- Report: Osama Alive And Plotting -- July 1
- Road Map Needs A 'Friendly Presence' In Mideast, Says Vatican -- July 1
- Cleanup Begins As Bill Leaves Gulf Coast -- July 1
- North Korea Warns Of Retaliation -- July 1
- Extreme Weather On The Rise In The United States -- July 3
- Bush Taking Heat For 'Bring Them On' Remark -- July 3
- U.S. Offers $25m For Saddam Capture -- July 4
- U.S. Envoy Says Bush 'Twisted' Iraq Intelligence -- July 5
- Report Calls U.S. Agencies Understaffed For Bioterror -- July 6
- In Iraq, A 'Totally Ugly Incident' Between U.S. And Turkey -- July 6
- Saddam Recording Deemed Probably Authentic by CIA -- July 7
- Mideast Peace Process In Danger Of Collapse -- July 8
- White House Admits Iraq Uranium Claim Was 'An Error' -- July 8
- No Let Up In Attacks On U.S. Troops -- July 9
- Democrats Want Uranium Claim Probed -- July 9
- North Korea 'Closer To Nuclear Goal - Black Clouds Of Nuclear War Gathering' -- July 9
- Confidence In Bush Slips Further -- July 9
- Senator Kerry Challenges Bush On Iraq -- July 10

- Bush: CIA Cleared State Of The Union Speech -- July 10
- Bush Team United Iraq Front Unravels -- July 11
- Bush Stands By CIA's Tenet -- July 12
- CIA Got Uranium Mention Cut In October Why Bush Cited It In January Is Unclear -- July 13
- Ari Fleischer's Final Briefing Is Not Quite A Grand Slam -- July 14
- Kennedy Assails Bush's Iraq policy -- July 15
- $455 Billion Budget Shortfall Seen: Bush Administration Projects Biggest Deficits Ever -- July 15
- U.S., N. Korea Drifting Toward War, Perry Warns -- July 15
- Hurricane Claudette Bearing Down On Texas -- July 15
- Dems Demand Probe Of Prewar Intelligence -- July 15
- N. Korea Nuclear Crisis Getting More Serious By The Week -- July 17
- U.S. Commander Calls Iraq Conflict A Guerrilla War -- July 17
- U.S. Troops On High Alert As New Saddam Tape Aired -- July 17
- North Korea Likely Boosting Effort To Build Nukes -- July 20
- Saddam's Sons Odai & Qusai Confirmed Dead - Killed Today -- July 22
- President Bush Discusses Progress In Iraq -- July 23
- North Korea Threatens To Build Tactical Nuclear Arms -- July 24

Bush Meets with Mahmoud Abbas at the White House

The following material will give you an idea of what was discussed in the U.S.-Palestinian peace talks of July 25.

Thoughts on the Rose Garden Event

I was at the White House Rose Garden Friday for the Bush - Abbas meeting. I watched as President Bush spoke and then observed him as he listened to Abbas. I really sensed he thought he could "will" peace into place with rhetoric, charm, creativity, military might and money.

It appeared Bush believed he could use his diplomatic skills to reverse thousands of years of hatred, and bring peace to the Middle East. Sadly, the United States continues to be the main perpetrator of the "land for peace" and is using her assets to manipulate the participants.

The Main Points from President Bush's Friday Rose Garden Address:

- Bush stated the government of Israel recognizes that its own interests will be served when the Palestinians govern themselves in their own state: a peaceful democratic state where the forces of terror have been replaced by the rule of law.
- He stated Prime Minister Abbas is committed to a complete end to violence and terrorism, and he recognizes that terror against Israelis, wherever they might be, is a dangerous obstacle to the achievement of a Palestinian state.
- Bush stated he is committed to meet the goal that has been set. To accomplish that, the President believes that the daily lives of ordinary Palestinians must be improved. Therefore, the President approved a grant of $20 million dollars to be directed to the Palestinian Authority.
- The President announced that the United States and Palestinian Authority would establish a joint Palestine Economic Development Group. This group of American and Palestinian officials will meet regularly and be charged with finding practical ways to bring jobs, growth and investment to the Palestinian economy.
- Treasury Secretary John Snow and Commerce Secretary Don Evans will report directly to him on the steps that need to be taken to build a solid economic

foundation for a free and sovereign Palestinian state.

The Main Points from Prime Minister Mahmoud Abbas' Rose Garden Address:

- Abbas promised to remain committed to the Road Map and to implement the security and reform obligations.
- Security for all Palestinians and Israelis is an essential element in progress, and they will achieve security based on the rule of law.
- Abbas said that the Palestinians have succeeded significantly, where Israel, with its military might, has failed in reducing violence, but the Palestinians will continue.
- Reform and institution building are an internal Palestinian priority. They do not merely seek a state, but they desire a state that is built on the solid foundations of the modern constitution, democracy, transparency, the rule of law, and the market economy.
- Abbas willcontinue to negotiate with Israel on the implementation of its obligations. Some progress has been made, but movement needs to be made in terms of freeing prisoners, lifting the siege on President Arafat, Israeli withdrawal from Palestinian areas, and easing up freedom of movement to Palestinians.
- The establishment of a sovereign, independent Palestinian state, with East Jerusalem as its capital.
- Just, agreed solution of the refugee question on the basis of the UN Resolution 194.
- This vision cannot be realized if Israel continues to grab Palestinian land.
- If the settlement activities in Palestinian land and construction of the so-called separation wall on confiscated Palestinian land continue, Palestinians might soon find themselves at a situation where the

foundation of peace, a free Palestine state, living side-by-side in peace and security in Israel is a factual impossibility.

- Nothing less than a full settlement freeze will do because nothing less than a full settlement freeze will work. Abbas believes that for the sake of peace, and for the sake of future Palestinian and Israeli generations, all settlement activities must be stopped now, and the wall must come down.

The Main Points from President Bush and Prime Minister Abbas' talks:

- Prime Minister Abbas and President Bush covered a range of issues in their talks. This included the impact of the limits on the freedom of movement on the Palestinian people and the need to reduce the network of checkpoints and barriers.
- Prime Minister Abbas shared his concerns about Israeli settlements, confiscation of land, and the building of a security fence. He also expressed his strong desire to see the release of many more Palestinian prisoners, which currently number over six thousand.
- The government of Israel announced that it would take down more of the checkpoints that are making it difficult for Palestinians to travel to their jobs and schools.
- In addition, Israel will consider ways to reduce the impact of the security fence on the lives of the Palestinian people.
- Bush stated Prime Minister Sharon has demonstrated that he is also a partner committed to reaching a peace settlement. Sharon has also pledged to transfer to the Palestinian Authority the security responsibility for two additional cities in the West Bank and to make further progress in removing settlement outposts.

- Bush stated that this is a time of great possibility in the Middle East. The people of the region are counting on all leaders involved to seize opportunities for peace and progress. Too many lives have been lost through resentment and violence. The Palestinian people, like people everywhere, deserve freedom. They deserve an honest government and they deserve peace.

Review of the Bush Administration Plan and Involvement:

- President Bush allowed the Palestinians to state to the world from the White House that an independent Palestinian state would have East Jerusalem as its capital; that UN Resolution 194 would address the refugee situation; and stated that settlement activities on Palestinian land must be frozen. [Note: The White House event further legitimized the Palestinians claims; the East Jerusalem capital and the refugee issues are deal-breakers.]
- President Bush gave Abbas the opportunity to call on Israel to stop building the West Bank security fence. He said it is not helpful to the peace process. [Note: Why the fence? To keep the Palestinians from killing Israelis.]
- President Bush in his June 24, 2002, Middle East message said there would be no more dealing with Arafat. [Note: Arafat is still calling the shots. He defined the role and provided the script for Mahmoud Abbas. In the Rose Garden, Abbas called on Arafat to be released from his Ramallah compound. Bush stated (thirteen months earlier) that his government was finished dealing with Arafat.]
- According to the *Washington Times*, the Bush administration, in a gesture to visiting Palestinian Prime Minister Mahmoud Abbas, softened its stance on the

militant group Hamas, saying it could survive if it transformed into a purely political organization. Secretary of State Colin L. Powell -- who said last month that "It is no longer possible to separate one part of Hamas from another part of Hamas" and called Hamas an "enemy of peace" -- told reporters in Washington on Thursday, July 24, 2003: "If an organization that has a terrorist component to it, a terrorist wing to it, totally abandons that, gives it up, and there is no question in anyone's mind that is part of its past, then that is a different organization." [Note: Bush stated numerous times in the last two months that the terror infrastructure in Israel has to be dismantled. Again, Powell and the State Department have entered the mix. In essence they are saying that the terror groups will be acceptable if the militants turn in their weapons and become political organizations instead.]

- The Council on Foreign Relations (CFR) remains in the political loop. Abbas addressed them on Thursday, July 14. [Note: The CFR farms people into State Department positions. Every U.S. Secretary of State since World War II has been a CFR member, Powell included.]
- After pressure from the White House and in preparation for Sharon's departure for Washington, Israel agreed to release 210 militants from Israeli prisons [Note: Sharon's Cabinet voted 13 to 10 to release the militants. This is a complete change of course from earlier in the week and it is due to White House pressure.]
- Bush planned to send Treasury Secretary John Snow and Commerce Secretary Don Evans to the region. [Note: The President is using U.S. financial might and ingenuity to induce the Palestinians and the Israelis to parcel God's covenant land.]
- The CIA has peace monitors in Israel. [Note: The CIA has trained Palestinian sharpshooters to keep order

within their own communities, they have also turned their guns on Israelis.]

Bush and Sharon Meet - Not a Good Day at the White House - July 29, 2003

I was also in attendance for the Bush - Sharon White House Rose Garden event. Bush and Sharon gave brief speeches and then they took a few questions from the U.S. and Israeli press.

I could tell from the very beginning that the interaction between the two was very tentative, the worse by far in Sharon's eight trips to the White House.

Bush kept attempting to get a positive response from Sharon but it wasn't forthcoming. Sharon acknowledged Bush a few times only out of politeness, but he was reluctant. Sharon couldn't hide his dismay and he seemed very troubled.

What a contrast to the exuberance we witnessed in Sharon's last visit to the White House on October 16, 2002. Sharon stated that Israel has never had a better friend in the White House than Bush. Later that night Sharon and his staff were singing Israeli songs at the Blair House. (He did not stay at the Blair House this time.)

The Israeli media was also very exuberant on October 16, but Tuesday, July 29 there was no life - you could sense their dismay. I spoke to two friends with the Israeli media, they tried to be positive but they couldn't hide their inner feelings. Also, after Sharon's meetings, Israeli journalists tried to put a positive spin in their commentaries.

Additionally, in my opinion, Sharon, who is a genius strategist, knew the White House has maneuvered him into a very dangerous position. The sad irony is that this is the result of the White House and State Department's desire to help prop up Palestinian Prime Minister Mahmoud Abbas. Abbas had been under great political pressure imposed by PLO Chairman Yasser Arafat, the heads of Hamas and other terror groups.

The White House made sure that both the Abbas and Sharon meetings and speeches started at the same time. The Oval office meetings both commenced at 11:20 AM. The Rose Garden events both began at 11:50 AM (they both began a few minutes late). Both Bush and Abbas and Bush and Sharon took a few questions from the U.S. and Palestinian and Israeli media before they left for lunch with their combined staffs.

There was energy in the Bush-Abbas meeting; there was not in the Bush - Sharon meeting. Abbas was all smiles Sharon seemed dejected. Bush went out of his way to be friendly to both leaders, Abbas responded, Sharon was reluctant.

I even noticed Bush nudge next to Sharon for a smiling photo-op when Sharon smiled for a brief second when he then lost his place in his speech and Bush helped him recover. Even the photos on the White House web site showed smiles, but don't let those or any other reports fool you; this was not a good day.

Sharon Pressured as Bush Feels the Repercussions July 29, 2003

On the very same day President George W. Bush applied pressure on Ariel Sharon to surrender Israel's covenant land and to stop the construction of the security fence, he too faced some serious pressure.

Bush's people came under intense Senate questioning for the billions of dollars spent in Iraq and the almost daily loss of American lives. President Bush met for two hours with an angry Saudi Foreign Minister who had rushed to the United States over the 9-11 report. He also faced scrutiny over the involvement of the role the Saudis played in 9-11. Moreover, the President refused to release additional information either to the American public or to the Saudi Foreign Minister about the oil-rich kingdom's involvement. U.S. security was heightened over a potential Al Qaeda terror attack and consumer confidence plummeted in July catching many economists and the White House by surprise.

As usual when the Bush Administration applies pressure on Israel they experience increased pressure and we observe disruption in America.

Here are some key headlines from July 29-30, 2003.

- Bush Meets With Sharon At The White House
- Saudi Minister Rushes To U.S.
- U.S. Senators Rap Administration On Iraq Policies
- U.S. Warns Of Possible Al Qaeda Plane Attacks
- Bush Meets Saudi Foreign Minister On Terror Report
- Scrutiny Rises Over Saudi Ties To Al-Qaeda
- U.S. Consumer Confidence Plummets In July
- Saudi Foreign Minister Condemns Nine-Eleven Report

Other major news headlines from July 25 to September 6, 2003

- White House To Heap Royal Honors On Mahmoud Abbas -- July 25
- President Bush Welcomes Prime Minister Abbas To White House -- July 25
- Bush Nominee For Secretary Of Navy Commits Suicide-- July 25
- U.S. Sends Troops To Liberian Coast -- July 26
- White House Criticized For Censoring September 11 Report -- July 27
- Congress Pushes To Release Classified Parts Of Report On September 11 Terrorist Attacks -- July 27
- Saudi Foreign Minister Comes To D.C. To Meet Bush Over 9-11 Controversy -- July 28
- Bush Meets With Sharon At The White House -- July 29
- Congress Pushes To Release Classified Parts Of

Report On September 11 Terrorist Attacks -- June 29

- U.S. Senators Rap Administration On Iraq Policies -- July 29
- U.S. Warns Of Possible Al Qaeda Plane Attacks -- July 29
- Bush Meets Saudi Foreign Minister On Terror Report -- July 29
- Scrutiny Rises Over Saudi Ties To Al-Qaeda -- July 29
- U.S. Consumer Confidence Plummets In July -- July 29
- Saudi Foreign Minister Condemns Nine-Eleven Report -- July 30
- Pentagon Says China Refitting Missiles To Hit Okinawa, U.S. Troops -- July 31
- Mystery Disease Afflicting U.S. Soldiers In Iraq -- July 31
- U.S. Ferries Warned Of Terror Plots -- July 31
- North Korea Says No Talks If Nuclear Issue Taken To UN -- August 2
- U.S. Presses Program For New Atom Bombs -- August 3
- Ashcroft: Al-Qaeda Could Strike Again -- August 3
- State Proposes Cut In Israel Loans -- August 4
- Feds To Warn Airlines On Carry-Ons -- August 4
- U.S. Looking To Keep Up Mideast Momentum -- August 5
- U.S. Eyes Cutting Israel Loan Guarantees Over Fence -- August 5
- U.S. Warns Of Weapons, Bombs Hidden In Electronics -- August 5
- July Warmest Month On Record For Phoenix, Arizona -- August 4
- U.S. Teams In Iraq Investigate Mystery 'Pneumonia-Like' Illness; 2 U.S. Soldiers Dead -- August 5
- Episcopalian Church USA Officially Confirms 1st Openly Gay Bishop -- August 6
- Judge Orders 10 Commandments & History Monument Taken Out Of Alabama Judicial Building -- August 6
- Relentless Heat Wave Plagues Europe -- August 7

- World's 1st Cloned Horse Born -- August 7
- U.S. Episcopal Churches Vote Allows Blessings Of Gay Unions -- August 8
- N.O.A.A. Raises Hurricane Predictions -- August 8
- West Nile Human Cases Triple In One Week -- August 8
- Record Heat Bakes Much Of Texas -- August 8
- Record London Temps Break 100 For 1st Time Ever -- August 10
- Europe Having Record-Breaking Heat -- August 10
- Israel To Continue Building Fence, Despite U.S. Objections -- August 11
- Terror Link To West Nile Virus? Saddam, Castro Suspect In Spread -- August 11
- Suspected Missile Smuggler To U.S. Charged With Trying To Support Terrorists -- August 13
- Arms Race Fear Over New Gamma-Ray Bomb -- August 14
- Largest-Ever Blackout In U.S. History Hits North Eastern U.S. - Around 50 Million Without Power -- August 14
- FBI: Suspected Arms Dealer Planned To Smuggle 50 Missiles Into U.S. -- August 14
- Appeals Court Rejects Challenge To Ten Commandments Plaque: Only Remaining Avenue Of Appeal The U.S. Supreme Court -- August 14
- Alabama's Chief Justice Roy Moore Refuses To Remove Ten Commandments -- August 14
- Blackout Shows Vulnerability Of Nation -- August 15
- Blackout Not Terrorist Act Yet - MSNBC -- August 16
- Weird, Wild Weather From Denver To Delhi Stumps Climatologists -- August 16
- Report Calls U.S. A Top Target For Terror Attack Within A Year -- August 17
- Sabotage Threatens Iraq's Economy -- August 17
- Citadel Has Dropped Mealtime Prayers After A Federal Appeals Court Decision -- August 17

- U.S. Public May Face Bill Up To $50 Billion For Power Upgrade -- August 17
- U.S. Troops Shoot Dead Award - Winning Reuters Cameraman In Iraq -- August 17
- Iraqi Oil, Water Pipes Sabotaged, Officials Say -- August 18
- Bin Laden And Mullah Omar - 'Still Alive' -- August 18
- North Korea Talks Tough On Atomic Bombs Ahead Of Talks -- August 18
- Internet Virus Becomes The Fastest Spreading In History -- August 18-22
- Major Terror Bombings In Jerusalem And Baghdad Within Hours -- August 20
- Former White House Press Secretary And Democrat Start Group To Try To 'Recall' Bush -- August 20
- The 90-Day Cease-Fire In Israel Is Over -- August 21
- Israel Stated That No Militant Leader Is Safe -- August 22
- News That U.S. Gas Prices May Reach Highest Level In History -- August 22
- Bush: "We're Going To Stay The Course" -- August 23
- Hamas Calls Bush 'Islam's Biggest Enemy', Turning Point For Sharon -- August 23
- Bremer: U.S. Can't Go It Alone -- August 24
- Analysis: Is 'Perfect Storm' Brewing For Bush? -- August 24
- Pres Bush: U.S. Will Remain Steadfast In War Against Terror -- August 26
- Amid Tensions, Saudi Envoy Meets Bush Father, Cheney -- August 27
- The Deficit-How Big? - Even IMF Is Making A Fuss -- August 27
- Last U.S. Troops Left Saudi Arabia Soil Yesterday -- August 28
- Bush To Face Iraq Challenge On Return To Washington -- August 29

- U.S. Officials Tell The Palestinian Leadership That If Abbas' Government Falls, They Will Withdraw Support For The Road Map And For Palestinian State -- August 30
- Succumbing To Pressure From The United States, The Palestinian Legislative Council Decided Over The Weekend To Postpone The Vote Of Confidence In The Government Of Prime Minister Mahmoud Abbas From Monday To Thursday. -- August 31
- EU Will Continue Talking To Arafat, Solana Says -- August 31
- Israel Refuses To Deal With Arafat -- August 31
- Russia's Putin, Italy's Berlusconi And Bush Discuss Iraq By Phone -- August 31
- Israel's Defense Minister Shaul Mofaz Promised A War "To The Bitter End" Against Hamas -- September 1
- Abu Ala, The Speaker Of The Palestinian Legislative Council Says Arafat And Abbas Hate Each Other -- September 1
- At U.S. Gathering, Muslims Rally For Civil Rights -- September 1
- Looking For Help-Bush Administration To Propose Expanded International Force In Iraq -- September 2
- U.S. Rushed Post-Saddam Planning -- September 3
- FBI Warns Of Potential Poison Attacks -- September 3
- Advisory: Al Qaeda Planning New U.S. Attacks - Plan To Hijack International Airliners Flying Near Or Over The Continental U.S. -- September 4
- FBI Concerned About Threat Of Terror-Induced Blackouts -- September 4
- Terror Attack On Grid Would Collapse U.S. -- September 5
- Palestinian Prime Minister Mahmoud Abbas Resigns -- September 6

The Arafat Problem

The sudden resignation of Mahmoud Abbas as Prime Minister of the Palestinian Authority stunned Bush administration officials and raised fresh questions about the administration's strategy of trying to isolate Yasser Arafat and work with so-called moderate Palestinians.

The official White House reaction to Mr. Abbas's resignation was cautious, hiding the administration's deep disappointment. A statement called on the Palestinian legislature to "act in a way that empowers the Prime Minister" no matter who is selected, and said that "all parties" needed to "consider carefully the consequences of their actions."

Realistically it would be extremely difficult for any successor of Mahmoud Abbas to do that.

The position of Palestinian Prime Minister has become poisoned, and anyone who tries to stand up to Mr. Arafat is seen as a pawn of the United States and Israel.

Since President Bush took office, events in Israel have forced constant adjustments by the administration. First, administration officials were openly disdainful of the way President Clinton had become personally engaged in the Middle East peace effort. In the view of many, Bush's predecessor had actually made the situation worse by trying and failing to broker a deal in the waning weeks of his term.

Not until 2003, after the Iraq war, did the administration become more involved itself, in large part because of pressure from Britain's Tony Blair, European allies, Crown Prince Abdullah of Saudi Arabia and other Arab allies. Bush also needed their money, troops and support in Iraq.

But there was never any doubt in the minds of the Europeans, Arabs and others that Mr. Arafat would still be able to sabotage the process by preventing a crackdown by

Palestinians on Palestinian militant groups, the prerequisite demanded by Israel for taking actions of its own.

Indeed, the Bush administration has been angered with its Road Map partners over their rebuffing of American pleas to stop meeting with Arafat when they visit Israel.

The United States and Israel both reaffirmed their refusal to work directly with Arafat. The EU has specifically stated over and over that they will continue to work with Arafat.

On September 7, 2003, Chairman Yasser Arafat chose a senior official, Ahmed Qureia (Abu Ala), as his next Prime Minister. Qureia helped broker the 1993 Oslo accords between Israel and the PLO.

On the day of Queria's appointment U.S. Secretary of State Colin Powell and White House National Security Adviser Condoleezza Rice blamed Arafat for hindering progress towards Middle East peace and said he must relinquish control of security forces.

They opposed any expulsion of Arafat, which the Sharon government voted to do in the time of their choosing. They said expulsion could give the veteran Palestinian leader a wider stage from which to work.

We know the historicity of Arafat's involvement and time has proven he cannot negotiate with any tool other than terrorism.

Ironically, the White House stated they would not work with him, but in reality they were, because Arafat controlled the Palestinian Prime Ministers. It had also become a Bush vs. Arafat situation now that Abbas had resigned. On March 14, 2003 in the Rose Garden, Bush reaffirmed his personal commitment to an "Israel and Palestine" living side by side in peace and security, but Arafat was the major obstacle to that happening; amongst the other matters we have pointed out in this book.

U.S. Secretary of State Colin Powell said, "Israel would

incite rage not only among Arabs but also Muslims everywhere by exiling or executing Palestinian Authority Chairman Yasser Arafat." (Note: A prime example that terrorism is having an impact.)

Powell, speaking from Baghdad on Sunday, September 14, 2003, during a visit to Iraq, said that Israeli politicians are not helping the U.S.-sponsored peace process by making such statements as Vice Prime Minister Ehud Olmert's comment on Sunday. His comment said "killing (Arafat) is definitely one of the 'options' under consideration by Prime Minister Ariel Sharon's government."

On Tuesday, September 16 the U.S. vetoed a UN Security Council bill that called on Israel to guarantee Yasser Arafat's security. America's UN Ambassador John Negroponte stated that the United States does not support the elimination or forced exile of Arafat and believes that his diplomatic isolation is the best course. He said the United States was forced to use its veto because the resolution failed to name groups such as Hamas and the Al-Aqsa Martyrs Brigade, which have claimed credit for numerous suicide bombings and other attacks against Israelis.

Also on Tuesday, the U.S. told Israel they would deduct money spent on settlements from their $9 billion loan guarantee. The U.S. also stated they were considering whether to reduce money spent on the security fence from the loan guarantees. U.S. Treasury Secretary Jack Snow reminded Israeli Finance Minister Benjamin Netanyahu that Israel is required to reduce its debt as another contingency of their loan guarantees. Due to Bush Administration pressure, Israeli Prime Minister Ariel Sharon delayed his cabinet meeting on Wednesday. They would have discussed the course of the security fence.

Israel is Quick to Respond

Israel normally responded quickly to U.S. dictates

and objections due to the financial and public support from the only nation who continues to favor them. With this in mind, the U.S. would continue to use her money to maneuver Sharon only to the point of not angering Jewish and Christian voters. Most Jews want peace and had no problem using covenant land for it, but they also do not want to see Israel put in further danger. Sixty one percent of the members of Congress attend replacement theology churches and seven percent attend Jewish synagogues. This sixty eight percent favor peace using Israel's land, as long as there are peace and security guarantees.

President Bush Welcomes King Abdullah II to Camp David on September 18, 2003

"First, I'm so pleased to welcome my friend, King Abdullah and Queen Rania to Camp David. I want to thank them so very much for rearranging their schedules to get up here ahead of Hurricane Isabel. Laura and I look forward to spending some quality time with two really fine people."

"We're going to have some serious discussions today, then we'll have a nice lunch and then we'll batten down the hatches and spend a good evening with our friend."

President Bush Comments on Arafat in His and King Abdullah II Press Briefing from Camp David on Thursday, September 18, 2003

"Mr. Arafat has failed as a leader. And as I mentioned, Prime Minister Abbas was undermined at all turns by the old order, which meant Mr. Arafat. And the people of the Palestinian territory must understand if they want peace, they must have leadership who is absolutely 100 percent committed to fighting off terror. I believed Prime Minister Abbas when he told me at Sharm el-Sheikh, then at Aqaba, then in the Oval Office, he would do everything in his power to fight terror, that he would work to consolidate the security forces so that he could fight terror."

"And his efforts were undermined, and that's why we're now stalled. I'm still committed to peace, because I believe the vast majority of people want peace; I'm committed to the Road Map."

"But I'll remind those who focus on the Road Map that the first thing the Road Map said was that there must be security in order for peace to advance, that there must be a collective effort to fight off terror. Mr. Arafat has failed in that effort. And, hopefully, at some point in time, a leadership of the Palestinian Authority will emerge which will then commit itself 100 percent to fighting off terror. And then we'll be able to consolidate the power necessary to fight off terror."

"And when that happens, the world will come together to provide the conditions for hope. The world will come together to help an economy grow so that the Palestinian people can have a hopeful future. The first thing that must happen is an absolute condemnation and defeat of those forces who will kill innocent people in order to stop a peace process from going forward."

Analysis -- Bush vs. Arafat

To President Bush's credit, he has never invited Arafat to the White House. He has refused both to meet with him and to negotiate with him. He attempted to isolate him in his dealings with Mahmoud Abbas but Arafat continued to interfere until Abbas finally resigned in frustration.

President Bush has a lot riding politically in Israel and Iraq. He needs the world community's support for Iraq. Israel had been pressured previously due to that fact. At this stage, the emphasis looks like it may be the elimination or exiling of Arafat. The White House will be subtle so as not to anger the Muslim leaders.

What Will Give?

As Michael Ledeen, Contributing Editor to the *National Review*, stated recently in a 700 Club interview with Pat Robertson; no peace agreement has ever been agreed to that did not first have a war. In other words, until the terror infrastructure in Israel is dealt with (which could bring in other Arab nations per Psalm 83 and Isaiah 17) there will not be a Daniel 9:27 peace agreement or any other.

Yasser Arafat is the number one enemy of Israel and he wants a large chunk of God's covenant land. Ironically, Arafat has served a prophetic purpose, however, his days appear numbered.

Again, despite refusing to work directly with Arafat, the United States has publicly called on Israel to change its mind regarding the expulsion of Yasser Arafat.

News Headlines from September 6–November 16, 2003

- Palestinian Prime Minister Mahmoud Abbas Resigns As Palestinian Prime Minister -- September 6
- Tropical Storm Isabel Develops In The Atlantic -- September 6
- President Addresses The Nation On Iraq Asks For $87 Billion -- September 7
- Democrats Blast Bush's Iraq Funding Plan -- September 8
- Rumsfeld: Criticism Of Bush Strengthens U.S. Foes -- Washington Post -- September 8
- World Council Of Churches Call For War-Crimes Probe Committed By "Occupying Powers" Including The "Illegal Resort To War" -- September 8
- Al-Qaeda Issues A Chilling Warning For Americans -- September 8
- Two Suicide Bombings In Israel Kill 15 People Injure Scores -- September 9
- IDF Chief: Al-Qaeda Tried To Use Saudi F-15 For 9/11 Type Attack On Israel -- September 9

- Prelude Top 9-11: Who Aided Hijackers Is Still Mystery -- September 10
- Saddam Ordered Najaf Bombing: Postwar Sabotage Hit List Includes Infiltrating Shrine, Killing Clerics -- September 10
- France And Germany Seek Full UN Control Over Iraq -- September 10
- New Bin Laden Video Shown On Al Jazeera -- September 10
- What Bush Hopes To Buy For $87 Billion, From Vehicle Treads To Iraqi Hospitals, U.S. Aims For A Better Foothold In The Sand -- September 9
- Israel Security Cabinet: Arafat Obstacle To Peace, Must Be Removed -- September 11
- U.S. Blocks Cabinet Move To Exile Arafat -- September 11
- Mubarak: Expelling Arafat Would Be "Grave, Fatal Error" -- September 11
- Isabel Threatens U.S., Insurers: Hurricane May Be One Of The Most Powerful In History, Causing Billions In Insurance Claims -- September 11
- State Department Gives World Travel Advisory -- September 11
- U.S. Warns Al-Qaeda May Be Planning Chemical, Biological Attack - Bloomberg -- September 11
- Isabel, A Category 5 Hurricane, Maintaining 160 MPH Sustained Winds -- September 12
- France Urges Israel Not To Make The 'Mistake' Of Expelling Arafat -- September 12
- CIA Analysis Finds Tape Was Probably Bin Laden - Reuters September 12
- World Leaders Voice Concern Over Arafat Removal Decision -- September 12
- Atomic Board Gives Iran October 31 Deadline -- September 12
- Al-Aqsa Vows To 'Strike Everywhere' If Arafat

Expelled -- September 12

- FBI Says It Can't Infiltrate Al-Qaeda Agency, Focuses On Recruiting Informants -- September 12
- Saudis Move F-15s Near Israel's Border -- September 12
- North Korea Nixes Demand To End Nuke Program -- September 12
- U.S. Expected To Veto Arafat Protection Deal -- September 13
- Powell: Arafat's Elimination May Ignite Muslim Rage Against Israel -- September 14
- UN Security Council Meeting Vote Moved To Tuesday -- September 15
- U.S. To Cut Loan Package For Settlement Building, Undecided About Fence -- September 16
- U.S. Vetoes Resolution On Arafat At UN -- September 16
- Facing U.S. Ire, Sharon Postpones Cabinet Fence Debate -- September 17
- Powell To Determine How Much Of $9B To Be Withheld -- September 17
- U.S. Snow Warns Israel On Loan Backing, Urges Peace -- September 17
- White House Prepares For Hurricane -- September 17
- U.S. Wants Israel's Debt Reduced As Loan Guarantee Condition -- September 17
- Bush To Moves Up Camp David Meeting With King Abdullah Due To Hurricane Isabel -- September 17
- U.S. Capital On Crisis Footing For Hurricane Isabel -- September 18
- Bush Calls Arafat A "Failed Leader" Cause For Peace Failure -- September 18
- Bush And Abdullah Committed To Middle East Process -- September 18
- Hurricane Isabel Comes Ashore In North Carolina And Virginia -- September 18
- Bush Declares North Carolina And Virginia Disaster

Areas -- September 18
- Isabel Kills 29, 8 Million Without Power -- Thursday -- September 18
- Isabel Insurance Estimated At $1 Billion -- Friday -- September 19
- UN General Assembly Condemns Israel Over Arafat -- September 19
- U.S.: Won't Back Any Palestinian Government Run By Arafat – September 21
- Car Bomb Kills Iraqi Officer, Wounds 19 Near UN Headquarters – September 22
- Massive Clean-up In U.S. After Hurricane Isabel – September 22
- More Than 40 Terrorist Warnings In Israel Today – September 22
- High Temperatures Helped Spur Four Wildfires In Southern California – September 22
- Fatah Leaders Go To Washington – September 22
- Europe's Record Heat wave Caused Major Poultry Loss – September 23
- Portugal's Worst Wildfire Season In Memory – September 23
- New Tornadoes Leave Areas Hit By Isabel With More Damage – September 24
- Bush Says Palestinian Cause 'Betrayed By Leaders' – September 24
- Israel Considers Iran Nuke Strike – September 25
- Quartet: P.A. Must Act On Terror, Israel Must Halt Settlements – September 27, 2003
- Isolated Bush Takes UN Helm – September 28
- Russia Won't End Accord With Iran To Build Reactor – September 28
- Qureia Taps Arafat Loyalist Youssef As Security Chief – September 29
- EU Foreign Ministers To Meet, Discuss Mideast In Brussels – September 29

- White House Denies A Top Aide Identified An Officer Of The C.I.A – September 29
- Stymied Administration Slams Both Sides Bush Warns P.A. As Powell Raps The Settlements – September 29
- Ambassador Joseph Wilson: 'Neo-Conservatives And Religious Conservatives Have Hijacked Bush Administration – October 1
- North Korea Using Plutonium For Bomb Production – October 2
- Russia, France, & UN Head Annan Not Satisfied With U.S. Resolution On Iraq – October 2
- Annan Stance On Iraq Threatens U.S. Plan - October 3
- Palestinians To Seek UN Resolution On Separation Fence – October 4
- Suicide Bomber In Northern Israel Kills 19, Wounds 55 – October 4
- Israeli Warplanes Strike Islamic Jihad Base 50 Km From Damascus – October 4
- UN Security Council Discussing Israeli Strike Inside Syria – October 5
- U.S. Won't Condemn Israel's Syria Attack - October 6
- Sharon: Israel Will Strike At Enemies – October 7
- U.S. Issues Alert In Saudi Arabia – October 8
- Sharon: Left Wing Is Collaborating With The Palestinians – October 8
- Syria Criticizes Proposed U.S. Sanctions – October 9
- Sharon Warns He May Block Palestinian State Plans – October 9
- Arafat's Health Is Failing – October 9
- Officials: Al Qaeda Actively Planning Terror Attacks On U.S. – October 13
- Report: U.S. Seeking Arafat Ouster With 'Ill Health' As Reason – October 13
- Israelis Heap Scorn On Beilin 'Peace Plan' – October 13
- Yasser Arafat, Shimon Peres Support Unofficial

Israeli-Palestinian Peace Treaty - October 14
- U.S. Supreme Court Accepts Pledge Of Allegiance Case - October 15
- Rumsfeld Defends General Who Commented On War And Satan - October 16
- U.S. General, Under Fire, Says He's Not 'Anti-Islam' - October 17
- Feds Order All Commercial Aircraft Searched After Box Cutters & Notes Found In Planes - October 17
- New Front In Mid-East Conflict? Gaza Attack On U.S. Convoy - October 17
- General: We're In A 'Spiritual Battle': Says 'Christian Army' Fights Satan, Muslims Worship 'Idol' - October 17
- Archbishop: 'Huge Crisis Looming' Over U.S. Gay Bishop - October 17
- Sharon To Tell Knesset: Road Map Is Sole Diplomatic Option - October 19
- White House Adviser Takes Issue With U.S. General - October 19
- Army Lt. General William Boykin's Formal Press Q&A To Quell Fears Of Military Insensitivity - October 20
- Pentagon To Probe General's Islam Comments - October 21
- Bush Repudiates Comments By Top General - October 22
- California Fires Begin - October 23
- Rumsfeld: He Meant Every Word Of Leaked Memo - October 23
- President Bush Gives Ramadan Message - October 24
- Al Qaeda Sends Message To Sleepers - October 24
- 'Under God' Foe Vows More Challenges Ahead - October 24
- Rumsfeld Draws Republicans' Ire - October 24
- Republicans Fret Over Rumsfeld's Drag On His Party

- October 26

- Powell: Fence's Disruption Of Palestinian Life Is 'Troublesome' - Haaretz - October 26 -
- Rockets Hit Wolfowitz's Iraq Hotel; U.S. Soldier Dies -October 26
- 'The Perfect Non-Storm': Why Southern California Is Burning - October 27
- Many Dead As Ramadan Rampage Starts With Red Cross Bombing - October 27 -
- Holy Month Begins In Anger And Ruin - October 27
- Suicide Bomber Strikes Iraqi Town - October 28
- Exhausted Crews Fight Deadly Calif. Fires - October 28
- Powell Asks Red Cross To Stay In Iraq- October 28
- Political Threat To Bush Growing - October 28
- U.S. Calls Tenders For West Bank Housing Units 'Provocation' - October 28
- President Bush Hosts Ramadan Dinner At White House - October 28
- Bush: Fence Will Impede Emergence Of Palestinian State - October 28
- Fire Roars Through San Bernardino Mountains - October 29
- Second Huge Solar Storm Hits Earth - October 30
- Al-Qaeda Warns Of Devastating Attacks Against Americans During Islamic Holy Month Ramadan - October 31
- Wolfowitz supports Ayalon-Nussiebeh peace plan - October 31
- Al-Qaeda Ramadan Plot Targets Western Airliners - November 1
- U.S. Helicopter Shot Down In Iraq: 16 Soldiers Killed And 20 Wounded - November 2
- American Spy Chiefs Want More Pressure On Settlements - November 3
- Sun On Fire, Unleashes 3 More Major Flares - November 3

- The Sun's Intense Activity In The Past Week Will Go Into The Record Books - November 4
- Bush Visits Scorched California - November 4
- Explosions Rock Baghdad; Three Wounded - November 4
- Religious Fervor Behind Iraqi Fighting: Fallujah Residents Routinely Refer To Americans As 'Crusaders' - November 5
- U.S. Officials: Iraq's Prewar Offers Not Legitimate - November 5, 2003
- Sun Produces Monster Solar Flare, Biggest Ever - November 5
- Muslims Told To Leave Washington, D.C., New York City And Los Angeles Because Of Implied Imminent Terrorist Attacks - November 5
- 'Map' Leads To U.S. Dilemma In Russia-Israel Conflict - November 6
- Bush Signs $87.5 Billion Bill For Iraq, Afghanistan - November 6
- Possible Anthrax At White House Mail Center - November 6
- Anthrax Scare Shuts 11 Washington Postal Buildings - November 6
- Bush: Mideast Must Move Toward Democracy - November 6
- Rumsfeld: 85,000 Troops Going To Iraq - November 7
- Six Killed As U.S. Helicopter Crashes Near Tikrit - November 7
- Powell Sends Letter Of Support To Initiators Of Geneva Accord - November 7
- U.S. Suffers Bloodiest Week Since Victory - November 8
- Suicide Car Bomb Rocks Saudi capital - November 8
- U.S. Turns Wrath On Resistance Fighters: Report Claims Bush Team Has Bungled Peace - November 8
- Saudis Blame al-Qaida As Bomb Kills 17 - November 8
- Al-Qaeda set to launch psychological warfare in Iraq -

November 9

- Western Embassies on High Alert: U.K., U.S. and France urge staff to restrict movement – November 9
- Senator: U.S. Intelligence Feels More Attacks Probable – November 9
- New Palestinian Cabinet Casts Uncertainty on Peace Process – November 10
- Falluja's Unruliness Proves Tough To Tame – November 11
- Soros Blames U.S., Israel For Anti-Semitism – November 11
- Billionaire Soros Takes On Bush: Ousting President 'Central Focus' Of My Life,' He Says – November 11
- Blasts Rock Baghdad Near Coalition Headquarters – November 11
- Bremer Summoned To D.C. For Talks On Iraq – November 11
- America's Top General In The Middle East Warns Iraqis Of Stern Measures Unless They Curb Attacks – November 11
- Soros Blames U.S., Israel For Anti-Semitism: Jewish Billionaire Says Mideast Policies Need To Change - WND - – November 11
- Billionaire Soros Takes On Bush: Ousting President 'Central Focus Of My Life,' He Says - MSNBC – November 11
- Freak Storm Dumps Hail, Rain On Southern California – November 14
- 'Unprecedented' Security For Bush Visit - Guardian – November 14
- After 40 Hours, Democrats Succeed In Blocking 3 Nominees - N.Y.Times – November 14
- Near Hurricane Strength Winds More Than 1.4 Million Customers Lost Power – November 14
- Winds Rock Air Force One - CNN - – November 14
- U.S. Steps Up Offensive In Iraq – November 14

- CIA Says Experts See 'Darker Bioweapons Future' - November 14
- Unofficial Mideast Plan Gains Ground - November 14
- Bombings At Istanbul Synagogues Kill 23 - November 15
- Black Hawks Crash In Northern Iraq, Killing 17 - November 15
- Expected Solar Fireworks Could Disrupt Air Travel-November 15
- Purported Saddam Tape Calls For Increased Resistance - November 16
- Report: Al Qaeda Behind Synagogue Bombings - November 16

The Eighth Disruptive Period: December 17, 2003 to January 10, 2004

From November 24 to December 18, 2003 President Bush, Secretary of State Colin Powell, the U.S. State Department, the EU, the UN, Russia, the Palestinians, the Egyptians, the Jordanians, members of the Arab League, the Vatican, members of the World Council of Churches, the National Council of Churches, Israeli peace activists, all applied significant pressure on Israeli Prime Minister Ariel Sharon to return to the negotiating table and to make painful land concessions.

In the same time period Israel's "hard-line" Likud party reevaluated their position on the disputed land. Moreover, the Yesha council, which represents Israeli settlers, stated Sharon's government would fail if he tampers with the settlements.

Plans Coming from Many Directions

The Geneva Accord was signed on December 1 in Geneva, Switzerland. It was an attempt by the French influenced EU to use the Accord to forge a compromise position between the Quartet's Road Map and the

Geneva Accord, and to stir sentiment in Israel.

Israeli and Palestinian opposition groups brokered the Geneva Accord after two years of secret negotiations.

Information about the Accord was circulated to Israeli and Palestinian households in an effort to drum up support.

The Israeli government stated they firmly opposed the Accord, and Jewish groups criticized Switzerland for "interfering" in internal Israeli affairs.

U.S. Secretary of State Colin Powell wrote a letter to Geneva Accord sponsors Israeli Yossi Beilin and Palestinian Yasser Abed Rabbo expressing appreciation for their effort, and then met with them on December 5th.

Washington Post columnist Charles Krauthhammer stated eloquently that the Geneva Accord was scandalous. Israel is a democracy, and this agreement was negotiated in defiance of the democratically elected government of Israel. If a private U.S. citizen negotiated a treaty on his own, he could go to jail under the Logan Act. If an Israeli does it, he gets a pat on the back from the U.S. Secretary of State.

The U.S. State Department sent an official observer from the U.S. Embassy in the Swiss capital Bern to attend the signing of the Geneva Accords in Geneva.

Former US President Jimmy Carter unleashed a fierce attack against the Israeli and American governments in his speech at the Geneva Initiative's ceremony in Switzerland.

Carter blamed US President George W. Bush for anti-American sentiment and worldwide terror.

"Bush's inordinate support for Israel allows the Palestinians to suffer," Carter said. "This is a source of anti-American sentiment in the world and encourages terror."

Carter said Israel's settlements in the West Bank and Gaza Strip and the security fence are the main obstacles to peace. He called repeatedly for the return of Palestinian refugees to the territories, beyond what is called for in the Geneva Initiative.

"Settlements prevent the return of the refugees who left their homes after the 1948 and 1967 wars," Carter said. "No matter what leaders the Palestinians may choose, Israel must choose between peace and settlements."

UN Secretary General Kofi Annan also stated his approval of the Geneva Accord.

New Phase – New Pressure

Ominously, the new attempted siege of the Holy Land by Israel's enemies has entered a new phase. Peace proposals designed to undermine Israeli security appear with the endorsement of past Israeli politicians, past sponsors of obsolete agreements, and most disconcerting, the EU and the U.S. Government, whose continued support, and ultimate guarantee of Israel security, looks more and more critical to any final peace agreement.

A quick review of the most perilous provisions of the recently signed Geneva Accord arouse deep concern:

- Reserve Maj.-Gen Yaakov Amidror is quoted as saying the Accord *conceded almost all the security arrangements for the West Bank and Gaza Strip sought by past Israeli governments* and would leave Israel without a *safety net* if the Palestinians violated the agreement
- Israel will be forced to turn over sovereignty of the Jerusalem Temple Mount, closing the door to the rebuilding of the Third Holy Temple, and effectively sabotaging Jewish aspirations of resuming the Temple-based worship of God
- Accord terms will be dictated by an Arab-biased, group of nations (International Crisis Group) operating a European (Brussels- based) conflict resolution organization
- UN Resolution 194 (and others) shall be the basis for solution of the refugee problem. Its financial impact

is potentially ruinous. 194 does not speak of the 'right' of return, but carries its own seed of discord to determine financial responsibility:

Secretary Powell spoke on December 2: I have an obligation...to listen to Individuals who have interesting ideas.

President Bush spoke on December 4: The Geneva Accord was productive, as long as terror is fought, there is security, and a free and democratic Palestinian state emerges.

Senators and Congressman Present Plan

A group of 18 American congressmen and five senators submitted a draft resolution in both houses of Congress, urging President George Bush to adopt and promote two initiatives for an Israeli-Palestinian agreement formulated by members of the Israeli opposition and Palestinian interlocutors.

The two initiatives are The Peoples' Voice, launched by Ami Ayalon and Sari Nusseibeh, and the Geneva Understandings, drafted by Yossi Beilin and Yasser Abed Rabbo.

The resolution's sponsors included two Jewish senators, Frank Lautenberg and Dianne Feinstein, as well as veteran senator Patrick Leahy.

Clergy Urge More Active White House Effort for Mideast Peace *(Washington Post)*

Thirty-two religious leaders representing many of the nation's largest Christian, Jewish and Muslim groups were jointly urging the Bush administration to make more "active and determined" efforts to forge peace between Israel and the Palestinians.

In a November 25 letter to the White House, the bishops, cardinals, rabbis and imams called for "renewed high-level U.S. engagement . . . to help both sides take the bold steps necessary to rebuild hope that peace is possible."

While praising President Bush's peace plan, known as the "road map," they were critical of the administration's effort to carry it out. So far, they said, the steps taken by Israel and the Palestinian Authority have been "far too timid" and the U.S.-led monitoring process has been "practically invisible."

The letter's signers include the presiding bishops of the Methodist, Lutheran, Presbyterian and Episcopal churches; the Roman Catholic cardinals of Washington and Baltimore; the Greek Orthodox primate in the United States; three prominent evangelical ministers; the heads of the Conservative, Reform and Reconstructionist rabbinical associations; and directors or founders of seven U.S. Muslim groups.

World Pressure

Putting this intense time period into perspective, the nations of the world dramatically increased their pressure on Israel to divide God's covenant land. Again, these entities called on the dismantling of Israeli settlements, condemned the construction of Israel's new security fence (the U.S. deducted $289 million from Israel's loan guarantees), called for Jerusalem to be divided, called on Israel to leave most of the West Bank (Judea and Samaria), called on Israel to deal with the Palestinian refugee situation, while the Palestinian terror groups threatened to renews their suicide bombings against Israel.

Sharon Responds with His Own Plan *(Jerusalem Post)*

In response to enormous pressure, especially from the United States, Israeli Prime Minister Ariel Sharon provided a major policy speech on December 18, 2003 pertaining to Israel's land and the peace talks. He made these major points:

Israel may begin to take unilateral steps to detach itself from the Palestinians while implementing the US-backed road map peace initiative.

"According to circumstances, it is possible that parts of the 'Disengagement Plan' that are supposed to provide maximum security to the citizens of Israel will be undertaken while also attempting to implement the road map," Sharon said during his speech at the Herziliya Conference.

Sharon said that Israel would initiate "unilateral security steps' should the Palestinians not take the road map seriously. "The steps we will take are security-based and not diplomatically-based," he added.

Sharon said that in the meantime, Israel would begin to take security measures in order to protect its citizens.

"The 'Disengagement Plan' will include the redeployment of IDF forces along new security lines and a change in the deployment of settlements, which will reduce as much as possible the number of Israelis located in the heart of the Palestinian population," Sharon said. "We will draw provisional security lines and the IDF will be deployed along them."

"The government, under my direction, adopted and is committed to the road map peace process. But I will not wait indefinitely for the Palestinians to fulfill their obligations," Sharon told participants at the Herzliya Conference.

The Prime Minister's speech comes after weeks of buildup. Sharon began speaking of undefined "unilateral steps" last month, indicating that he might consider moving West Bank Jewish settlements.

Calling on the Palestinians, Sharon said "I use this opportunity to turn to the Palestinian and say: We are not interested in controlling you but rather wish upon you a Palestinian state which has a normal relationship with Israel."

Sharon reiterated his recent statements whereby Israelis "would not stay in every place they are now."

"This reduction of friction will require the extremely

difficult step of changing the deployment of some of the settlements," Sharon said. "In the framework of a future agreement, Israel will not remain in all the places where it is today."

Sharon said he had made a commitment to the Bush administration to remove illegal settlement outposts, and "I plan to stand by that commitment."

Speaking of the road map peace plan, Sharon said, "This is a balanced plan with a progressive staged process to achieve peace and it is the best way to achieve real peace."

"The road map is a clear and logical plan and therefore it must be implemented," he said.

Sharon said, "The perception, according to which the very signing of a peace agreement will produce security out of thin air, has already been tried in the past and failed miserably."

Sharon said that Israel has taken and will continue to take steps to improve the Palestinian's living conditions.

"We will take away roadblocks and will ease passage for Palestinians." he said. "All these steps are meant to create a better life for the Palestinians who are not involved in terror."

Israel will only detach from the Palestinians under full coordination with the United States. "We cannot hurt the strategic coordination with the US," he said.

"If in a few months the Palestinians still don't begin to follow the road map then Israel will initiate a unilateral plan in order to give Israel maximum security," he said.

Sharon said that Israel wants to hold direct negotiations with the Palestinians "but we will not allow ourselves to be held hostage by the Palestinians."

"As I said before, we will not wait for them forever." Referring to the controversial construction of the security fence, the prime minister said, "The security fence will not be the permanent border for Israel."

Calling out to the Israeli people, Sharon said, "My life

experience has taught me that peace like war, requires complete unity."

"I believe that this path of unity must be continued today. Whether we will be able to advance the Roadmap, or will have to implement the "Disengagement Plan", experience has taught us that, together, through broad national consensus, we can do great things," he said.

EU's Solana warns Israeli PM against unilateral action

EU foreign affairs chief Javier Solana warned on Friday, December 19, there was no "unilateral solution" to the Middle East conflict after Israel's leader threatened to take action of his own to bring about peace.

"There is no unilateral solution to this conflict. Any statements pointing in that direction will certainly not help to move the process forward," Solana said in a statement.

"I welcome PM Sharon's acknowledgement that a full and genuine implementation of the road map is the best way to achieve true peace between Israelis and Palestinians.

"This important statement fully coincides with the EU's well-known position on this issue," Solana said.

"But what is urgently required is that courageous and bold steps be taken in parallel by both sides for the effective implementation of the road map."

NRP: Sharon's speech harms Israel

National Religious Party (NRP) leader Effi Eitam said in response to Prime Minister Ariel Sharon's Herziliya Conference speech that the prime minister is inviting terror and harms the goals of the Jewish settlement movement.

"Unfortunately Sharon is continuing to make statements that invite continued terror, and harm the goal of Jewish settlement," Eitam said. "The NRP will judge Sharon according to his actions."

Eitam said that the NRP would not be partners to a

government that uproots Jewish communities and endangers the Zionist enterprise as a whole.

"Sharon's threat to unilaterally disconnect from the Palestinians is an Israeli surrender to the war waged against it by Arafat for the past three years," he said. "Israel should learn from the Americans that the only key to achieve quiet and peace in the region is by militarily defeating terror, along with economic and diplomatic pressure."

NRP faction chairman Shaul Yahalom said, "The NRP will do every effort to assassinate the idea of unilateral separation."

Housing and Construction Minister Effi Eitam (NRP) said his party could not sit in a government that uprooted Jewish settlements.

Pinhas Wallerstein, a veteran leader of Israeli settlers, complained about the possible moving of settlements and warned that disengagement would create the "imposition of a siege on the Jewish settlements" inside the barrier.

MK Shimon Peres said that he was very disappointed with Sharon's speech. According to Peres, "Instead of a decision, we were handed another delay, and a delay that is not necessarily in our favor."

Palestinian Prime Minister: Sharon, in speech, 'threatening' Palestinians

Palestinian Prime Minister Ahmed Qureia reacted to a speech given by Prime Minister Ariel Sharon at a security conference in Herzliya saying he was "disappointed" that Sharon's speech included "threats" to the Palestinians, in the form on unilateral steps.

Qureia said that if Sharon would negotiate with the Palestinians, peace could come "sooner than expected."

Asked by CNN what he would do if Israel started unilateral moves, Erekat said: "With this unilateral approach, they may make peace with Israelis and Israelis; they'll not make peace with Palestinians".

Erekat urged the Israeli prime minister to stick to the "road map" for peace, a blueprint backed by a Quartet that includes the United States, the European Union, Russia and the United Nations.

"We invite Mr. Sharon to come immediately with no conditions to the negotiating table on the basis of the road map and let the Americans, Europeans, Russians and the UN - the Quartet members - to be the judges of both of us," he said.

Revealing News Headlines

The following news headlines illustrate how the world's leaders pressured Israel from November 24 to January 10, 2004. There are also headlines that show the emotion of those who are opposed to giving land to the Palestinians:

- Sharon Comes Under Fire For Plans To Take 'Unilateral Steps' - November 24
- Israel To Label EU Exports Made In Territories – November 24
- Geneva Accord Maps Out New Road To Peace: To Be Signed On December 1, Amid Opposition From The Israeli – November 24
- Al Qaeda Terrorists to Gas U.S. Subways? – November 25
- Israel Mum On Germany's Reported Refusal To Sell Subs - November 26
- U.S. To Trim $289.5M Israeli Loan Package Over Settlements, Fence – November 26
- Powell To Meet With Ayalon, Nusseiba And Geneva Pact Partners - November 26
- Palestinians Criticize U.S. Loan Decision: Insufficient To Deter Israel – November 26
- Far-Right Mounts Campaign To Defeat Settlers' 'Peace Plan'- November 26
- Israel Admits Land Concessions A Must – November 27

- UN, Int'l Agencies Warn Of Halting Operations In Territories - November 27
- U.S. Lawmakers Urge Bush To Adopt Unofficial Peace Plans - November 28
- UN's Annan: Israel Violating Resolution On Fence - November 28
- Powell Urges Start Of Mideast Peace Plan - November 28
- Qureia: Israeli Fence Destroying Peace Chances - November 29
- Israel Braces For UN Anti-Fence Move - November 29
- Sharon Rejects Palestinian Condition For Talks - November 30
- Carter Slams Israel, Bush In Geneva Speech - December 1
- Geneva Ceremony Becomes Forum For Slamming Israel - December 1
- Clergy Urge More Active White House Effort For Mideast Peace - December 1
- Bush Confers With Egyptian Leader On Mideast - December 2
- White House Backs Powell Meeting With Geneva Architects - December 3
- U.S. To Israel: Don't Harm Arafat Or Foil Future Palestinian State- December 3
- Report: Bush Administration "Disappointed" With Sharon - December 4
- Middle East Peace Spotlight Moves To Washington With Bush-Abdullah Meeting - December 4
- Bush And Jordanian King Confer On Palestinian Plan - December 5
- Israel's Sharon Under Pressure At Home Amid U.S. Rift - December 5
- Bush: Geneva Accord Could Be 'Productive' To Peace Process - December 5
- Geneva Plan Has No 'Safety Net' For Israel, Military Expert Says - December 5

- UN Takes Fence To The Hague World Court - December 6
- Annan Says Quartet Will Discuss Geneva Accord In Early 2004- December 6
- EU Pledges Emergency Aid To Palestinian Government – December 6
- Sharon: Cabinet Will Debate Unilateral Steps When The Time Comes - December 7
- Israel Slams UN Decision To Refer West Bank Fence To Hague – December 8
- Rabbi Calls For Charges Against Geneva Architects – December 9
- Yesha Council: PM Who Evacuates Settlements Will Be Ousted – December 10
- Fatah Movement Planning More Suicide Attacks Against Israelis – December 11
- Bush: "Palestinian State Is In Israel's Interest" - December 12
- Likud Debates A Palestinian State To Save Israel – December 12
- UN Nuclear Watchdog Urges Israel To Jettison Any Weapons – December 12
- Israel, Vatican Talk After Pope's Criticism Of Fence – December 12
- Arafat's Mufti: No Such Thing As A 'Wailing Wall' – December 13
- EU Calls On Israel To Dismantle Outposts, Slams Anti-Semitism – December 14
- Powell Hints U.S. Will Pressure Israel If Palestinians Seal Truce – December 15
- Israel Assures U.S.: Nothing Decided On Unilateral Steps – December 16
- CBN Chief: It's A Religious War – December 17
- Shalom: Israel Should Explore Assad's Offer Of Talks – December 17

Major increase in U.S. and World terror warnings, U.S. mad-cow outbreak, major earthquakes in California and Iran, chaos in Iraq, and a suicide bombing in Israel

On December 17, U.S. Secretary of State Colin Powell stated to the Palestinians, that a cease-fire deal would seal statehood.

On December 18, Israeli Prime Minister Ariel Sharon gave a major policy address on the future of Israel's land.

On December 19, President Bush's spokesman Scott McClellan reacted warmly to much of Israeli Prime Minister Ariel Sharon's latest plan for dealing with the Palestinians.

"We were very pleased with the overall speech," spokesman Scott McClellan said in an apparent effort to offset published accounts that focused on his admonition Thursday that Sharon should not try to impose a settlement without negotiations.

"We believe that the road map is the way to get to the president's two-state vision" of a democratic Palestinian state existing alongside Israel by 2005, McClellan said, referring to a blueprint for peacemaking that has the backing of the United States, the United Nations, the European Union and Russia.

These political statements were immediately followed by a significant increase in U.S. and world terror warnings, the U.S.'s first mad-cow case on record, a major 6.5 earthquake in Central California and a 6.3 earthquake in Iran, an increase in insurgent chaos in Iraq and a tragic suicide bombing in Tel Aviv, Israel.

On December 25, 2003: Israeli Prime Minister Ariel Sharon stated he would allow Likud members to vote on his plan for disengagement from the Palestinians, which included the replacement of settlements and the approval of a Palestinian state. The move was intended to bypass the hawkish Likud central committee and the troublesome

Likud Knesset faction and instead turn to the party's relatively moderate 300,000 grassroots members, who would be more likely to give the "Disengagement Plan" the party's stamp of approval. (A major suicide bombing occurred at a bus stop at the Geha Junction, east of Tel Aviv. The Popular Front for the Liberation of Palestine claimed responsibility for the attack.)

The headlines below will illustrate the major period of disruption that immediately followed Powell's statement, Sharon's speech and the White House's reaction to Sharon's speech:

- Powell Tells Palestinians Cease-Fire Would Seal Statehood, Israel Prepares To Give Up All Gaza, Much Of West Bank - December 17
- U.S. Urges Citizens to Leave Saudi Arabia - December 17
- Justice Minister Lapid Slams 'Barbaric' Behavior Of Settlers - December 18
- Sharon: Israel May 'Disengage' During Road Map Execution - December 18
- NRP: Sharon's Speech Harms Israel - December 18
- Israel Prepares For A Mass Move If Road Map Fails - December 18
- Palestinian PM: Sharon, In Speech, 'Threatening' Palestinians - December 18
- Qaeda Leader Says Chasing Americans In 'Homeland' - December 19
- U.S. Intelligence Learn Of Possible Threats To New York And Other Cities -December 19
- EU's Solana Warns Sharon Against Unilateral Action - December 19
- Jewish Settlers Attack Sharon Plan As Betrayal - December 19
- Sharon Comes Under Heavy Fire For Separation Plan - December 19
- Jerusalem Issues Christmas Terror Alert For Israelis Abroad - December 19

- U.S. Urges Vigilance At Christmas On Terror, Qaeda Threats - December 19
- White House 'Very Pleased' With Sharon's Speech - December 19
- Peres Says He Doesn't Believe Sharon Will Implement New Plan - December 19
- International Court Hearings On Separation Fence To Begin February 23 - December 20
- PA Calls On Quartet To Make Israel Implement Road Map - December 20
- Arafat: Sharon Coordinated 'Disengagement Plan' With U.S. - December 21
- Opposition Growing In Likud Over Sharon's Unilateral Speech - December 21
- U.S. Raises The Terror Alert To 'High'... Possible Attack To "Rival Or Exceed 9/11' - December 21
- Olmert: Tens Of Thousands Of Settlers May Be Relocated - December 21
- Israel Considers Sending Judges To Hague - December 21
- Mubarak Says Discussed Dismantling Nukes With Peres - December 21
- San Francisco Blackout Leaves 1/3 Without Electricity - December 21
- U.S. Army Is Warning Of Fresh Iraq Violence - December 22
- Bush Urges People To Go On With Holiday Plans - December 22
- 6.5 Earthquake Rocks Central California - December 22
- California Earthquake Rang Planet 'Like A Bell' - December 22
- Mideast Rife With Rumors Of America's 'Jihad' - December 22
- NBC: U.S. Terror Threat To Extend Through January - December 23
- Pentagon To Conduct Terror Drill: Operation Aimed

At Protecting Officials During Attack - December 23
- Airports To Fingerprint, Photograph Foreigners: - December 23
- Security Plan To Include U.S. Seaports, Land Border Crossings - December 23
- More Aftershocks Rattle California - December 23
- National Security Adviser Condoleezza Rice Is Apparently Not Keen On Going Under Oath For The Kean 9/11 Commission - December 23
- Israel Accepts U.S. Demand Of Palestinian State In 2004 - December 23
- Israel, U.S. Disagree On Definition Of Settlement Freeze - December 23
- A Global Glut Of Greenbacks: A Great Drama Is Now Unfolding In The World's Money Markets - December 23
- Pentagon: War Planes To Patrol Some U.S. Cities To Counter New Terror Threats - December 23
- Intelligence: Bin Laden Behind New Terror Threat: U.S. Ferreting Out Plot In Significant Detail, Officials Tell NBC News - December 23
- U.S. Blurs Aerial Shots Of Washington: Rooftops Obscured Due To Homeland Security Concerns - December 24
- U.S. Braces For Impact Of Mad Cow Disease - December 24
- Nations Block U.S. Beef Imports - December 24
- Rumsfeld: 'Bet Your Life' Threat To U.S. Is Serious - December 24
- Surface-To-Air Missiles Being Deployed Around Washington - December 24
- Six Paris-To-L.A. Flights Canceled Over Security: NBC: U.S. Officials Raise Concerns; More Flights Could Be Scrapped- December 24
- Muslims Warned To Leave U.S. Cities: Al-Qaida Websites Claim New York, Washington, Los Angeles

Are Targets - December 24

- Insurgents Hit Baghdad Hotel After Deadly Attacks - December 24
- LA Airport Raises Security To Highest Level In Two Years - December 24
- Sharon To Bring His Plan To Likud Vote - December 25
- IDF Clamps Full Closure On Territories After Suicide Attack, 4 Killed 15 Wounded - December 25
- U.S., Fearing Terror Attack, Seeks Global Cooperation - December 26
- A London-Based Arab Magazine Says Qaeda Vows 'Back-Breaking' Strike By February - December 26
- New FBI Warning Cites Biochem Threat: Feds Advise Security To Be On Alert For 'Unusual Powders, Liquids, Odors' - December 26
- Did Canceled Flights Avert Terror Attack? U.S. Thinks L.A.-Bound Air France Jet Was Set For Crash-Landing In Las Vegas - December 26
- Concerns Rising With Dollar's Continued Fall - December 26
- CIA Leaks Probe Is Gathering Momentum - December 26
- Terrorists Plan To Pose As Disabled Travelers: Pakistani Nationals Behind U.S. Plot - December 26
- Second Herd Quarantined In Mad Cow Scare - December 26
- Bush Still Eating Beef Despite Scare, Aide Says - December 26
- U.S. Enhances Air Monitors in 30 Cities - December 26
- Iraq Insurgents Make Christmas Week A Deadly One For The Americans - December 26
- Feds Eye New Year's Terror Possibilities - December 27
- Bush Spends 2nd Half Of Vacation In Texas: Shadowed By Troubles On Both The Global And Domestic Fronts - December 27
- U.S. Loses 90 Percent Of Beef Exports - December 27

- 13 Dead, 172 Wounded In Iraq Terror Attacks - December 27
- Mad Cow Is Tough For Bush Administration - December 28
- Meat Of Infected Cow Found In More States - December 28
- Report: Al Qaeda Targeting Oceanliners, $1.3 Billion Queen Mary II A Target - December 28
- Gadhafi Armed Al-Qaida With Bio-Chem Weapons: U.S. Raised Terror Alert Largely Due To New Libyan Intelligence - December 28
- If Musharraf Is Assassinated, The War On Terror Will Also Be A Victim - December 29
- U.S. Asks Int'l Air Carriers For Officers - December 29
- U.S. Says It Is Considering Expanded Mad Cow Testing - December 29
- Warning Of Imminent U.S. Terrorist Attack: Islamic Website Claims 'Final Blows' In 'Crucial Battle' About To Begin - December 30
- Al Qaeda Links Seen In Attacks On Top Saudi Security Officials: New Effort To Destabilize The Saudi Government - December 30
- Israel To Tweak Route Of Barrier Under Pressure - December 30
- Fed Helicopters To Patrol NYC On New Year's Eve - December 30
- Ashcroft Drops Out Of CIA Leak Probe - December 30
- New Year's Security Highest Ever - December 31
- U.S. Cancels, Delays London-D.C. Flights: Terror Concerns Prompt Disruption Of More Than A Half-Dozen New Year's Holiday Flights - January 1
- Bush Appoints James Baker To Visit Middle East As Special U.S. Envoy - January 1, 2004
- U.S. Calls For Halt To Golan Settlement - January 1
- Capital Threat: Al Qaeda Concerns Led To Cancellations Of London- Washington Flights -

January 2

- The CIA Agent Flap: FBI Asks For Reporters To Talk - January 2
- Terror Alerts Cause International Air Disruption - January 2
- FBI Seeks Confidentiality Waivers From Bush Staffers - December 3
- Al-Jazeera Airs Purported Bin Laden Tape; U.S. 'Occupation Of Gulf States' And Road Map Emphasized - January 4
- British Pilots See BA Flight Holdups As "Warning Shot" By U.S. - January 5
- Dollar Tumbles Again To Begin Year - January 5
- U.S. Begins Foreign Visitor-Tracking Program - January 5
- Sharon: Israel Will Have To Give Up Settlements In Final Peace Deal - January 5
- Bush Administration: Three Firms To Develop Anti-Missile Systems For U.S. Commercial Planes Vs. Shoulder-Fired Rockets- January 5
- Ex-Mossad Chief: Road Map Cannot Be Implemented - December 6
- 'Dirty Bomb' Was Major New Year's Worry - January 7
- Al Qaeda's D.C. Death Jet Plot - January 7
- IMF Researchers: U.S. Budget Gaps Endanger Global Economy- January 7
- Experts Seeking 'Dirty Bombs' In U.S. Cities: Government Teams Working Undercover Throughout Country - December 9
- Oil Hits Fresh Post-War Highs On U.S. Cold: Crude Stocks Seen Lowest Since 1975 - January 9
- Powell: U.S. Opposes One-State Solution - January 9
- U.S. Lowers National Terror Threat Level - January 9
- Terror Alert Level Lowered Except for Aviation and Airline Industry - January 9

Again, as the nation of Israel was pressured to divide her land, the world experienced a major increase in terror warnings.

CHAPTER 6

The Washington Times

www.washingtontimes.com TUESDAY, MAY 20, 2003 25 cents

Saudi warns of more attacks

Kingdom, U.S. said to be targets

Bush vows to stick with 'road map'

Fifth suicide bomb blast in 48 hours kills 3 Israelis

see BOMB, page A13

Backs Mideast peace plan despite suicide bombings

see PEACE, page A13

U.S. AND ISRAEL "LAND FOR PEACE" STATEMENTS AND EFFORTS

According to various Israeli government officials an estimated 90% of planned terror events in Israel have been averted. Frequently, we hear about the large ones that have been miraculously prevented by the Lord's hand. Tragically, there are occasional suicide bombings or shootings where there is a large loss of life and multiple injuries.

Bush Administration Middle East statements and efforts that coincide with major suicide bombings

Our research conclusively shows that from the point that President George W. Bush intensified his involvement in the Middle East peace efforts and backed a Palestinian state (late November 2001 through January 29, 2004), 26 out of 31 major suicide bombings (large loss of life with many injuries) occurred on the same day or within 24 hours of a major U.S. presidential announcement, statements or activities by Israel's leadership.

President Bush sees the suicide bombings as an attempt to disrupt the peace process. However, research shows that when President Bush or his top level people are not actively involved in high-level meetings with Israel concerning land issues, a large majority of suicide bombings are averted; only small bombing events occur with very little loss of life and a few injuries; or there are periods of calm.

President Bush Condemns June 11, 2003 Terrorist Attacks

> Today there was a terrible bombing in Jerusalem. I send my heartfelt condolences to those who suffered and lost life.
>
> It is clear there are people in the Middle East who hate peace; people who want to kill in order to make sure that the desires of Israel to live in secure and peace don't happen; who kill to make sure the desires of the Prime Minister of the Palestinian Authority and others of a peaceful state, living side-by-side with Israel, do not happen.
>
> To the people in the world who want to see peace in the Middle East, I strongly urge all of you to fight off terror, to cut off money to organizations such as Hamas, to isolate those who hate so much that they're willing to kill to stop peace from going forward. I strongly condemn the killings, and I urge and call upon all of the free world, nations which love peace, to not only condemn the killings, but to use every ounce of their power to prevent them from happening in the future.

What causes this phenomenon? Is the Lord lifting His

restraining hand of protection for a brief moment as His Covenant Land is being negotiated? Through these tragedies is the Lord protecting His people in Israel from even greater terror events? Is He keeping Israel from agreeing to a dangerous peace deal, which would place her in indefensible borders with an enemy who is committed to her destruction?

Furthermore, the world community has bought the Arab line that the key to world peace is the land of Israel. How absurd! Moreover, no nation in the world should require Israel to negotiate with terrorist regimes, and she should not be kept from being allowed to defend herself and/or be kept from eliminating the terror infrastructure within her country.

Additionally, the God of Israel does not want to see His covenant land given to His enemy or the enemy of the nation of Israel and the Jewish people.

Below is an outline of specific activity concerning Bush Administration intervention in Israel's affairs, and corresponding major suicide bombings during the period of December 1, 2001-- January 29, 2004.

- November 30 -- December 2, 2001: General Zinni was in Israel negotiating a cease-fire agreement between the Israelis and the Palestinians. (Two major suicide bombings occurred on December 1 and December 2, 2001.)
- March 8, 2002: President Bush stated he was sending General Zinni back to the Middle East. (A major suicide bombing occurred on March 9, 2002.)
- March 20-21, 27-29, 2002: General Zinni was in Israel twice to negotiate a cease-fire agreement. (Major suicide bombings occurred on March 20-21,27,29, 2002.)
- March 30, 2002: The UN and the U.S. called on Israel to withdraw from Palestinian cities. (Two major suicide bombings occurred on March 30-31, 2002.)
- April 10-12, 2002: Secretary of State Colin Powell went to Israel to jump-start peace talks. (Two major suicide

bombings occurred on April 10 and April 12, 2002.)

- May 7, 2002: President Bush met with Israeli Prime Minister Ariel Sharon at White House. (A major suicide bombing occurred during their meeting in the Oval Office.)
- June 5, 2002: CIA Director George Tenet was in Israel negotiating a cease-fire deal. (A major suicide bombing occurred on June 5, 2002.)
- June 18-19, 2002: President Bush's Middle East address was postponed two days in a row by two major suicide bombings. (Major suicide bombings occurred on June 18 and 19, 2002, in Jerusalem.)
- July 18, 2002: Powell stated the CIA was working on a plan to protect Israel from terror. (Two major suicide bombings occurred on July 18-19, 2002.)
- October 20, 2002: U.S. Assistant Secretary of State William Burns was in the Middle East to gain Road Map input. (A major suicide bombing occurred on October 21, 2002.)
- November 7, 2002: Revised "Road Map" asked for immediate Israeli acceptance of Palestinian state (a major suicide bombing occurred on November 7, 2002.)
- January 5, 2003: U.S. Rejected Israel's Objections to the Road Map. (A major suicide bombing occurred on the same day.)
- May 11, 2003: U.S. Secretary of State Colin Powell was on the way to Riyadh, Saudi Arabia to meet with Crown Prince Abdullah of Saudi Arabia, the sponsor of the Saudi Middle East peace plan. They were to discuss the Israeli-Palestinian peace talks. (Four bombings occurred late Monday evening May 12, 2003, in Riyadh within hours of Powell's arrival targeting American, the largest terror event directed towards Americans since 9-11-2001.)
- June 9-10, 2003: President Bush reiterated his commitment to the Middle East peace process following

Israel's attempted assassination of the Hamas leader. (A major suicide bombing occurred in the center of Jerusalem on June 11.)

- August 18, 2003: Under White House pressure, Israel was in the final stage of negotiations with the Palestinians before turning over security responsibility to four West Bank cities. (A major suicide bombing occurred on a bus in Jerusalem the next day.)
- September 6-9, 2003: Palestinian Prime Minister Mahmoud Abbas resigned on Saturday, September 6. The next day PLO Chairman Yasser Arafat selected Ahmed Qureia as the new Palestinian Prime Minister. On Tuesday, September 9, after pressure from the United States Prime Minister Ariel Sharon's aides said, that Qureia could be a partner if he carried out the Palestinians' obligations under a U.S.-backed peace plan, including disarming militants. (Late that afternoon there was a major suicide bombing at the Tzrifin army base near Tel Aviv, five hours later there was another major suicide bombing at the entrance to the Cafe Hillel restaurant on Emek Refaim Road in the German Colony in southern Jerusalem.)
- January 28, 2004: In Jerusalem, U.S. State Department envoys John Wolf and David Satterfield pressed Ahmed Qureia and Ariel Sharon to hold a long-delayed summit to help revive the quartet's road map. (A major suicide bombing occurred in Jerusalem near Prime Minister Sharon's residence within 24-hours, Al Aqsa Martyrs' Brigades claimed responsibility.)

Statements by Israeli leaders and peace efforts that coincide with major suicide bombings and terror events

Between October 21, 2001, and January 29, 2004, as Israeli Foreign Minister Shimon Peres or Israeli Prime Minister Ariel Sharon confirmed Israel's approval of a

Palestinian state, or when Sharon was elected or supported as leader of his political party for his Palestinian state position, or stated Israel would be leaving land, there were corresponding terror events the same day or within 24-hours:

- October 21, 2001: Sharon stated he may accept a Palestinian state if Israel's security is guaranteed. (The Minister of Tourism Rechavam Ze'evi was fatally shot in the head in the Jerusalem Hyatt Hotel the same morning of Sharon's public statement.)
- May 18, 2002: Peres called for an accelerated Palestinian state. (A major suicide bombing occurred in Netanya within 24 hours.)
- June 17, 2002: Sharon told U.S. he envisioned two states living in peace. (A major suicide bombing occurred within 24 hours at Patt junction between Gilo and Jerusalem. A major suicide bombing occurred in the French Hill intersection in northern Jerusalem within 48 hours.)
- July 31, 2002: Israel transferred cash to Palestinian Authority at U.S. insistence. (A major suicide bombing occurred in the student center cafeteria on the Hebrew University's Mt. Scopus campus.)
- September 18, 2002: Peres told UN that Israel was for a Palestinian state. (A major suicide bombing occurred in Tel Aviv within 24 hours.)
- October 21, 2002: Peres told EU that Israel was in favor of a Palestinian state. (A major suicide bombing occurred on bus from Kiryat Shmona to Tel-Aviv, within 24 hours.)
- November 14, 2002: Sharon said a Palestinian state was all but a given. (A major shooting occurred in Hebron within 24 hours.)
- November 20, 2002: Jerusalem Mayor Olmert backed Ariel Sharon for the leader of the Likud Party. (A major suicide bombing occurred in Jerusalem within 24 hours.)

- November 28, 2002: Sharon won Likud election over Netanyahu, who was not in favor of a Palestinian state. (A bombing in Mombassa, Kenya; two missiles missed Israeli plane leaving Mombassa; a shooting attack on a Likud branch in Beit She'an all occurred on the same day.)
- January 5, 2003: Israel in secret statehood talks. (A major double suicide bombing occurred near the old Central Bus Station in Tel-Aviv.)
- March 5, 2003: Sharon agreed to painful concessions for peace. (A major suicide bombing of a bus in Haifa, en route to Haifa University occurred within 24 hours.)
- April 29, 2003: Sharon stated "we will do whatever we have to, to bring peace to Israel"; the Quartet Road Map was delivered on April 30, 2003. (A major suicide bombing occurred in Tel Aviv the day the Road Map is delivered.)
- May 17, 2003: Sharon met with new Israeli Prime Minister Mahmoud Abbas. (A major suicide bombing occurred near French Hill in Jerusalem on May 18, 2003; a major suicide bombing occurred May 19, 2003 in Afula.)
- June 10, 2003: Israel attempted to assassinate Hamas leader. (A major suicide bombing occurred in a building on Jaffa Road in the center of Jerusalem within 24 hours.)
- August 18, 2003: Israel was in final negotiations with Palestinian negotiators prior to turning over security responsibility to four West Bank cities. (A major suicide bombing occurred in Jerusalem's Shmuel Hanavi neighborhood.)
- September 9, 2003: Israel indicated it would be willing to work with Ahmed Qureia as the new Palestinian prime minister, despite his close ties with veteran leader Yasser Arafat. Israel initially said after the weekend resignation of Palestinian Prime Minister Mahmoud

Abbas that it would not deal with a successor hand-picked by Arafat. However, Israeli Prime Minister Ariel Sharon's aides said on Tuesday that Qureia could be a partner if he carries out the Palestinians' obligations under a U.S.-backed peace plan, including disarming militants. (A major suicide bombing occurs in at Tzrifin army base, within five hours a suicide bombing occurred at the entrance to the popular Cafe Hillel restaurant on Emek Refaim Rd. in the German Colony in southern Jerusalem.)

- December 25, 2003: Israeli Prime Minister Ariel Sharon stated he would allow Likud members to vote on his plan for disengagement from the Palestinians, which included the replacement of settlements and the approval of a Palestinian state. The move was intended to bypass the hawkish Likud central committee and the troublesome Likud Knesset faction and instead turn to the party's relatively moderate 300,000 grassroots members, who would be more likely to give the "Disengagement Plan" the party's stamp of approval. (A major suicide bombing occurs at a bus stop at the Geha Junction, east of Tel Aviv. The Popular Front for the Liberation of Palestine claimed responsibility for the attack.)
- January 13, 2004: Prime Minister Ariel Sharon raised the possibility Tuesday January 13, 2004, that the Israel Defense Forces would one day leave the Gaza Strip, captured by Israel in the 1967 Six-Day War. "I hope the day will come when we will not have to sit in the Strip," Sharon said in a speech to Bedouin soldiers, which was broadcast on Army Radio. Sharon's comments followed his recent statements that Israel will have to yield some land for peace either in a deal with Palestinians or as part of go-it-alone steps to end years of violence. (Wednesday, January 14, 2004, four Israelis are killed and ten injured when a female suicide

bomber associated with Hamas blows herself up at the Erez checkpoint in the Gaza Strip.)

- January 29, 2004: On Sunday, January 25, Israel and Hezbollah finalized terms of an exchange of prisoners and soldiers' remains for Israeli businessman Elhanan Tennenbaum, and the bodies of three Israel Defense Forces soldiers kidnapped in October 2000. On Thursday, January 29, Israel freed 400 Palestinian prisoners as well as prisoners from Lebanon, Syria and other Arab states; Israel also returned to Lebanon several dozen bodies. Israeli Foreign Ministry spokesman Jonathan Peled said in Jerusalem, "We are releasing another 400 Palestinians with a very heavy heart, because we know that these 400 will return very quickly to the cycle of violence." (A major suicide bombing occurred when a suicide bomber exploded inside a bus in Jerusalem near the Prime Minister's residence in Jerusalem's Rehavia neighborhood, Al Aqsa Martyrs' Brigades claimed responsibility.)

The Cycle of Violence Continues

Presented below is the Israeli-Palestinian pattern that repeated itself from late November 2001, to January 29, 2004:

- The U.S. and the world community called for a stop of violence in Israel and for new meetings between the Israelis and the Palestinians.
- The U.S. would sponsor a meeting between Israelis and Palestinians in Israel; a Bush-Sharon meeting would occur at the White House; Shimon Peres-Ariel Sharon would state Israel's approval of a Palestinian state, Mayor Olmert of Jerusalem and/or the Likud Party would back Sharon for leadership of the Likud Party based on his pro-Palestinian state position; or Israel would agree to a large Palestinian prisoner release. As these events occurred, a major suicide

bombing (or a major shooting event) would occur within the same day or within 24 hours. A radical Islamic terror group would take "credit" for the act.

- President George W. Bush or his senior officials would condemn the killings in strong language, encourage the sides to get back to the table and ask Israel not to respond too harshly for the sake of peace.
- The world leaders would condemn the suicide bombings in strong terms and call for the Israelis and the Palestinians to go back to talks. The leaders would call on Israel to not respond too harshly in the spirit of peace and to leave the occupied land.
- Israel would respond forcefully to the tragedy by hitting on the militant targets within the Palestinian neighborhoods and tighten up their defenses. At times they would call for the exiling of Yasser Arafat, the World community would disapprove.
- If Israel responded too harshly, the U.S. State Department and the world community led by the UN and the EU would chastise Israel for their use of force. The greater the proportion of military response by Israel the greater the world leader's outcry.
- The cycle would repeat itself once again.

CHAPTER 7

U.S. ADMINISTRATIONS AND MIDDLE EAST LEADERS INVOLVED IN THE MIDDLE EAST PROCESS AND DEFINING EVENTS

United States Administrations have been very active with the nation of Israel during her history.

It was Harry Truman who favored Israel becoming a nation. His endorsement of Israel being recognized as a nation was key to receiving UN approval. However, he also withheld military aid when it was most needed, during Israel's War of Independence.

Dwight Eisenhower took the Arabs side in the 1956 Suez crisis. It was reported that John Kennedy traveled to New York to meet Israeli Prime Minister David Ben Gurion because he didn't want to greet him at the White House.

The first pro-Israel President was Lyndon Johnson.

Richard Nixon didn't particularly care for Jews but he did provide support for Israel in the 1973 war. His Secretary of State William Rogers was best known for his proposals for Israeli withdrawal from the West Bank to its 1967 borders. The Rogers plan, as it became known, was rejected by Israel and Egypt, when it was put to them in 1970, but has formed the basis of more recent peace initiatives, including swapping land for peace and shared control of Jerusalem. Nixon's second Secretary of State Henry Kissinger was directly responsible in the drafting and approval of UN Resolution 338, which is part of today's Quartet Road Map.

Jimmy Carter was the main sponsor of the Camp David Accords. This was first time the Palestinians were recognized by the U.S. and Israel in an agreement, which connected them to the land mentioned in UN Resolutions 242 and 338, and which is the foundation of the Quartet's Road Map.

George H. W. Bush was very tight with the House of Saud in Saudi Arabia. In 1991 he and Secretary of State James Baker applied major pressure on Israel to participate and comply with the "land for peace" process.

Bill Clinton spent a tremendous amount of time on the peace process with PLO Chairman Yasser Arafat the most frequent visitor of world leaders to the White House. Clinton applied a lot of pressure on Israel in search of a legacy, which intensified right after the Lewinsky affair became public.

George W. Bush wanted to be a facilitator and not an active participant in the Middle East process but the volatile situation in Israel, the Middle East and the war on terror has forced him to be more active than any other previous U.S. President. His calling for a Palestinian state were words no other U.S. President had uttered.

I reviewed previous U.S. Administration's role in the Middle East peace process and studied the defining events that greatly influenced their time in office, by doing this I found a distinct connection between the two. I discovered as the Presidents and their administrations became involved with the Middle East peace process, major events developed that ultimately impacted and curtailed their future peace efforts.

What Happened to the U.S. Presidents Who Were Actively Involved in the Dividing of Israel's Land?

- Richard Nixon -- Watergate -- resignation
- Gerald Ford -- After effect of Nixon's resignation, energy crisis and a campaign
- Jimmy Carter -- Economic crisis after the Camp David Accords and a campaign
- Ronald Reagan -- Iran-Contra
- George H. W. Bush -- National recession and a close election and defeat due to H. Ross Perot's candidacy
- Bill Clinton -- Lewinsky scandal, Whitewater land, Kosovo war and Chinese espionage allegations
- George W. Bush -- 9-11 terror event, the war on terror and Iragi freedom

Richard Nixon's Administration 1968 - 1974

- U.S. Secretary of State William Rogers, who served under President Nixon between 1969-1973, was best known for his proposals for Israeli withdrawal from the West Bank to its 1967 borders. The Rogers plan, as it became known, was rejected by Israel and Egypt when it was put to them in 1970, but has formed the basis of more recent peace initiatives, including swapping land for peace and shared control of Jerusalem. While Rogers was Nixon's secretary of state he often found himself sidelined by Henry A. Kissinger, the President's national security assistant who played a secret and prominent role in advancing Nixon's foreign policy - especially an opening to communist China.
- Five burglars were arrested in the early morning hours of June 17, 1972, at the Democratic National Committee offices. The Watergate scandal has broken and interrupted the Nixon Middle East peace efforts and led to President Nixon's resignation.
- September 10, 1973 - Secretary of State William P.

Rogers resigned and was replaced by National Security Advisor Henry A. Kissinger.

- October 10, 1973 - Vice President Spiro T. Agnew resigned after pleading nolo contendre to tax evasion and bribery charges. House Minority Leader Gerald R. Ford, Jr. replaced him.
- October 20-21, 1973 in the later stages of the Yom Kippur War -- after Israel repulsed the Syrian attack on the Golan Heights and established a bridgehead on the Egyptian side of the Suez Canal - international efforts to stop the fighting were intensified. U.S. Secretary of State Kissinger flew to Moscow on October 20, and, together with the Soviet Government, the U.S. proposed a cease-fire resolution in the UN Security Council. The Council met on 21 October at the urgent request of both the U.S. and the U.S.S.R, and by 14 votes to none, adopted UN Resolutions 338 and others.
- On Saturday, October 20 the infamous Saturday Night Massacre occurred when Nixon fired Watergate special prosecutor Archibald Cox and abolished his office. Attorney General Richardson and Deputy Attorney General William D. Ruckelshaus resign. Pressure for impeachment mounts in Congress. This was a hugely defining day, which led into the final months of Richard Nixon's political career ending in his resignation on August 8, 1974.
- The Watergate crisis paralyzed the Middle East peace efforts and the introduction and implementation of major programs.

Gerald Ford's Administration 1974 - 1976

- Vice President Gerald Ford became President of the United States following Nixon's resignation and served the final year and a half of Nixon's term. His administration was focused on the upcoming 1976

U.S. presidential election with very little effort in the Middle East peace process. He was defeated by Jimmy Carter.

- Ford pardoned Nixon of all charges related to the Watergate case.

Jimmy Carter's Administration 1977 - 1980

- November 2, 1976: Jimmy Carter is elected President of the United States
- August 23, 1976: The price of gold hits modern era low of under $104/oz.
- 1978: Crude oil prices were in the $14 per barrel range
- September 17, 1978: Jimmy Carter, Anwar Saddat and Menachem Begin signed the Camp David Accords. The agreement gave Egypt the land Israel obtained in the 1967 Six Day War, a war Israel did not plan.
- March 26, 1979: Carter sponsors the Israel-Egypt peace treaty.
- January 20, 1980: The price of gold hits all time high of over $850/oz.
- March 27, 1980: The Hunt Brothers of Texas' attempt to corner the world silver market finally ends. Price of silver plunged to $10.80 an ounce from $21.62 an ounce the day before, a 50% single day decline. Two months before, silver changed hands at a high of $52 an ounce. The silver crisis touched off the Panic of 1980, which sent the Dow down from 903.84 in February to 759.13 in April.
- November 2, 1980: Ronald Reagan received 489 electoral and President Jimmy Carter received only 49 electoral votes in the 1980 Presidential election.
- December 19, 1980: Prime rate hits all time high at 21%.
- December 1980: Spot oil price hit all time high of over $40/bbl.
- January 20, 1981: Ronald Reagan sworn in as

President of the United States
- 1981: Crude oil prices were in the $35 per barrel range in 1981

Ronald Reagan's Administration 1981 - 1988
- Reagan's Middle East peace plan was released in September 1982 in his first term, with preliminary work by Secretary of State George Schultz.
- His Middle East peace efforts increased in the first year (1985) of his second term.
- The Israeli government was approached by the United States in August 1985 with a proposal to act as an intermediary by shipping 508 American made TOW anti-tank missiles to Iran in exchange for the release of the Reverend Benjamin Weir, an American hostage being held by Iranian sympathizers in Lebanon, with the understanding that the United States would then ship replacement missiles to Israel. Robert McFarlane, the Assistant to the President for National Security Affairs, approached United States Secretary of Defense Caspar Weinberger and arranged the details. The transfer took place over the next two months. (from Wikipedia.org)
- In January of 1986, Reagan allegedly approved a plan whereby an American intermediary, rather than Israel, would sell arms to Iran in exchange for the release of the hostages, with profits funnelled to the Contras. In February, 1,000 TOW missiles were shipped to Iran. From May to November, there were additional shipments of miscellaneous weapons and parts. The proceeds from the arms sales were diverted, via Colonel Oliver North, aide to the U.S. National Security Advisor John Poindexter, to provide arms for the Contras (from Spanish contrarevolucionario, "counter-revolutionary"). The Sandinistas' eventual loss of power in national elections was seen by some

as stemming from U.S. support for the contras as well as the effects of a U.S. trade embargo initiated in May 1985. (from Wikipedia.org)

- The November 1986 Iran-Contra Affair complicated the Reagan Administration's Middle East peace efforts and occupied much of their time and focus in 1987 leading into the election year of 1988. However, in early December 1987 the Palestinians living in the West Bank and Gaza initiated the intifadah, or uprising. This forced Secretary of State George Shultz to become reengaged in the peace process. Among others, Shimon Peres, Israeli foreign minister at the time, thought the only way to achieve a breakthrough in the peace process was to involve Jordan's King Hussein, under the context of an international conference. Shultz made three visits to the area in February, April and June 1988, trying to gain support for a revised Middle East peace plan.
- The "Shultz Plan" drew upon the provisions of the Camp David accords and the September 1, 1982, Reagan peace plan, and was based on the well-known "land for peace" formula laid out in UN Resolution 242. The plan called for an international conference and implied that Israel would have to give up some of the territory it occupies. Contained in the peace plan was an accelerated version of the time frame set out in the Camp David accords, particularly the period required for autonomy before a permanent negotiated settlement could be reached. Shultz' efforts to meet the Arabs' need for an accelerated peace process and the Israeli need for an interim arrangement before handing territory back ran into predictable trouble.
- On December 24, 1992, President George H. W. Bush pardoned all the principals charged in the Iran-Contra scandal. Walsh's eventual report, released in 1994, absolved Presidents Reagan and Bush for their

roles in events.

George Herbert Walker Bush Administration 1989 - 1992

- As a payback to the Arab nations and European allies who joined his ally base in the Desert Storm war with Iraq, Bush cosponsored the Madrid Conference with Russia on October 30-31, 1991.
- Bush and his hard-line Secretary of State James Baker threatened to freeze $10 billion in loan guarantees if Israeli Prime Minister Yitzhak Shamir did not join the Madrid peace talks and called on him to freeze settlement construction. On September 6, in a televised White House Oval Office appearance with the secretary of state, the President made his request: "It is in the best interest of the peace process and of peace itself that consideration of this absorption aid question be deferred for simply 120 days. And I think the American people will support me on this." The funds were to be a "humanitarian measure" to provide housing for Soviet Jewish immigrants.
- President Bush went from experiencing the highest approval rating in history (in the spring of 1991) to defeat by Bill Clinton in the November 1992 presidential election. The 1992 election was complicated by Ross Perot's candidacy, which helped consume Bush's focus. From October 1991, the only other significant Middle East peace meeting took place in Washington D.C. when a Madrid Conference convened on August 24, 1992.
- Soviet President Mikhail Gorbachev, co-sponsor of the Madrid Conference with President George H. W. Bush, survived an attempted coup (August 18--22, 1991), less than eight weeks from the beginning of the Madrid Conference. The unsuccessful anti-Gorbachev coup by hard-liners shifted greater authority to the

Russian Republic's President, Boris Yeltsin, and greatly accelerated change. Gorbachev dissolved the Communist party, granted the Baltic States independence, and proposed a much looser, chiefly economic federation among the remaining republics. With the formation of the Commonwealth of Independent States (CIS) on December 8, 1991, the federal government of the Soviet Union became superfluous, and on December 25, less than eight weeks after the Madrid Conference, Gorbachev resigned as President.

Bill Clinton's Administration 1993 - 2000

- Clinton was one of the key sponsors of the Oslo I Agreement, which was signed on the South Lawn of the White House on September 13, 1993.
- The Israeli - Jordanian peace deal was agreed to on October 26, 1994
- The Wye Plantation Agreement was agreed to on October 23, 1998
- On January 21, 1998 the Lewinsky sex scandal is picked up by major news services and complicates Clinton's Middle East peace efforts. Bill Clinton fights for his political life that was already embroiled in Special Prosecutor Ken Starr's Whitewater inquiry and the Paula Jones sexual harassment case.
- Clinton became the second American President to be impeached by the U.S. House on December 19, 1998.
- On February 12, 1999 Clinton was cleared of all charges in his U.S. Senate impeachment trial, leaving him free to carry on as the American President.
- Clinton increased his peace efforts dramatically after his acquittal, in his words, in an effort at atonement for the Lewinsky sex scandal. He also was after a lasting legacy to help offset his very tainted two terms as President.

- Clinton and James Carville, his campaign director, coordinated Ehud Barak's successful May 1999 election as Prime Minister of Israel. During 2000, Barak offered more land than any other Israeli leader to the Palestinians and the Syrians. Barak negotiated with Syria in January 2000, and with Yasser Arafat at Camp David in July 2000. Both Assad and Arafat turned down enormously generous offers.

George W. Bush's Administration 2001 - Present

- Bush approved of the Mitchell Plan, a "land for peace" plan prepared by former U.S. Senator George Mitchell and others.
- Bush initiated the Tenet Cease-fire Agreement between the Israelis and the Palestinians, it was agreed to by the parties but never signed or implemented.
- Bush was preparing the most comprehensive address ever by an American President when the 9-11-2001 World Trade Center and Pentagon terror events occurred.
- Bush gave his vision for Middle East peace in the White House Rose Garden on June 24, 2002. It became a key part of the Quartet Road Map.
- Bush was the key player in the Quartet Road Map, which was presented to the Israelis and the Palestinians on April 30, 2003.

Iraqi Freedom has been very costly to the United States. The situation in Iraq worsened considerably on May 30, 2003, when President Bush left Washington for his G8 meetings in France. He then had meetings with Arab leaders on June 3 in Egypt, followed by his Middle East peace summit in Aqaba, Jordan on June 4, 2003.

Our research shows that when President Bush applies political pressure on Israel that events on the Iraq front worsens. Congress approved $67 billion for Iraqi Freedom and approved an additional $87 billion dollars.

What happened to the Middle East leaders who have been directly involved in the Middle East peace process?

- **Egyptian President Anwar Sadat** was assassinated on October 6, 1981, during an annual military parade celebrating the "successful" campaigns during the 1973 Egypt-Israeli war. Among those in the reviewing stand who weren't injured were future UN Secretary-General Boutros Boutros-Ghali and future Egyptian President Hosni Mubarek. Mubarek was sitting just to the right of Sadat and miraculously escaped injury.
- **Israeli Prime Minister Yitzhak Shamir's** former hardline image appeared to moderate. He was reelected Prime Minister of Israel in 1989. He and Shimon Peres formed a new coalition government in 1990. In 1991 the Shamir government took part in the Madrid peace talks after intense pressure and financial threats by U.S. President George H. W. Bush and Secretary of State James Baker. Although long a hardliner, Shamir left office after his government fell amid charges that Likud was too conciliatory toward the Palestinians. Shamir stepped down from Likud leadership in March 1993. He was a sharp critic of his Likud successor, Benjamin Netanyahu, as being too soft and indecisive in dealing with the Palestinians.
- **Israeli Prime Minister Yitzhak Rabin** was elected Israel's Prime Minister in 1992. On November 4, 1995 a right-wing Israeli, Yigal Amir, who objected to the peace process and the handing over of territories to the Palestinians, assassinated Yitzhak Rabin.
- **Jordan's King Hussein** died of lymph cancer in 1999 four and a half years after signing the Israeli-Jordanian peace agreement in 1994.
- **Syria's President Haffez Assad** died of a heart attack in June 2000 less than three months after refusing

Israeli Prime Minister Ehud Barak's generous peace offer.

- **Minister of Foreign Affairs Shimon Peres**, The father of Oslo has refused to voice regret for the failed accords, and has been unwilling to acknowledge the error of his peace efforts. There have been countless victims of his policies.

  Peres has been the most responsible for continuing the "land for peace" folly, while the enemies of Israel have been developing weapons of mass destruction.

  He was the first Israeli leader to tell the UN and the EU that Israel favors a Palestinian State in 2002. He has been the number one proponent of dismantling Israeli settlements.

  He is a pawn of European and U.S. one-world order forces. He has also been a key advisor to the principals involved in the Geneva Accord of December 1, 2003.

- **Israeli Prime Minister Benjamin Netanyahu** signed two accords with the Palestinians: the Hebron Agreement in January 1997 and the Wye River Memorandum of October 1998. On Monday, December 21, 1998, eight weeks from the signing of the Wye River deal, the Israeli Knesset voted to dissolve and hold early elections after Benjamin Netanyahu failed to win support for his peacemaking policy with the Palestinians. His Likud Party was in total disarray. He lost to Ehud Barak in May 1999.

- **Israeli Prime Minister Ehud Barak** government collapsed in the fall of 2000. Barak officially resigned as Israel's Prime Minister on December 9 and called for new elections for February 2001. The violence in Israel had made his pro-negotiation stance difficult to defend. He lost in a landslide election to Ariel Sharon.

- **Israeli Prime Minister Ariel Sharon** defeated Ehud Barak on February 6, 2001. Sharon survived a no-confidence vote in November 2002 and then resigned and called for a new election. He was reelected Israeli Prime Minister on January 31, 2003. He has accepted the Quartet's Road Map.

Sharon refuses to quit over bribe scandal despite waning popular trust

On January 21, 2004, despite the threat of indictment over a bribe scandal, Israel's Prime Minister Ariel Sharon insisted he would not resign though opinion polls showed that a majority of Israelis believe he is guilty and, if proven so, should step down.

"I will continue to be prime minister next year, all the rumors about my eventual resignation or about a voluntary suspension of my functions are just foolishness," Sharon was quoted as saying after Wednesday', January 21, 2004, indictment of property developer David Appel.

Appel was charged with trying to bribe then foreign minister Sharon through his son Gilad, along with deputy Prime Minister Ehud Olmert, then mayor of Jerusalem, in exchange for their help in securing a major Greek property deal.

If indicted, Sharon could be forced to step down before his mandate ends in 2007.

Some Jewish Orthodox commentators are saying that Sharon's possible downfall is divine retribution for his recent announcement–under intense United States and European Union pressure–that he is now ready to permanently hand over many parts of Judaism's biblical heartland, Judea and Samaria, to the Palestinian Authority

- **Palestinian Prime Minister Mahmoud Abbas** resigned September 6, 2003, over conflict with Palestinian Chairman Yasser Arafat.

CHAPTER 8

CONCLUSION, ADDENDUMS AND LETTERS

Conclusion

Many warnings have been issued about giving or trading away God's covenant land, Israel, in exchange for a peace, which would be tenuous and temporary at best.

Letters have been delivered to government leaders and officials in both the United States and Israel. Our book, "Israel: The Blessing or the Curse" and accompanying documentation about the past, present, and future implications of tampering with Israel's covenant land have been widely distributed to those involved in policy decisions for both nations.

Realistically, we never completely believed that this information would change the course of current events in Israel. However, it was our prayers and hope that both the Bush Administration and the Sharon government would understand and react to the importance of taking a strong biblically based position regarding the covenant land.

These two countries, both of them democracies and allies, were founded on Biblical principles. Israel is primarily a Jewish nation, and the U.S.A. is primarily a Christian nation. By historical and spiritual standards alike, both nations serve the one true God of the Bible.

Just as our fair and just God of the Bible has done, in both documented prophetic history and in stated promises, both governments have been warned about dealing with His covenant land.

Since the first "land for peace" proposals were introduced at the Middle East peace talks in Madrid, Spain in 1991, the Lord has warned those involved, time after time, through these events.

During this time, Israel's leaders have reluctantly bought into the "land for peace" dream and some even yielded to the enormous pressure being exerted by the world powers. No one could ever totally comprehend the pressures that the Prime Ministers of Israel have had to face.

However, yielding to those pressures has led Israel into the most dangerous position in her history. The United States, her ally and benefactor, has been complicit in this scenario.

The bottom line is that only an American President and an Israeli Prime Minister, who will stand firm on God's covenant land, can offer any hope. As long as any proposals or plans call for giving away covenant land, there is no solution, and God's judgment will continue to intensify.

Collision Course with the God of Israel

As the Bible has prophesied, the nations of the world are rapidly moving towards a major collision course with the God of Israel. For those who have not accepted the Lord, the scenario isn't going to be pretty.

"And it shall come to pass in that day that I will seek to destroy all the nations that come against Jerusalem" (Zechariah 12:9).

Up until the present time, the many prayers of Christians for Israel and for God's mercy have helped to hold off God's judgment on an unsuspecting secular world. What is yet to come, for those who come against

Israel, is going to be devastating.

To know where the world is headed in the coming days and weeks, keep your ears and eyes on the words and actions of the world leaders as they pertain to Israel. Most, if not all of them, do not even suspect what could await them. They have a divine appointment with the God of Israel, the God of the Bible. His fury is building.

The ultimate solution, of course, lies with the return of the Messiah, the Lord Jesus Christ, who will begin His 1,000-year millennial reign in Jerusalem.

"Behold the tabernacle of God is with men, and He will dwell with them, and they shall be His people, and God Himself shall be with them and be their God. And God shall wipe away all tears from their eyes, and there shall be no more death, neither sorrow, nor crying, neither shall there be any more pain: for the former things are passed away" (Revelation 21:3-4).

Addendum
Open Letter to Israel

To the Nation of Israel from William Koenig

June 28, 2002

An open letter to the people of Israel and to Jewish people everywhere:

We want you to know that your best friend in the world is the passionate Christian who would live and die for you. Please call on us and we will be there for you whenever you need us. Just look next to you, and you will see that we are there also!

God is allowing the current world events to bring our times to completion and to bring many more to Him. Yes, all that is happening does have a purpose in His plan; our prayers for the Peace of Jerusalem are about to be answered.

Please know that the Lord is speaking to you these days. It is time for you to get your life right with the Lord, Israel.

If you keep sinning, you will keep paying the price, because sin does have consequences!

If you keep denying Him, you will also continue paying the price, because many are called but very few are chosen!

If you keep subscribing to the "land for peace" mantra of "peace and security," you must know that there will be no lasting peace. Your only peace is in the Messiah!

Man has not been given the ability to comprehend or understand the purpose of death and the tragedies that you are facing, but know that your God, the God of the Bible, loves you. Nothing in the world happens over which He does not have control.

The God of Israel is not millions of miles away. To the contrary, He exists in those who have called on Him, and He will come into your life if you will ask Him.

If you have doubts about His existence, ask Him to show Himself. He will answer your petition just like He has many others who have doubted Him but who have reached out and were given proof of His existence.

Out of His love for you and His desire to be everything in your life, He wants you to reach out your hand, and then He will take yours. Learn to walk in His presence, because there is nothing like it. Trust me, your life will never be the same!

It is time to press into the power, which can only come through Jesus Christ.

I am not here to evangelize you, but I do want to tell you about the One who can deliver you, and to tell you about those Christians who would put their lives on the line to be there for you.

It is the existence of Jesus Christ in us that has given us this love for you and for your nation. Those who have the heart of Jesus Christ will also have a heart for Israel and for the Jewish people.

Please read these words spoken by Jesus Christ 2,000 years ago alongside the Sea of Galilee. Take time to ponder and pray over these words because they will bless you and give you the hope for today, for the future, and for eternity.

Matthew 5: 1-12

The Sermon on the Mount--The Beatitudes

Now when he saw the crowds, he went up on a mountainside and sat down. His disciples came to him, and he began to teach them saying:

"Blessed are the poor in spirit, for theirs is the kingdom of heaven. Blessed are those who mourn, for they will be

comforted. Blessed are the meek, for they will inherit the earth. Blessed are those who hunger and thirst for righteousness, for they will be filled. Blessed are the merciful, for they will be shown mercy. Blessed are the pure in heart, for they will see God. Blessed are the peacemakers, for they will be called sons of God. Blessed are those who are persecuted because of righteousness, for theirs is the kingdom of heaven. Blessed are you when people insult you, persecute you, and falsely say all kinds of evil against you because of me. Rejoice and be glad, because great is your reward in heaven, for in the same way they persecuted the prophets who were before you."

Our God loves us all, but He is especially fond of you, the nation of Israel and His Chosen People, because you are the "apple of His eye" (Zechariah 2:8).

In the New Testament Letter to Romans, Paul (formerly Saul, a Jew and a Pharisee who was devoted to serving the God of Israel by strict adherence to the Law) wrote that followers of Jesus Christ have been grafted into the olive tree of Jewish inheritance and blessing (Romans 11:17). We are your brothers and sisters, and we are there for you too!

I won't expound or attempt to share Jesus Christ with you, but if you ever want to know more about Him, please ask!

For now, we will continue to stand by you, to comfort you and to be there for you... in the bad times and in the good times... in the Spirit of His love for you! We are your best friends!

We love you, Israel. We love the Jewish people! We love Jesus Christ! All to His Glory!

Addendum
Land Grant Scriptures

God gave the land to Abram; from Abram will come a great nation:

Genesis 12

[1]Now the LORD had said unto Abram, Get thee out of thy country, and from thy kindred, and from thy father's house, unto a land that I will shew thee: [2]And I will make of thee a great nation, and I will bless thee, and make thy name great; and thou shalt be a blessing:

[7]And the LORD appeared unto Abram, and said, Unto thy seed will I give this land...

Genesis 13

[14]And the LORD said unto Abram, after that Lot was separated from him, Lift up now thine eyes, and look from the place where thou art northward, and southward, and eastward, and westward: [15]For all the land which thou seest, to thee will I give it, and to thy seed for ever. [16]And I will make thy seed as the dust of the earth: so that if a man can number the dust of the earth, then shall thy seed also be numbered. [17]Arise, walk through the land in the length of it and in the breadth of it; for I will give it unto thee.

God creates an everlasting covenant with Abram

Genesis 15

[7]And he said unto him, I am the LORD that brought thee out of Ur of the Chaldees, to give thee this land to inherit it. [8]And he said, LORD God, whereby shall I know that I shall inherit it? [9]And he said unto him, Take me an heifer of three years old, and a she goat of three years old,

and a ram of three years old, and a turtledove, and a young pigeon. [10]And he took unto him all these, and divided them in the midst, and laid each piece one against another: but the birds divided he not. [11] And when the fowls came down upon the carcasses, Abram drove them away. [12]And when the sun was going down, a deep sleep fell upon Abram; and, lo, an horror of great darkness fell upon him.

God creates a land covenant

Genesis 15

[17]And it came to pass, that, when the sun went down, and it was dark, behold a smoking furnace, and a burning lamp that passed between those pieces. [18]In the same day the LORD made a covenant with Abram, saying, Unto thy seed have I given this land, from the river of Egypt unto the great river, the river Euphrates:

God reinforces that the covenant is forever

Genesis 17

[1]And when Abram was ninety years old and nine, the LORD appeared to Abram, and said unto him, I am the Almighty God; walk before me, and be thou perfect. [2] And I will make my covenant between me and thee, and will multiply thee exceedingly. [3]And Abram fell on his face: and God talked with him, saying, [4]As for me, behold, my covenant is with thee, and thou shalt be a father of many nations. [5]Neither shall thy name any more be called Abram, but thy name shall be Abraham; for a father of many nations have I made thee. [6]And I will make thee exceeding fruitful, and I will make nations of thee, and kings shall come out of thee. [7]And I will establish my covenant between me and thee and thy seed after thee in their generations for an everlasting covenant, to be a God

unto thee, and to thy seed after thee. [8]And I will give unto thee, and to thy seed after thee, the land wherein thou art a stranger, all the land of Canaan, for an everlasting possession; and I will be their God.
[15]And God said unto Abraham, As for Sarai thy wife, thou shalt not call her name Sarai, but Sarah shall her name be. [16]And I will bless her, and give thee a son also of her: yea, I will bless her, and she shall be a mother of nations; kings of people shall be of her
[19]And God said, Sarah thy wife shall bear thee a son indeed; and thou shalt call his name Isaac: and I will establish my covenant with him for an everlasting covenant, and with his seed after him.
[21]But my covenant will I establish with Isaac...

God testifies that He gave the surrounding countries to Abraham

Genesis 26
[2]And the LORD appeared unto him, and said, Go not down into Egypt; dwell in the land which I shall tell thee of: [3]Sojourn in this land, and I will be with thee, and will bless thee; for unto thee, and unto thy seed, I will give all these countries, and I will perform the oath which I sware unto Abraham thy father; [4]And I will make thy seed to multiply as the stars of heaven, and will give unto thy seed all these countries; and in thy seed shall all the nations of the earth be blessed;

Genesis 35
[11] And God said unto him, I am God Almighty: be fruitful and multiply; a nation and a company of nations shall be of thee, and kings shall come out of thy loins; [12]And the land which I gave Abraham and Isaac, to thee I will give it, and to thy seed after thee will I give the land.

God defines the boundaries of the inherited land

Exodus 23

[30]By little and little I will drive them out from before thee, until thou be increased, and inherit the land. [31]And I will set thy bounds from the Red sea even unto the sea of the Philistines, and from the desert unto the river: for I will deliver the inhabitants of the land into your hand; and thou shalt drive them out before thee.
God specifically states "no peace deals" [32]Thou shalt make no covenant with them, nor with their gods. [33]They shall not dwell in thy land, lest they make thee sin against me: for if thou serve their gods, it will surely be a snare unto thee.

God again restates borders of the inherited land

Numbers 34

[1]And the LORD spake unto Moses, saying, [2]Command the children of Israel, and say unto them, When ye come into the land of Canaan; (this is the land that shall fall unto you for an inheritance, even the land of Canaan with the coasts thereof:) [3]Then your south quarter shall be from the wilderness of Zin along by the coast of Edom, and your south border shall be the outmost coast of the salt sea eastward: [4]And your border shall turn from the south to the ascent of Akrabbim, and pass on to Zin: and the going forth thereof shall be from the south to Kadeshbarnea, and shall go on to Hazaraddar, and pass on to Azmon: [5]And the border shall fetch a compass from Azmon unto the river of Egypt, and the goings out of it shall be at the sea. [6]And as for the western border, ye shall even have the great sea for a border: this shall be your west border. [7]And this shall be your north border: from the great sea ye shall point out for you mount Hor: [8]From mount Hor ye shall point out your border unto the

entrance of Hamath; and the goings forth of the border shall be to Zedad: [9]And the border shall go on to Ziphron, and the goings out of it shall be at Hazarenan: this shall be your north border. [10]And ye shall point out your east border from Hazarenan to Shepham: [11]And the coast shall go down from Shepham to Riblah, on the east side of Ain; and the border shall descend, and shall reach unto the side of the sea of Chinnereth eastward: [12]And the border shall go down to Jordan, and the goings out of it shall be at the salt sea: this shall be your land with the coasts thereof round about.

Deuteronomy 1
[7]Turn you, and take your journey, and go to the mount of the Amorites, and unto all the places nigh thereunto, in the plain, in the hills, and in the vale, and in the south, and by the sea side, to the land of the Canaanites, and unto Lebanon, unto the great river, the river Euphrates. [8]Behold, I have set the land before you: go in and possess the land which the LORD sware unto your fathers, Abraham, Isaac, and Jacob, to give unto them and to their seed after them.

God commands the Jews to possess the land

Deuteronomy 1
[20]And I said unto you, Ye are come unto the mountain of the Amorites, which the LORD our God doth give unto us. [21]Behold, the LORD thy God hath set the land before thee: go up and possess it, as the LORD God of thy fathers hath said unto thee; fear not, neither be discouraged.

Deuteronomy 2
[24]Rise ye up, take your journey, and pass over the river Arnon: behold, I have given into thine hand Sihon the Amorite, king of Heshbon, and his land: begin to possess

it, and contend with him in battle.

God's judgment concerning the land

Deuteronomy 4

[25]When thou shalt beget children, and children's children, and ye shall have remained long in the land, and shall corrupt yourselves, and make a graven image, or the likeness of any thing, and shall do evil in the sight of the LORD thy God, to provoke him to anger: [26]I call heaven and earth to witness against you this day, that ye shall soon utterly perish from off the land whereunto ye go over Jordan to possess it; ye shall not prolong your days upon it, but shall utterly be destroyed. [27]And the LORD shall scatter you among the nations, and ye shall be left few in number among the heathen, whither the LORD shall lead you. [28]And there ye shall serve gods, the work of men's hands, wood and stone, which neither see, nor hear, nor eat, nor smell. [29]But if from thence thou shalt seek the LORD thy God, thou shalt find him, if thou seek him with all thy heart and with all thy soul. [30]When thou art in tribulation, and all these things are come upon thee, even in the latter days, if thou turn to the LORD thy God, and shalt be obedient unto his voice; [31](For the LORD thy God is a merciful God;) he will not forsake thee, neither destroy thee, nor forget the covenant of thy fathers which he sware unto them.

God again confirms the covenant land boundaries

Joshua 1

[1]Now after the death of Moses the servant of the LORD it came to pass, that the LORD spake unto Joshua the son of Nun, Moses' minister, saying, [2]Moses my servant is dead; now therefore arise, go over this Jordan, thou, and all this people, unto the land which I do give to them, even to the children of Israel. [3]Every place that the sole of

your foot shall tread upon, that have I given unto you, as I said unto Moses. [4]From the wilderness and this Lebanon even unto the great river, the river Euphrates, all the land of the Hittites, and unto the great sea toward the going down of the sun, shall be your coast.

Psalm 105

[7]He is the LORD our God: his judgments are in all the earth. [8]He hath remembered his covenant for ever, the word which he commanded to a thousand generations. [9]Which covenant he made with Abraham, and his oath unto Isaac; [10]And confirmed the same unto Jacob for a law, and to Israel for an everlasting covenant: [11]Saying, Unto thee will I give the land of Canaan, the lot of your inheritance:

Ezekiel 47

[13]Thus saith the Lord GOD; This shall be the border, whereby ye shall inherit the land according to the twelve tribes of Israel: Joseph shall have two portions. [14]And ye shall inherit it, one as well as another: concerning the which I lifted up mine hand to give it unto your fathers: and this land shall fall unto you for inheritance. [15]And this shall be the border of the land toward the north side, from the great sea, the way of Hethlon, as men go to Zedad; [16]Hamath, Berothah, Sibraim, which is between the border of Damascus and the border of Hamath; Hazarhatticon, which is by the coast of Hauran. [17]And the border from the sea shall be Hazarenan, the border of Damascus, and the north northward, and the border of Hamath. And this is the north side. [18]And the east side ye shall measure from Hauran, and from Damascus, and from Gilead, and from the land of Israel by Jordan, from the border unto the east sea. And this is the east side. [19]And the south side southward, from Tamar even to the waters of strife in Kadesh, the river to the great sea. And

this is the south side southward. [20]The west side also shall be the great sea from the border, till a man come over against Hamath. This is the west side. [21]So shall ye divide this land unto you according to the tribes of Israel. [22] And it shall come to pass, that ye shall divide it by lot for an inheritance unto you, and to the strangers that sojourn among you, which shall beget children among you: and they shall be unto you as born in the country among the children of Israel; they shall have inheritance with you among the tribes of Israel. [23]And it shall come to pass, that in what tribe the stranger sojourneth, there shall ye give him his inheritance, saith the Lord GOD.

God states not to give the land away

Ezekiel 48

[14]And they shall not sell of it, neither exchange, nor alienate the firstfruits of the land: for it is holy unto the LORD.

[29]This is the land which ye shall divide by lot unto the tribes of Israel for inheritance, and these are their portions, saith the Lord GOD.

Addendum

The Error Of Replacement Theology

by Clarence H. Wagner, Jr.

Perhaps you have heard of the term Replacement Theology. However, if you look it up in a dictionary of Church history, you will not find it listed as a systematic study. Rather, it is a doctrinal teaching that originated in the early Church. It became the fertile soil from which Christian anti-Semitism grew and has infected the Church for nearly 1,900 years.

What Is Replacement Theology?

Replacement Theology was introduced to the Church shortly after Gentile leadership took over from Jewish leadership.

What are its premises?

1. Israel (the Jewish people and the land) has been replaced by the Christian Church in the purposes of God, or, more precisely, the Church is the historic continuation of Israel to the exclusion of the former.
2. The Jewish people are now no longer a "chosen people." In fact, they are no different from any other group, such as the English, Spanish, or Africans.
3. Apart from repentance, the new birth, and incorporation into the Church, the Jewish people have no future, no hope, and no calling in the plan of God. The same is true for every other nation

and group.

4. Since Pentecost of Acts 2, the term "Israel," as found in the Bible, now refers to the Church.
5. The promises, covenants and blessings ascribed to Israel in the Bible have been taken away from the Jews and given to the Church, which has superseded them. However, the Jews are subject to the curses found in the Bible, as a result of their rejection of Christ.

What Happens When the Church Replaces Israel?

1. The Church becomes arrogant and self-centered.
2. It boasts against the Jews and Israel.
3. It devalues the role of Israel or has no role for Israel at all.
4. These attitudes result in anti-Semitism in word and deed.
5. Without a place for Israel and the Jewish people today, you cannot explain the Bible prophecies, especially the very specific ones being fulfilled in Israel today.
6. Many New Testament passages do not make sense when the Church replaces the Jewish people.
7. You can lose the significance of the Hebrew Scriptures, the Old Testament, for today. Many Christians boast of being a New Testament (NT) Christian or a NT Church as in the Book of Acts. However, the Bible of the early Church was not the New Testament, which did not get codified until the 4th century, but rather the Hebrew Scriptures.
8. You can lose the Hebraic/Judaic contextualization of the New Testament, which teaches us more about Yeshua and how to become better disciples.

9. The Church loses out on the opportunity to participate in God's plan and prophecy for the Church, Israel and the world today.

What Happens When the Church Relates to Israel?

1. The Church takes its proper role in God's redemptive plan for the world, appreciating God's ongoing covenant relationship and love for Israel and the Jewish people.
2. We can see the consistency of God's redemptive plan from Genesis to Revelation as an ongoing complementary process, not as disconnected snapshots.
3. We show love and honor for God's covenant people, not contempt.
4. We value the Old and New Testaments as equally inspired and significant for the Church today.
5. Bible prophecy makes sense for today and offers opportunities for involvement in God's plan for Israel.
6. We become better disciples of Yeshua [Jesus] as we are able to appreciate the Hebraic/Judaic roots that fill in the definitions, concepts, words and events in the New Testament that are otherwise obscured. Why? The Jewish writers of the New Testament did not explain many, because they did not feel the need to fill in all the details that were already explained in the Old Testament.

Had the Church understood this very clear message from the beginning, and then the sad legacy of anti-Semitic hatred from the Church may have been avoided. The error of Replacement Theology is like a cancer in the

Church that has not only caused it to violate God's Word concerning the Jewish people and Israel, but it made us into instruments of hate, not love in God's Name. Yet, it is not too late to change our ways and rightly relate to the Jewish people and Israel today. Through Bridges for Peace you can read, study and learn more, and also give to demonstrate God's exhortation to us to bless His Covenant People, whom He still loves. Not only do we need to learn and do for ourselves, but also we need to teach others so as to counteract the historical error that has been fostered in the Church for nearly 2,000 years.

Thank God, He is a God of mercy, redemption and second chances.

For full commentary go to:
http://www.bridgesforpeace.com/publications/teaching/Article-18.html

Addendum
Resolutions, Agreement, Letters, and Speeches

- UN Security Council Resolution 242 -- November 22, 1967
- UN Security Council Resolution 338 -- October 22, 1973
- Remarks by Mr. George Bush, President of the United States -- October 30, 1991
- Quartet Road Map: A Performance-Based Road Map to a Permanent Two-State Solution to the Israeli-Palestinian Conflict -- April 30, 2003
- President George W. Bush's Speech at Aqaba Summit -- June 04, 2003

UN Security Council Resolution 242
November 22, 1967

Source: http://www.mfa.gov.il/mfa/go.asp?MFAH00p40

Following the June '67, Six-Day War, the situation in the Middle East was discussed by the UN General Assembly, which referred the issue to the Security Council. After lengthy discussion, a final draft for a Security Council resolution was presented by the British Ambassador, Lord Caradon, on November 22, 1967. It was adopted on the same day.

This resolution, numbered 242, established provisions and principles which, it was hoped, would lead to a solution of the conflict. Resolution 242 was to become the cornerstone of Middle East diplomatic efforts in the coming decades.

The Security Council,

Expressing its continuing concern with the grave situation in the Middle East,

Emphasizing the inadmissibility of the acquisition of territory by war and the need to work for a just and lasting peace in which every State in the area can live in security,

Emphasizing further that all Member States in their acceptance of the Charter of the United Nations have undertaken a commitment to act in accordance with Article 2 of the Charter,

1. Affirms that the fulfillment of Charter principles requires the establishment of a just and lasting peace in the Middle East which should include the application of both the following principles:
   - Withdrawal of Israeli armed forces from territories occupied in the recent conflict;
   - Termination of all claims or states of belligerency and respect for and acknowledgement of the sovereignty, territorial integrity and political independence of every State in the area and their right

to live in peace within secure and recognized boundaries free from threats or acts of force;

2. Affirms further the necessity:
   - For guaranteeing freedom of navigation through international waterways in the area;
   - For achieving a just settlement of the refugee problem;
   - For guaranteeing the territorial inviolability and political independence of every State in the area, through measures including the establishment of demilitarized zones;

3. Requests the Secretary General to designate a Special Representative to proceed to the Middle East to establish and maintain contacts with the States concerned in order to promote agreement and assist efforts to achieve a peaceful and accepted settlement in accordance with the provisions and principles in this resolution;

4. Requests the Secretary-General to report to the Security Council on the progress of the efforts of the Special Representative as soon as possible.

UN Security Council Resolution 338
October 22, 1973

In the later stages of the Yom Kippur War -- after Israel repulsed the Syrian attack on the Golan Heights and established a bridgehead on the Egyptian side of the Suez Canal -- international efforts to stop the fighting were intensified. U.S. Secretary of State Kissinger flew to Moscow on October 20, and, together with the Soviet Government, the U.S. proposed a cease-fire resolution in the UN Security Council. The Council met on 21 October at the urgent request of both the U.S. and the USSR, and by 14 votes to none, adopted the following resolution:

The Security Council,

1. Calls upon all parties to present fighting to cease all firing and terminate all military activity immediately, no later than 12 hours after the moment of the adoption of this decision, in the positions after the moment of the adoption of this decision, in the positions they now occupy;

2. Calls upon all parties concerned to start immediately after the cease-fire the implementation of Security Council Resolution 242 (1967) in all of its parts;

3. Decides that, immediately and concurrently with the cease-fire, negotiations start between the parties concerned under appropriate auspices aimed at establishing a just and durable peace in the Middle East.

The Madrid Conference Opening Speech October 30-31, 1991 Remarks By President George H.W. Bush

Source: http://www.mfa.gov.il/mfa/go.asp?MFAH0dg10

Prime Minister Gonzalez and President Gorbachev, Excellencies. Let me begin by thanking the Government of Spain for hosting this historic gathering. With short notice, the Spanish people and their leaders stepped forward to make available this magnificent setting. Let us hope that this Conference of Madrid will mark the beginning of a new chapter in the history of the Middle East.

I also want to express at the outset my pleasure at the presence of our fellow co-sponsor, President Gorbachev. At a time of momentous challenges at home, President Gorbachev and his senior associates have demonstrated their intent to engage the Soviet Union as a force for positive change in the Middle East. This sends a powerful signal to all those who long for peace.

We come to Madrid on a mission of hope - to begin work on a just, lasting, and comprehensive settlement to the conflict in the Middle East. We come here to seek peace for a part of the world that in the long memory of man has known far too much hatred, anguish, and war. I can think of no endeavor more worthy - or more necessary.

Our objective must be clear and straightforward. It is not simply to end the state of war in the Middle East and replace it with a state of non-belligerency. This is not enough; this would not last. Rather, we seek peace, real peace. And by real peace I mean treaties. Security. Diplomatic relations. Economic relations. Trade. Investment. Cultural exchange. Even tourism.

What we seek is a Middle East where vast resources are no longer devoted to armaments. A Middle East where young people no longer have to dedicate and, all too often, give their lives to combat. A Middle East no longer victimized by fear and terror. A Middle East where normal men and women lead normal lives.

Let no one mistake the magnitude of this challenge. The struggle we seek to end has a long and painful history. Every life lost - every outrage, every act of violence - is etched deep in the hearts and history of the people of this region. Theirs is a history that weighs heavily against hope. And yet, history need not be man's master. I expect that some will say that what I am suggesting is impossible. But think back. Who back in 1945 would have thought that France and Germany, bitter rivals for nearly a century, would become allies in the aftermath of World War II? And who two years ago would have predicted that the Berlin Wall would come down? And who in the early 1960s would have believed that the Cold War would come to a peaceful end, replaced by cooperation - exemplified by the fact that the United States and the Soviet Union are here today - not as rivals, but as partners, as Prime

Minister Gonzalez pointed out.

No, peace in the Middle East need not be a dream. Peace is possible. The Egyptian-Israeli Peace Treaty is striking proof that former adversaries can make and sustain peace. And moreover, parties in the Middle East have respected agreements, not only in the Sinai, but on the Golan Heights as well.

The fact that we are all gathered here today for the first time attests to a new potential for peace. Each of us has taken an important step toward real peace by meeting here in Madrid. All the formulas on paper, all the pious declarations in the world won't bring peace if there is no practical mechanism for moving ahead.

Peace will only come as the result of direct negotiations, compromise, give-and-take. Peace cannot be imposed from the outside by the United States or anyone else. While we will continue to do every thing possible to help the parties overcome obstacles, peace must come from within. We come here to Madrid as realists. We do not expect peace to be negotiated in a day, or a week, or a month, or even a year. It will take time; indeed, it should take time - time for parties so long at war to learn to talk to one another, to listen to one another. Time to heal old wounds and build trust. In this quest, time need not be the enemy of progress.

What we envision is a process of direct negotiations proceeding along two tracks, one between Israel and the Arab states; the other between Israel and the Palestinians. Negotiations are to be conducted on the basis of UN Security Council Resolutions 242 and 338. The real work will not happen here in the plenary session, but in direct bilateral negotiations. This Conference cannot impose a settlement on the participants or veto agreements; and just as important, the Conference can only be reconvened with the consent of every participant. Progress is in the hands of the parties who must live with the consequences.

Soon after the bilateral talks commence, parties will convene as well to organize multilateral negotiations. These will focus on issues that cross national boundaries and are common to the region: arms control, water, refugee concerns, economic development. Progress in these fora is not intended as a substitute for what must be decided in the bilateral talks; to the contrary, progress in the multilateral issues can help create an atmosphere in which long-standing bilateral disputes can more easily be settled.

For Israel and the Palestinians, a framework already exists for diplomacy. Negotiations will be conducted in phases, beginning with talks on interim self-government arrangements. We aim to reach agreement within one year. And once agreed, interim self-government arrangements will last for five years; beginning the third year, negotiations will commence on permanent status.

No one can say with any precision what the end result will be; in our view, something must be developed, something acceptable to Israel, the Palestinians and Jordan, that gives the Palestinian people meaningful control over their own lives and fate and provides for the acceptance and security of Israel.

We can all appreciate that both Israelis and Palestinians are worried about compromise, worried about compromising even the smallest point for fear it becomes a precedent for what really matters. But no one should avoid compromise on interim arrangements for a simple reason: nothing agreed to now will prejudice permanent status negotiations. To the contrary, these subsequent negotiations will be determined on their own merits.

Peace cannot depend upon promises alone. Real peace - lasting peace - must be based upon security for all states and peoples, including Israel. For too long the Israeli people have lived in fear, surrounded by an unaccepting Arab world. Now is the ideal moment for the Arab world to demonstrate that attitudes have changed that the Arab world is willing to live in peace with Israel and make allowances for Israel's reasonable security needs.

We know that peace must also be based on fairness. In the absence of fairness, there will be no legitimacy - no stability. This applies above all to the Palestinian people, many of whom have known turmoil and frustration above all else. Israel now has an opportunity to demonstrate that it is willing to enter into a new relationship with its Palestinian neighbors; one predicated upon mutual respect and cooperation. Throughout the Middle East, we seek a stable and enduring settlement. We've not defined what this means; indeed, I make these points with no map showing where the final borders are to be drawn. Nevertheless, we believe territorial compromise is essential for peace. Boundaries should reflect the quality of both security and political arrangements. The United States is prepared to accept whatever the parties themselves find accept able. What we seek, as I said on March 6, is a solution that meets the twin tests of fairness and security.

I know - I expect we all know - that these negotiations will not be easy. I know, too, that these negotiations will not be smooth. There will be disagreement and criticism, setbacks - who knows - possibly interruptions. Negotiation and compromise are always painful. Success will escape us if we focus solely upon what is being given up. We must fix our vision on what real peace would bring. Peace, after all, means not just avoiding war and the costs of preparing for it. The Middle East is blessed with great resources: physical, financial, and, yes, above all, human. New opportunities are within reach - if we only have the vision to embrace them.

To succeed, we must recognize that peace is in the interest of all parties - war, absolute advantage of none. The alternative to peace in the Middle East is a future of violence and waste and tragedy. In any future war lurks the danger of weapons of mass destruction. As we learned in the Gulf War, modern arsenals make it possible to attack urban areas to put the lives of innocent men, women, and children at risk, to transform city streets, schools, and children's playgrounds into battlefields.

Today, we can decide to take a different path to the future to avoid conflict. I call upon all parties to avoid unilateral acts, be they words or deeds that would invite retaliation or, worse yet, prejudice or even threaten this process itself. I call upon all parties to consider taking measures that will bolster mutual confidence and trust steps that signal a sincere commitment to reconciliation. I want to say something about the role of the United States of America. We played an active role in making this conference possible; both the Secretary of State, Jim Baker, and I will play an active role in helping the process succeed. Toward this end, we've provided written assurances to Israel, to Syria, to Jordan, Lebanon, and the Palestinians. In the spirit of openness and honesty, we will brief all parties on the assurances that we have provided to the other. We're prepared to extend guarantees, provide technology and support, if that is what peace requires. And we will call upon our friends and allies in Europe and in Asia to join with us in providing resources so that peace and prosperity go hand in hand.

Outsiders can assist, but in the end, it is up to the peoples and governments of the Middle East to shape the future of the Middle East. It is their opportunity and it is their responsibility to do all that they can to take advantage of this gathering, this historic gathering, and what it symbolizes and what it promises.

No one should assume that the opportunity before us to make peace will remain if we fail to seize the moment. Ironically, this is an opportunity born of war - the destruction of past wars, the fear of future wars. The time has come to put an end to war - the time has come to choose peace.

Speaking for the American people, I want to reaffirm that the United States is prepared to facilitate the search for peace, to be a catalyst, as we've been in the past and as we've been very recently. We seek only one thing, and this we seek not for ourselves, but for the peoples of the area and particularly the children: that this and future generations of the Middle East may know the meaning and blessing of peace.

We have seen too many generations of children whose haunted eyes show only fear - too many funerals for their brothers and sisters, the mothers and fathers who died too soon - too much hatred, too little love. And if we cannot summon the courage to lay down the past for ourselves, let us resolve to do it for the children. May God bless and guide the work of this Conference, and may this Conference set us on the path of peace.

Thank you.

A Performance-Based Road Map to a Permanent Two-State Solution to the Israeli-Palestinian Conflict Press Statement

Office of the Spokesman
Washington, D.C.
April 30, 2003

Source: http://www.state.gov./r/pa/prs/ps/2003/20062.htm

The following is a performance-based and goal-driven roadmap, with clear phases, timelines, target dates, and benchmarks aiming at progress through reciprocal steps by the two parties in the political, security, economic, humanitarian, and institution-building fields, under the auspices of the Quartet [the United States, European Union, United Nations, and Russia]. The destination is a final and comprehensive settlement of the Israel-Palestinian conflict by 2005, as presented in President Bush's speech of 24 June, and welcomed by the EU, Russia and the UN in the 16 July and 17 September Quartet Ministerial statements.

A two-state solution to the Israeli-Palestinian conflict will only be achieved through an end to violence and terrorism, when the Palestinian people have a leadership acting decisively against terror and willing and able to build a practicing democracy based on tolerance and liberty, and through Israel's readiness to do what is necessary for a democratic Palestinian state to be established, and a clear, unambiguous acceptance by both parties of the goal of a negotiated settlement as described below. The Quartet will assist and facilitate implementation of the plan, starting in Phase I, including direct discussions between the parties as required. The plan establishes a realistic timeline for implementation. However, as a performance-based plan, progress will require and depend upon the good faith efforts of the parties, and their compliance with each of the obligations outlined below. Should the parties perform their obligations rapidly, progress within and through the phases may come sooner than indicated in the plan. Non-compliance with obligations will impede progress.

A settlement, negotiated between the parties, will result in the emergence of an independent, democratic, and viable Palestinian state living side by side in peace and security with Israel and its other neighbors. The settlement will resolve the Israel-Palestinian conflict, and end the occupation that began in 1967, based on the foundations of the Madrid Conference, the principle of land for peace, UNSCRs 242, 338 and 1397, agreements previously reached by the parties, and the initiative of Saudi Crown Prince Abdullah -- endorsed by the Beirut Arab League Summit -- calling for acceptance of Israel as a neighbor living in peace and security, in the context of a comprehensive settlement. This initiative is a vital element of international efforts to promote a comprehensive peace on all tracks, including the Syrian-Israeli and Lebanese-Israeli tracks.

The Quartet will meet regularly at senior levels to evaluate the parties' performance on implementation of the plan. In each phase, the parties are expected to perform their obligations in parallel, unless otherwise indicated.

Phase I: Ending Terror And Violence, Normalizing Palestinian Life, and Building Palestinian Institutions -- Present to May 2003

In Phase I, the Palestinians immediately undertake an unconditional cessation of violence according to the steps outlined below; such action should be accompanied by supportive measures undertaken by Israel. Palestinians and Israelis resume security cooperation based on the Tenet work plan to end violence, terrorism, and incitement through restructured and effective Palestinian security services. Palestinians undertake comprehensive political reform in preparation for statehood, including drafting a Palestinian constitution, and free, fair and open elections upon the basis of those measures. Israel takes all necessary steps to help normalize Palestinian life. Israel withdraws from Palestinian areas occupied from September 28, 2000 and the two sides restore the status quo that existed at that time, as security performance and cooperation progress. Israel also freezes all settlement activity, consistent with the Mitchell report.

At the outset of Phase I:

- Palestinian leadership issues unequivocal statement reiterating Israel's right to exist in peace and security and calling for an immediate and unconditional cease-fire to end armed activity and all acts of violence against Israelis anywhere. All official Palestinian institutions end incitement against Israel.

- Israeli leadership issues unequivocal statement affirming its commitment to the two-state vision of an independent, viable, sovereign Palestinian state living in peace and security alongside Israel, as expressed by President Bush, and calling for an immediate end to violence against Palestinians everywhere. All official Israeli institutions end incitement against Palestinians.

Security

- Palestinians declare an unequivocal end to violence and terrorism and undertake visible efforts on the ground to arrest, disrupt, and restrain individuals and groups conducting and planning violent attacks on Israelis anywhere.
- Rebuilt and refocused Palestinian Authority security apparatus begins sustained, targeted, and effective operations aimed at confronting all those engaged in terror and dismantlement of terrorist capabilities and infrastructure. This includes commencing confiscation of illegal weapons and consolidation of security authority, free of association with terror and corruption.
- GOI takes no actions undermining trust, including deportations, attacks on civilians; confiscation and/or demolition of Palestinian homes and property, as a punitive measure or to facilitate Israeli construction; destruction of Palestinian institutions and infrastructure; and other measures specified in the Tenet work plan.
- Relying on existing mechanisms and on-the-ground resources, Quartet representatives begin informal monitoring and consult with the parties on establishment of a formal monitoring mechanism and its

implementation.

- Implementation, as previously agreed, of U.S. rebuilding, training and resumed security cooperation plan in collaboration with outside oversight board (U.S.--Egypt--Jordan). Quartet support for efforts to achieve a lasting, comprehensive cease-fire.
- All Palestinian security organizations are consolidated into three services reporting to an empowered Interior Minister.
- Restructured/retrained Palestinian security forces and IDF counterparts progressively resume security cooperation and other undertakings in implementation of the Tenet work plan, including regular senior-level meetings, with the participation of U.S. security officials.
- Arab states cut off public and private funding and all other forms of support for groups supporting and engaging in violence and terror.
- All donors providing budgetary support for the Palestinians channel these funds through the Palestinian Ministry of Finance's Single Treasury Account.
- As comprehensive security performance moves forward, IDF withdraws progressively from areas occupied since September 28, 2000 and the two sides restore the status quo that existed prior to September 28, 2000. Palestinian security forces redeploy to areas vacated by IDF.

Palestinian Institution-Building

- Immediate action on credible process to produce draft constitution for Palestinian statehood. As rapidly as possible, constitutional committee circulates draft Palestinian constitution, based on strong parliamentary democracy and cabinet with empowered Prime Minister, for public comment/debate. Constitutional committee proposes draft document for submission after elections for approval by appropriate Palestinian institutions.

- Appointment of interim Prime Minister or cabinet with empowered executive authority/decision-making body.
- GOI fully facilitates travel of Palestinian officials for PLC and Cabinet sessions, internationally supervised security retraining, electoral and other reform activity, and other supportive measures related to the reform efforts.
- Continued appointment of Palestinian ministers empowered to undertake fundamental reform. Completion of further steps to achieve genuine separation of powers, including any necessary Palestinian legal reforms for this purpose.
- Establishment of independent Palestinian election commission. PLC reviews and revises election law.
- Palestinian performance on judicial, administrative, and economic benchmarks, as established by the International Task Force on Palestinian Reform.
- As early as possible, and based upon the above measures and in the context of open debate and transparent candidate selection/electoral campaign based on a free, multi-party process, Palestinians hold free, open, and fair elections.
- GOI facilitates Task Force election assistance, registration of voters, movement of candidates and voting officials. Support for NGOs involved in the election process.
- GOI reopens Palestinian Chamber of Commerce and other closed Palestinian institutions in East Jerusalem based on a commitment that these institutions operate strictly in accordance with prior agreements between the parties.

Humanitarian Response

- Israel takes measures to improve the humanitarian situation. Israel and Palestinians implement in full all recommendations of the Bertini report to improve humanitarian conditions, lifting curfews and easing restrictions on movement of persons and goods, and allowing full, safe, and unfettered access of international and humanitarian personnel.
- AHLC reviews the humanitarian situation and prospects for economic development in the West Bank and Gaza and launches a major donor assistance effort, including to the reform effort.
- GOI and PA continue revenue clearance process and transfer of funds, including arrears, in accordance with agreed, transparent monitoring mechanism.

Civil Society

- Continued donor support, including increased funding through PVOs/NGOs, for people to people programs, private sector development and civil society initiatives.

Settlements

- GOI immediately dismantles settlement outposts erected since March 2001.
- Consistent with the Mitchell Report, GOI freezes all settlement activity (including natural growth of settlements).

Phase II: Transition -- June 2003-December 2003

In the second phase, efforts are focused on the option of creating an independent Palestinian state with provisional borders and attributes of sovereignty, based on the new constitution, as a way station to a permanent status settlement. As has been noted, this goal can be achieved when the Palestinian people have a leadership acting decisively against terror, willing and able to build a practicing democracy based on tolerance and liberty. With such a leadership, reformed civil institutions and security structures, the Palestinians will have the active support of the Quartet and the broader international community in establishing an independent, viable, state.

Progress into Phase II will be based upon the consensus judgment of the Quartet of whether conditions are appropriate to proceed, taking into account performance of both parties. Furthering and sustaining efforts to normalize Palestinian lives and build Palestinian institutions, Phase II starts after Palestinian elections and ends with possible creation of an independent Palestinian state with provisional borders in 2003. Its primary goals are continued comprehensive security performance and effective security cooperation, continued normalization of Palestinian life and institution-building, further building on and sustaining of the goals outlined in Phase I, ratification of a democratic Palestinian constitution, formal establishment of office of prime minister, consolidation of political reform, and the creation of a Palestinian state with provisional borders.

- International Conference: Convened by the Quartet, in consultation with the parties, immediately after the successful conclusion of Palestinian elections, to support Palestinian economic recovery and launch a process, leading to establishment of an independent Palestinian state with provisional borders.
- Such a meeting would be inclusive, based on the goal of a comprehensive Middle East peace (including between Israel and Syria, and Israel and Lebanon), and based on the principles described in the preamble to this document.
- Arab states restore pre-Intifada links to Israel (trade offices, etc.).

- Revival of multilateral engagement on issues including regional water resources, environment, economic development, refugees, and arms control issues.
- New constitution for democratic, independent Palestinian state is finalized and approved by appropriate Palestinian institutions. Further elections, if required, should follow approval of the new constitution.
- Empowered reform cabinet with office of Prime Minister formally established, consistent with draft constitution.
- Continued comprehensive security performance, including effective security cooperation on the bases laid out in Phase I.
- Creation of an independent Palestinian state with provisional borders through a process of Israeli-Palestinian engagement, launched by the international conference. As part of this process, implementation of prior agreements, to enhance maximum territorial contiguity, including further action on settlements in conjunction with establishment of a Palestinian state with provisional borders.
- Enhanced international role in monitoring transition, with the active, sustained, and operational support of the Quartet.
- Quartet members promote international recognition of Palestinian state, including possible UN membership.

Phase III: Permanent Status Agreement and End of the Israeli-Palestinian Conflict -- 2004 -- 2005

Progress into Phase III, based on consensus judgment of Quartet, and taking into account actions of both parties and Quartet monitoring. Phase III objectives are consolidation of reform and stabilization of Palestinian institutions, sustained, effective Palestinian security performance, and

Israeli-Palestinian negotiations aimed at a permanent status agreement in 2005.

- **Second International Conference**: Convened by Quartet, in consultation with the parties, at beginning of 2004 to endorse agreement reached on an independent Palestinian state with provisional borders and formally to launch a process with the active, sustained, and operational support of the Quartet, leading to a final, permanent status resolution in 2005, including on borders, Jerusalem, refugees, settlements; and, to support progress toward a comprehensive Middle East settlement between Israel and Lebanon and Israel and Syria, to be achieved as soon as possible.
- Continued comprehensive, effective progress on the reform agenda laid out by the Task Force in preparation for final status agreement.
- Continued sustained and effective security performance, and sustained, effective security cooperation on the bases laid out in Phase I.
- International efforts to facilitate reform and stabilize Palestinian institutions and the Palestinian economy, in preparation for final status agreement.
- Parties reach final and comprehensive permanent status agreement that ends the Israel-Palestinian conflict in 2005, through a settlement negotiated between the parties based on UNSCR 242, 338, and 1397, that ends the occupation that began in 1967, and includes an agreed, just, fair, and realistic solution to the refugee issue, and a negotiated resolution on the status of Jerusalem that takes into account the political and religious concerns of both sides, and protects the religious interests of Jews, Christians, and Muslims worldwide, and fulfills the vision of two states, Israel and sovereign, independent, democratic and viable Palestine, living side-by-side in peace and security.

- Arab state acceptance of full normal relations with Israel and security for all the states of the region in the context of a comprehensive Arab-Israeli peace.
  [End]

President George W. Bush's Speech at Aqaba
Wednesday, June 04, 2003

GEORGE W. BUSH, PRESIDENT OF THE UNITED STATES: King Abdullah, thank you for hosting this event.

Her Majesty, thank you for your hospitality.

It is fitting that we gather today in Jordan. King Abdullah is a leader on behalf of peace, and is carrying forward the tradition of his father, King Hussein.

I'm pleased to be here with Prime Minister Sharon. The friendship between our countries began at the time of Israel's creation. Today, America is strongly committed and I am strongly committed to Israel's security as a vibrant Jewish state.

I'm also pleased to be with Prime Minister Abbas. He represents the cause of freedom and statehood for the Palestinian people. I strongly support that cause as well.

Each of us is here because we understand that all people have the right to live in peace. We believe that with hard work and good faith and courage it is possible to bring peace to the Middle East. And today we mark important progress toward that goal.

Great and hopeful change is coming to the Middle East.

In Iraq, a dictator who funded terror and sowed conflict has been removed, and a more just and democratic society is emerging.

Prime Minister Abbas now leads the Palestinian cabinet. By his strong leadership, by building the institutions of Palestinian democracy and by rejecting terror, he is serving the deepest hopes of his people.

All here today now share a goal: The Holy Land must be shared between the state of Palestine and the state of Israel, living at peace with each other and with every nation of the Middle East.

All sides will benefit from this achievement and all sides have responsibilities to meet. As the Road Map accepted by the parties makes clear, both must make tangible immediate steps toward this two-state vision.

I welcome Prime Minister Sharon's pledge to improve the humanitarian situation in the Palestinian areas and to begin removing unauthorized outposts immediately. I appreciate his gestures of reconciliation on behalf of prisoners and their families, and his frank statements about the need for territorial contiguity.

As I said yesterday, the issue of settlements must be addressed for peace to be achieved. In addition, Prime Minister Sharon has stated that no unilateral actions by either side can or should prejudge the outcome of future negotiations. The Prime Minister also recognizes that it is in Israel's own interest for Palestinians to govern themselves in their own state.

These are meaningful signs of respect for the rights of the Palestinians and their hopes for a viable, democratic, peaceful Palestinian state.

Prime Minister Abbas recognizes that terrorist crimes are a dangerous obstacle to the independent state his people seek.

He agrees that the process for achieving that state is through peaceful negotiations. He has pledged to consolidate Palestinian institutions, including the security forces, and to make them more accountable and more democratic.

He has promised his full efforts and resources to end the armed intifadah. He has promised to work without compromise for a complete end of violence and terror.

In all these efforts, the Prime Minister is demonstrating

his leadership and commitment to building a better future for the Palestinian people.

Both Prime Ministers here agree that progress toward peace also requires an end to violence and the elimination of all forms of hatred, and prejudice and official incitement, in schoolbooks, in broadcasts and in the words used by political leaders. Both leaders understand that a future of peace cannot be founded on hatred and falsehood and bitterness.

Yet these two leaders cannot bring about peace if they must act alone. True peace requires the support of other nations in the region.

Yesterday in Sharm el-Sheik we made a strong beginning. Arab leaders stated that they share our goal of two states, Israel and Palestine, living side by side in peace and in security. And they have promised to cut off assistance and the flow of money and weapons to terrorist groups and to help Prime Minister Abbas rid Palestinian areas of terrorism.

All sides have made important commitments, and the United States will strive to see these commitments fulfilled.

My government will provide training and support for a new, restructured Palestinian security service. And we'll place a mission on the ground, led by Ambassador John Wolf. This mission will be charged with helping the parties to move toward peace, monitoring their progress and stating clearly who is fulfilling their responsibilities.

And we expect both parties to keep their promises.

I've also asked Secretary of State Colin Powell and National Security Adviser Dr. Condoleezza Rice to make this cause a matter of the highest priority. Secretary Powell and Dr. Rice, as my personal representative, will work closely with the parties, helping them move toward true peace as quickly as possible.

The journey we're taking is difficult, but there is no

other choice. No leader of conscience can accept more months and years of humiliation, killing and mourning. And these leaders of conscience have made their declarations today in the cause of peace. The United States is committed to that cause. If all sides fulfill their obligation, I know that peace can finally come.

Thank you very much and may God bless our work.

Koenig's International News

"Monitor of World Events" William R. Koenig

October 22, 2001

Mr. George W. Bush
President of the United States
The White House
1600 Pennsylvania Avenue
Washington D.C. 20500

Re: God's Covenant Land (Israel)

Dear President Bush,

In the Bible, God speaks to Abraham, father of the Jews and the nation of Israel, and directs him to the land of Canaan (Israel);

I will make you into a great nation, and I will bless you,
I will make your name great, and you will be a blessing.
I will bless those who bless you,
and whoever curses you I will curse;
and all peoples on earth will be blessed through you.
(Genesis 12:1-3, NIV)

With all due respect, America is now experiencing the consequences (curses) of Middle East policies which have been opposed to God's Word and the preservation of His covenant land. Ever since the Madrid Conference over ten years ago, this country's participation in Israel's destiny has been flawed when put in the context of Holy Scripture.

The events of September 11 were a national wake-up call. However, this nation continues to support the Mitchell Plan, affirming a "land for peace" approach, and if Secretary of State Colin Powell proclaims your Middle East "vision" for a Palestinian state, with a foothold in Jerusalem, to the United Nations General Assembly, America can expect to experience the lifting of the Lord's protective hand in an even greater measure.

It is a fact that Israel's very existence is in grave danger, because of our nation's sponsorship of "land for peace" plans which have led her to the brink of war.

What is happening in the world, and especially in the Middle East, these days is truly remarkable. But then again, Bible believers (like yourself) shouldn't be surprised, because the Old Testament prophet, Zachariah, pre-warned us about these times over 2,500 years ago:

"On that day, when all the nations of the earth are gathered against her, I will make Jerusalem an immovable rock for all the nations. All who try to move it will injure themselves" (Zechariah 12:3 NIV).

"On that day, I will set out to destroy all the nations that attack Jerusalem" (Zechariah 12:9 NIV).

The attached documents lists five examples of warning events which have taken place since you have been in office. These events all happened at or near times when you were involved in dialogue or decisions pressuring Israel to trade her Covenant land for peace, contrary to the Word of God. These warnings are examples of the Lord trying to get your attention.

May I suggest, Mr. President, that the way in which you are currently responding while the United States homeland is at risk is not unlike the manner in which the Lord responds when His promised land (Israel) and His chosen people (the Jews) are at risk.

The land of Israel is unique and special, like no other land in the world. It is God's land, and this fact is well documented throughout the Old Testament. "O descendants of Israel his servant, O sons of Jacob, his chosen ones. He is the Lord our God; his judgments are in all the earth. He remembers his covenant forever, the word he commanded, for a thousand generations, the covenant he made with Abraham, the oath he swore to Isaac. He confirmed it to Jacob as a decree, to Israel as an everlasting covenant: "To you I will give the land of Canaan as the portion you will inherit" (I Chronicles 16:13-18 NIV).

I realize that these words I have written will not likely change your decision, but I am hoping and especially praying that they will. Please understand, Mr. President, that I am fulfilling part of my calling, which is to warn you and those who advise you about the seriousness of your pressure on Israel to give up her Covenant land. The Bible is very clear that our loving and fair God will always warn His people before judgment comes.

You are a very good man with an enormous responsibility and a fine administration. It is obvious that you love the Lord and desire to do God's will. Many people, including myself, are praying for you.

In Christ,

William R. Koenig

William R. Koenig
Cc:
Mr. Dick Cheney
Mr. Andrew Card
Ms. Condoleezza Rice
Mrs. Karen Hughes
Mr. Carl Rove
Mr. Ari Fleischer

THE WHITE HOUSE

WASHINGTON

November 9, 2001

Mr. William R. Koenig
White House Correspondence
Koenig's International News
Post Office Box 671127
Dallas, Texas 75367-1127

Dear Mr. Koenig:

Thank you for your letter and the materials you sent.

I welcome information from Americans across the country, and I value your input.

Sincerely,

George W. Bush

THE VICE PRESIDENT
WASHINGTON

January 8, 2002

Dear Mr. Koenig:

Thank you for sending me a copy of your book " Israel: the Blessing or the Curse." I very much appreciate your thoughtfulness.

Lynne joins me in sending our best wishes to you.

Sincerely,

Dick Cheney

Mr. William R. Koenig
P.O. Box 25812
Alexandria, Virginia 22313-5812

Koenig's International News

"Monitor of World Events" William R. Koenig

March 25, 2002

Mr. George W. Bush
President of the United States
The White House
1600 Pennsylvania Avenue
Washington D.C. 20500

Re: God's Covenant Land (Israel)

Dear President Bush,

On October 22, I wrote you a letter about the importance of Israel's covenant land in the context of the Middle East Peace Process and our country's involvement in the "land for peace" proposals.

That letter cited same day events that have taken place when you or your administration made public comments or were actively involved in meetings that would have an adverse impact on God's covenant land of Israel.

Our new book, "*Israel: The Blessing or the Curse*," which deals specifically with this subject, was also sent to you by Ruth Mizell a friend of your parents and was sent to the First Lady by a friend of yours from Midland.

In addition, I was able to personally give a copy to Vice President Dick Cheney and to Karen Hughes and 450 copies of the book were distributed to legislators on Capitol Hill.

By now, you certainly must be aware of Sen. James M. Inhofe (R-OK) and his address on the Senate floor this week. Sen. Inhofe stood courageously in the face of world opinion and presented seven powerful reasons why Israel is entitled to possess her covenant land.

His seventh reason was and is, by all accounts, the most important. Quoting Scripture, he said that Israel has a right to the land, and that we ought to support her in this, because God said so. "This is not a political battle at all." he said. "It is a contest over whether or not the Word of God is true."

Surely you would agree, Mr. President, that Israel's very existence today is in grave danger, not only because of the Palestinian Authority and other Muslim states who seek her demise, but because of our nation's sponsorship of "land for peace" plans which have led her to the brink of war.

The Bible is very clear that our loving and fair God will always warn His people before judgment comes. He has warned our nation many times since the Madrid peace talks in which your father was an active party and participant. Those warnings are clearly documented in "Israel: The Blessing or the Curse."

However, the Lord is preparing to lift His protection on our nation and against those other nations who are pressuring the nation of Israel to give up her land (God's covenant land) according to United Nations Resolutions 242 and 338. Those resolutions are an affront to our Lord.

Allying with the enemies of Israel in a war against terrorism, in return for siding against Israel, is not only illogical and erroneous, but it will be a miserable failure. Most importantly, it will draw the Lord's anger and wrath. What is happening in the world, and especially in the Middle East these days, is truly remarkable. But then again, Bible believers (like yourself) should not be surprised, because the Old Testament prophet, Zechariah, pre-warned us about these times over 2,500 years ago:

"On that day, when all the nations of the earth are gathered against her, I will make Jerusalem an immovable rock for all the nations. All who try to move it will injure themselves" (Zechariah 12:3 NIV).

"On that day, I will set out to destroy all the nations that attack Jerusalem" (Zechariah 12:9 NIV).

Mr. President, you have been very clear about choosing sides in the battle of good versus evil. In that perspective, the world continues to side with the Palestinians and the Arab nations against Israel, the country that is called the Promised Land in the Bible and home to the Jews who are called God's Chosen People in the Word of God.

Millions of Bible-believing Christians and observant Jews around the world are currently lifting prayers to God on behalf of Israel, the integrity of her covenant land, and for the United States that you, your Administration, and members of Congress will choose to support Israel, with faith and courage, in the face of increasing pressure.

In my previous letter, I expressed my feeling that the words I have written may not affect or change your decisions regarding Israel, but I am hoping and especially praying that they will.

Please understand, Mr. President, that I am fulfilling part of my calling, which is to warn you, and those who advise you, about the seriousness of any pressure on Israel to give up her Covenant land.

Many people, including myself, are praying for you, and they will continue praying for you daily.

In His Service,

William R. Koenig

William R. Koenig

"And I will make of thee [Israel] a great nation, and I will bless thee, and make thy name great; and thou shalt be a blessing: And I will bless them that bless thee, and curse him that curseth thee: and in thee shall all families of the earth be blessed" (Genesis 12:2,3).

Washington Office: 400 Madison Street, Suite 209 — Alexandria, VA 22314

THE WHITE HOUSE

WASHINGTON

May 1, 2002

Mr. William R. Koenig
White House News Correspondent
Koenig's International News
Post Office Box 671127
Dallas, Texas 75367

Dear Bill:

Thank you for the copy of *Israel: The Blessing or the Curse*, forwarded by Ruth Mizell.

As we strive for lasting peace in the Middle East, I am continually impressed by the deep historical context of this conflict. I appreciate your gift of a book that addresses the different aspects of this situation.

I am grateful for your kind words of support and your prayers. Laura joins me in sending our best wishes.

Sincerely,

George W. Bush

Koenig's International News

"Monitor of World Events" William R. Koenig

June 5, 2002

Mr. George W. Bush
President of the United States
The White House
1600 Pennsylvania Avenue
Washington D.C. 20500

Re: God's Covenant Land (Israel)

Dear President Bush,

Thank you for your kind note acknowledging receipt of our book, "Israel: the Blessing or the Curse," which goes into great detail about what happens when the United States pushes on Israel to give up her covenant land. In our newly revised book we have added some additional words on your wonderful staff on (pages 149-151).

You are the man the Lord has chosen for this hour, it is incredible to see how our Lord has positioned you at the most crucial time in biblical history. The United States is so blessed to have you as our President and your administration representing us.

As you continue to call on Israel to accept UN Resolutions 242 and 338 and a Palestinian State I would like to warn you as a fellow Christian that the United States will reap major repercussions and magnitude as never before. The Lord has sent many warning signs as we outlined in our book since October 30, 1991 and due to the intensity and seriousness of the moment in Israel the future repercussions will be enormous.

In the October 21, 2001 *Washington Post* article, "Putting a Price on 'What Ifs' it mentioned the three largest insurance events in U.S. history. I might add all three of these events had a same day Israel component.

On September 11, 2001, the World Trade Center and Pentagon terror attacks produced the most expensive event in U.S. history ($30 to $50 billion estimate). Saudi Arabia Prince Bandar bin Sultan went from being "the happiest man in the world" on Monday night, 9-10, to experiencing the worst crisis of his career on 9-11. Dreams of a new Mid East peace initiative evaporated. The realization that most of the hijackers were Saudis "fell on me ... like the whole house collapsed over my head," Bandar said later. He couldn't imagine a way to "do more damage or worse damage to Islam or to Saudi Arabia."

On April 23, 1991, the $19.6 billion Hurricane Andrew the most expensive event in U.S. history, hit Florida at the very moment the Madrid talks convened in Washington.

On January 16, 1994, President Clinton and Syrian President Haffez Assad called on Israel to leave the Golan Heights. Within 24 hours the third largest event in U.S. insurance history the "Northridge Earthquake caused a loss of $16. 2 billion.

Please reconsider being the on sponsoring the "land for peace" efforts in Israel. They are contrary to God's word. If you don't stop the effort the United States is going to experience enormous repercussions.

As I have stated before, please understand Mr. President, that I am fulfilling part of my calling, which is to warn you, and those who advise you, about the seriousness of any pressure on Israel to give up her Covenant land.

Many people, including myself, are praying for you, and they will continue praying for you daily.

In His Service,

William R. Koenig

William R. Koenig
Cc:
Mr. Dick Cheney
Mr. Andrew Card
Ms. Condoleezza Rice
Mrs. Karen Hughes
Mr. Carl Rove
Mr. Ari Fleischer

"And I will make of thee [Israel] a great nation, and I will bless thee, and make thy name great; and thou shalt be a blessing: And I will bless them that bless thee, and curse him that curseth thee: and in thee shall all families of the earth be blessed" (Genesis 12:2,3).

Washington Office: 400 Madison Street, Suite 209 - Alexandria, VA 22314

President Bush Petition

Sign Petition

Please sign this declaration and proclaim your support for Israel and God's covenant land!

This petition will be given to the President of the United States.

*Your personal information will only be used for this petition and kept in complete confidence.

To: **George W. Bush, President of the United States**

WHEREAS, we the undersigned recognize the Bible as the Word of God – eternal, unchanging, and of the authority of God. (2 Timothy 3:16)
WE AFFIRM the steadfast and permanent love of God for Israel and the Jewish people, as clearly declared in the Word of God. (Jeremiah 31:3).
WE AFFIRM as stated in the Bible, which declares that those people, nations and leaders, who bless Israel shall be blessed, and those who curse her, shall be cursed. (Genesis 12:3; Zechariah 12:2-9).
WE AFFIRM the Abrahamic Covenant of God with Israel, and His promise and giving of the land of Israel to the Jewish people as their everlasting homeland, now and always as declared by His Word. (Genesis 17:7-9).
WE AFFIRM the regathering of the Jewish people to their ancient homeland and the rebirth of Israel as ordained and prophesied in the Scriptures, accomplished by His hand, and thus the right and Biblical mandate of Israel to exist in the land of Israel. (Ezekiel 36 and 37; Isaiah 11:11-12).
WE AFFIRM Jerusalem as the undivided eternal capital of Israel, and the biblical warning that any seeking to move or divide it shall do so at their peril. (Joel 3:16-21).
WE AFFIRM the resolve of Israeli citizens to stand and defend themselves against the onslaught of terror arrayed against them.
WE AFFIRM the call of God for all nations and governments, including all those of the Arab world, to recognize the right of Israel to exist, by His decree. (Zechariah 2:8).
WE AFFIRM our steadfast support of Israel, and her right to exist, to thrive, and to defend her people against all that is arrayed against her.

THEREFORE, WE PETITION the President and the United States Government to unequivocally support the state of Israel in her struggle against terrorism, to support her God given right to all of her land, to not call on Israel to stop settlement growth on God's covenant land, and a committment that Jerusalem, stand unmoved, undivided, as Israel's capital, and her "eternal city."

Mr. President, as a professing Christian, we pray you won't be remembered throughout eternity as one of those responsible for dividing up God's land against His promise (Joel 3:2) - The one who attempted to divide God's city (Zechariah 12:1-3) - The one who sacrificed Israel, the apple of God's eye, and compromised her security (Zechariah 2:8).

We will continue to pray **Psalm 91** for you, for your cabinet, for our military, for our nation, and for Israel during these biblically significant times.

This petition was prepared by Worthy News **(click here)** and modified by Bill Koenig.

September 30, 2003

Mr. George W. Bush
President of the United States
The White House
1600 Pennsylvania Avenue
Washington D.C. 20500

Re: Petition with 26,000 signatures

Dear President Bush,

We have submitted 26,000 signatures on the enclosed petition from people concerned about your role in the parceling of God's covenant land in Israel. Please remember your efforts will have eternal consequences.

Surely you would agree, Mr. President, that Israel's very existence today is in grave danger, not only because of the Palestinian Authority and other Muslim states who seek her demise, but because of our nation's sponsorship of "land for peace" plans which have led her to the brink of war.

What is happening in the world, and especially in the Middle East these days, is truly remarkable. But then again, Bible believers (like yourself) should not be surprised, because the Old Testament prophet, Zechariah, pre-warned us about these times over 2,500 years ago:

"On that day, when all the nations of the earth are gathered against her, I will make Jerusalem an immovable rock for all the nations. All who try to move it will injure themselves" (Zechariah 12:3 NIV).

"On that day, I will set out to destroy all the nations that attack Jerusalem" (Zechariah 12:9 NIV).

Israel, the country that is called the Promised Land in the Bible and home to the Jews who are called God's Chosen People in the Word of God is not to be parceled. The nations who parcel God's land will be judged harshly by our Lord (Joel 3:2).

Many people, including us, are praying for you.

In His Service,

William R. Koenig

William R. Koenig
Koenig's International News

George Whitten
Worthy News

ENDNOTES

Chapter 1

Catastrophe #1

Middle East Peace Chronology – 1989-1991
http://usinfo.state.gov/regional/nea/summit/chron2.htm

The Oakland-Berkeley Hills Fire: An Overview
http://www.sfmuseum.org/oakfire/overview.html

Drought in the United States
http://www.glaciermedicaled.com/Earthquake_html/Drought/draught6.html

Catastrophe #2

Bush opens historic Mid East peace conference - October 30, 1991
http://news.bbc.co.uk/onthisday/hi/dates/stories/october/30/newsid_2465000/2465725.stm

The Madrid Conference Speeches October/November 1991
http://www.mfa.gov.il/mfa/go.asp?MFAH0dg10

The Perfect Storm - October 1991
http://www.ncdc.noaa.gov/oa/satellite/satelliteseye/cyclones/pfctstorm91/pfctstorm.html

Bush Kennebunkport Home Damaged by Perfect Storm
http://wampum.wabanaki.net/archives/000349.html

Catastrophe #3

Chronology Of Events, June 1992-December 1994
http://www.mfa.gov.il/mfa/go.asp?MFAH0je60

Middle East Peace Chronology – 1992-1993
http://usinfo.state.gov/regional/nea/summit/chron3.htm

Hurricane history: Andrew
http://www.usatoday.com/weather/wandrew5.htm

Hurricane Andrew – Ten Years Later
http://www.noaa.gov/hurricaneandrew.html

Catastrophe #4

Ross Perot: Political Timeline
http://www.cnn.com/ALLPOLITICS/1996/conventions/long.beach/perot/political.timeline.shtml

H. Ross Perot
http://www.famoustexans.com/rossperot.htm

Only the stupid could think it'll be the economy: Comparing the Bushes - May 7, 2003
http://www.jewishworldreview.com/0503/blankley050703.asp

Catastrophe #5

1993: World Trade Center bomb Terrorizes New York - February 26, 1993

http://news.bbc.co.uk/onthisday/hi/dates/stories/february/26/newsid 2516000/2516469.stm

U.S. Secretary of States Visits to Israel - 1953-2002

http://www.state.gov/r/pa/ho/trvl/12924.htm

Catastrophe #6

Visits to the U.S. by Foreign Heads of State and Government—1993

http://www.state.gov/r/pa/ho/15737.htm

Chronology Of Events, June 1992-December 1994

http://www.mfa.gov.il/mfa/go.asp?MFAH0je60

Storm of the Century - The Blizzard of 1993, March 12-15, 1993

http://snrs.unl.edu/amet498/sherman/blizzard93.html

Catastrophe #7

The Oslo Peace Process

http://news.bbc.co.uk/1/shared/spl/hi/middle_east/03/v3_ip_timeline/html/1993.stm

Israel-Palestinian Negotiations

http://www.us-israel.org/jsource/Peace/ispal.html

Middle East Peace Chronology – 1992-1993

http://usinfo.state.gov/regional/nea/summit/chron3.htm

Effects of the Great Midwest Flood of 1993 on Wetlands

http://water.usgs.gov/nwsum/WSP2425/flood.html

Looking Back: The Great Midwest Floods of 1993

http://www.redcross.org/news/ds/floods/030806midwest93.html

Catastrophe #8

Opening statements by President al-Assad and President Bill Clinton at a news conference, Geneva, 16 January 1994 http://domino.un.org/UNISPAL.NSF/0/0ba7b126ad99f8c78525605b00722335?OpenDocument

Case Studies in Sanctions and Terrorism - US v. Syria

http://www.iie.com/research/topics/sanctions/syria.htm

Earthquake

http://www.eqe.com/publications/northridge/northridge.html

Catastrophe #9

Treaty Of Peace: Between The State Of Israel And The Hashemite

Kingdom Of Jordan - October 26, 1994 -
http://www.mfa.gov.il/mfa/go.asp?MFAH00pa0
Middle East Peace Chronology – 1994-1997
http://usinfo.state.gov/regional/nea/summit/chron4.htm
U.S. Flooding Disasters
http://snrs.unl.edu/amet351/oppenheim/disasters.html
One Hundred Years of Southeast Texas Weather (1900-2000)
http://www.srh.noaa.gov/hgx/climate/holidays/hundred.htm#2

Catastrophe #10

Israeli-Palestinian Interim Agreement on the West Bank and the Gaza Strip Washington, D.C., September 28, 1995 -
http://www.israel.org/mfa/go.asp?MFAH00qa0
Opal - 27 September - 5 October 1995
http://www.nhc.noaa.gov/1995opal.html

Catastrophe #11

Arafat arrives in Washington: Tensions rising between Israel and the Palestinians - March 2, 1997 -
http://www.cnn.com/WORLD/9703/02/arafat/
March 1997 Tornadoes and Flooding
http://www.ncdc.noaa.gov/oa/reports/marchflooding/marchflooding.html
Tornado outbreak, flood index
http://www.usatoday.com/weather/wmar0197.htm
March 1997 Tornadoes and Flooding
http://www.ncdc.noaa.gov/oa/reports/marchflooding/marchflooding.html
FEMA Highlights And Statistics For 1997
http://www.fema.gov/library/fact97.shtm

Catastrophe #12.

President Clinton And King Hussein Discuss Ways To Revive Middle East Peace Process - April 1, 1997 -
http://www.usembassyisrael.org.il/publish/peace/documents/clnt0401.htm
1997 Red River flood index
http://www.usatoday.com/weather/wsflood1.htm
1997 northern Plains flooding at a glance
http://www.usatoday.com/weather/wgredfld.htm
The Flood of the Century: A look into the 1997 Red River Flood
http://www.geo.mtu.edu/department/classes/ge404/mlbroder/during.html

Burns: U.S. Talks With Netanyahu "Serious" - April 7, 2004
http://www.usembassy-israel.org.il/publish/peace/documents/brns0407.htm
Transcript: Clinton/Netanyahu Oval Office Q&A With Reporters - April 7, 1997
http://www.usembassyisrael.org.il/publish/peace/documents/cln0407b.htm
Blizzard adds to weather woes in upper Midwest- April 7, 1997
http://www.cnn.com/WEATHER/9704/07/flood.update/

Catastrophe #13

Israel condemns UN vote on Har Homa - April 27, 1997
http://www.jpost.com/com/Archive/27.Apr.1997/News/Article-1.html
UN condemns new Israeli settlements in Jerusalem
http://southmovement.alphalink.com.au/southnews/July18.htm
Emergency Special Session Of General Assembly Condemns Israel's Failure To Cease Building
Of New Settlement In East Jerusalem: By 131-3-14 Vote, Assembly Also Demands That Israel Reverse Immediately All Illegal Actions against Palestinian Jerusalemites - July 15, 1997
http://domino.un.org/UNISPAL.NSF/0/4dfef4edb0bdae8585256c8b0072c05f?OpenDocument
Russia's Financial Crisis - June 8, 1998
http://csf.colorado.edu/students/Hosomi.Eiji/russian-crisis.html
"Contagion Indicators" for an Ailing Global Economy
http://www.rand.org/publications/randreview/issues/rr.winter98.9/market.html
Contagion
http://www.guardian.co.uk/globalisation/story/0,7369,768336,00.html

Catastrophe #14

Transcript: Ross January 7 Remarks To Press In Jerusalem - January 7, 1998
http://www.usembassyisrael.org.il/publish/peace/archives/1998/january/me0107a.html
Northeast ice storm index
http://www.usatoday.com/weather/wice98.htm

Catastrophe #15

Transcript: Clinton, Netanyahu Oval Office Q&A With Reporters - January 20, 1998
http://www.usembassyisrael.org.il/publish/peace/archives/1998/january/me0120b.html

Clinton Works To Move The Middle East Peace Process Forward - January 20, 1998
http://www.usembassyisrael.org.il/publish/peace/archives/1998/january/me0120c.html

Clinton Denies Affair With Intern, Cover-up Attempt - January 21, 1998
http://www.cnn.com/ALLPOLITICS/1998/01/21/clinton.starr.am/

Transcript: Clinton/Arafat Oval Office Q&A With Reporters - January 22, 1998
http://www.usembassyisrael.org.il/publish/peace/archives/1998/january/me0122c.html

Clinton Meets With Palestinian Authority Chairman Arafat - January 22, 1998
http://www.usembassyIsrael.org.il/publish/peace/archives/1998/january/me0122d.html

Firestorm Consumes White House - January 22, 1998
http://www.cnn.com/ALLPOLITICS/1998/01/22/clinton.main/

New Details Emerge About Sex Allegations Against Clinton - December 23, 1998
http://www.cnn.com/ALLPOLITICS/1998/01/23/clinton.main/

A Chronology: Key Moments In The Clinton-Lewinsky Saga
http://www.cnn.com/ALLPOLITICS/1998/resources/lewinsky/timeline/

Catastrophe #16

Transcript: Clinton, Netanyahu Oval Office Q&A With Reporters - January 20, 1998
http://www.usembassyisrael.org.il/publish/peace/archives/1998/january/me0120b.html

Clinton Meets With Palestinian Authority Chairman Arafat - January 22, 1998
http://www.usembassyisrael.org.il/publish/peace/archives/1998/january/me0122d.html

Transcript: Albright To Try Again To Jump-Start Mideast Peace- January 28, 1998
http://www.usembassyisrael.org.il/publish/peace/archives/1998/january/me0128a1.html

Us Must Find A Way To Continue Peace Process, Official States February 6, 1998 -
http://www.usembassyisrael.org.il/publish/peace/archives/1998/february/me0206a.html

Albright Reaffirms U.S. Commitment To Middle East Peace - February 10, 1998 -

http://www.usembassyIsrael.org.il/publish/peace/archives/1998/february/me0210a.html

1998 off to a very warm, wet start in USA
http://www.usatoday.com/weather/climate/warm98.htm

California Flooding and Florida Tornadoes - February, 1998
http://www.ncdc.noaa.gov/oa/reports/febstorm/february98storms.html#CMORE

Event #17

CHRONOLOGY OF EVENTS, 1998-1999
http://www.israel-mfa.gov.il/mfa/go.asp?MFAH0h1n0

Transcript: Gore, Netanyahu 5/1 Joint Press Conference - May 1, 1998
http://www.usembassyisrael.org.il/publish/peace/archives/1998/may/me0501b.html

VP GORE, SAUDI CROWN PRINCE JOINT STATEMENT, MAY 2
http://Www.UsembassyIsrael.Org.Il/Publish/Peace/Archives/1998/May/Me0504a.Html

Chinese Missile Allegations: Key Stories
http://www.washingtonpost.com/wpsrv/politics/special/missile/keystories.htm

Catastrophe #18

Transcript: Clinton Remarks After Meeting With Netanyahu, Arafat - September 28, 1998
http://usembassyaustralia.state.gov/hyper/WF980929/epf202.htm

Hurricane Georges comes ashore near Biloxi - September 28, 1998
http://www.cnn.com/WEATHER/9809/28/georges.02/

Revised Middle East peace deal gets Arafat's OK - September 29, 1998
http://www.cnn.com/WORLD/meast/9809/29/mideast.03/

Hurricane Georges
http://www.nhc.noaa.gov/1998georges.html

Catastrophe #19

Middle East Peace Talks Wye River October 16-23, 1998
http://www.usembassyisrael.org.il/publish/peace/october98/news.html

Texas reeling from tornadoes, floods - October 18, 1998
http://www.cnn.com/US/9810/18/texas.storms.03/

Rivers crest as Texas flood toll climbs- October 23, 1998
http://www.cnn.com/WEATHER/9810/23/texas.floods.02/

The Wye River Memorandum October 23, 1998
http://www.mfa.gov.il/mfa/go.asp?MFAH07o10

Event #20

Conference raises $3 billion for Palestinians: Arafat meets Clinton at White House - November 30, 1998 - http://www.cnn.com/WORLD/meast/9811/30/mideast.01/

Transcript: Clinton 11/30 Remarks To Mideast Donors Conference http://usembassy-australia.state.gov/hyper/WF981130/epf102.htm

Stock markets tumble worldwide as meltdown fears grow - December 2, 1998 http://archives.tcm.ie/irishexaminer/1998/12/02/fbhead.htm

Event #21

Judiciary approves three articles of impeachment - December 11, 1998 http://www.cnn.com/ALLPOLITICS/stories/1998/12/11/impeachment.01/

President Clinton's Trip to the Middle East - December 12-15, 1998 http://www.usembassyisrael.org.il/publish/president/photos.html

Clinton says he will not resign - December 13, 1998 http://www.cnn.com/ALLPOLITICS/stories/1998/12/13/impeachment.02/

Palestinians affirm Israel's right to exist - December 14, 1998 http://www.cnn.com/WORLD/meast/9812/14/clinton.gaza.03/

Arafat, Netanyahu, Clinton gather to seek Mideast peace - December 15, 1998 http://www.cnn.com/WORLD/meast/9812/15/mideast.03/

Judiciary Committee wraps up its case against Clinton - December 15, 1998 http://edition.cnn.com/ALLPOLITICS/stories/1998/12/12/impeachment.02/

Republicans skeptical of Iraq attack on eve of impeachment vote - December 16, 2003 http://edition.cnn.com/ALLPOLITICS/stories/1998/12/16/congresstional.react.02/

House impeaches Clinton: President will face Senate trial on perjury, obstruction of justice charges - December 19, 1998 http://edition.cnn.com/ALLPOLITICS/stories/1998/12/19/impeachment.01/

Israel to Hold Early Elections, Netanyahu Government Fails - December 21, 1998 http://www.cnsnews.com/indepth/archive/199812/IND19981221g.html

Netanyahu decries 'fantasies' of political rivals - December 22, 1998 http://www.cnn.com/WORLD/meast/9812/22/israel.01/

Event #22

Arafat meets with U.S. leaders to discuss statehood - March 23, 1999 http://www.cnn.com/WORLD/meast/9903/23/arafat.01/
Clinton urges Arafat to delay declaration of Palestinian state - March 24, 1999
http://www.cnn.com/ALLPOLITICS/stories/1999/03/24/clinton.arafat/

NATO attack on Yugoslavia begins - March 24, 1999
http://www.cnn.com/WORLD/europe/9903/24/kosovo.strikes/

Catastrophe #23

Oklahoma/Kansas Tornado Outbreak - May 3, 1999
http://www.nssl.noaa.gov/headlines/outbreak.shtml

US President Bill Clinton will send a message to Palestinian President Yasser Arafat, pushing him to postpone the declaration of the Palestinian state on May 4 - April 19, 1999
http://www.arabicnews.com/ansub/Daily/Day/990419/1999041909.html
Hillary Clinton: Eventual Palestinian State Important For Mideast Peace - May 6, 1999
http://www.usembassyisrael.org.il/publish/peace/archives/1998/may/me0506b.html

Mrs. Clinton backs Palestinian state- May 7, 1999
http://www.cnn.com/US/9805/07/palestinians.hillary/

Catastrophe #24

Transcript: Albright Remarks On Meeting With Palestinian Officials - August 30, 1999
http://www.usembassyisrael.org.il/publish/peace/archives/1999/august/me0830a.html

Hurricane Dennis Impact Studies; Peculiar Storm Path
http://coastal.er.usgs.gov/hurricanes/dennis/

Hurricane Dennis weakens, heads away from North Carolina coast - August 31, 1999
http://www.cnn.com/WEATHER/9908/31/storms.02/

Catastrophe #25

Israel, PA launch final-status talks tonight - September 13, 1999
http://www.jpost.com/com/Archive/13.Sep.1999/News/Article-0.html

Final Status Talks: 'Middle East Peace In The New Millennium?'- September 16, 1999
http://www.fas.org/news/israel/wwwh9s16.htm

Floyd's floods hit N.C., N.J. hardest - September 17, 1999
http://edition.cnn.com/WEATHER/9909/17/floyd.floods.01/

Hurricane Floyd 7 - 17 September, 1999
http://www.nhc.noaa.gov/1999floyd.html

Events #26

Barak Plans to Dismantle Some Settlements, Expand Others - October 12-13, 1999
http://www.us-israel.org/jsource/Peace/barakot.html

Hurricane Irene 13 - 19 October 1999
http://www.nhc.noaa.gov/1999irene_text.html

Hurricane Irene makes landfall in SW Florida- October 15, 1999
http://edition.cnn.com/WEATHER/9910/15/irene.05/

Greenspan fuels market meltdown: The Dow nose dives 267 points- Friday, October 15, 1999
http://starbulletin.com/1999/10/15/business/market.html

Barak lauds deal with settlers - October 15, 1999
http://www.jpost.com/com/Archive/15.Oct.1999/News/Article-0.html

The October 16, 1999 M7.1 Hector Mine Earthquake
http://pasadena.wr.usgs.gov/hector/index.html

Event #27

Wall Street Takes a Beating, Nation Burns, the Land in Drought

Washington's Role In The Syrian-Israeli Peace Talks: Do's And Don'ts- February 4, 2000
http://www.heritage.org/Research/MiddleEast/BG1345.cfm

Barak, Arafat holding third day of talks - March 9, 2000
http://www.cnn.com/2000/WORLD/meast/03/09/mideast.talks.02/

Remarks By The President And Prime Minister Ehud Barak Of Israel - April 11, 2000 http://www.usembassy-israel.org.il/publish/peace/archives/2000/april/me0412b.html

Clinton Meets Barak at White House - April 12, 2000
http://www.newsmax.com/articles/?a=2000/4/12/61439

$1,000bn wiped off US stocks - Saturday, 15 April, 2000
http://news.bbc.co.uk/1/low/business/711505.stm

Finance/Apr. 2000 - Stock Market Fluctuation - $2.1 Trillion /Nasdaq Fluctuation - 574.57 points -
http://mt.sopris.net/mpc/finance/$2.1.trillion.html

Remarks By The President In Photo Opportunity With Chairman Yasser Arafat Of Palestinian Authority - April 20, 2000
http://www.usembassyisrael.org.il/publish/peace/archives/2000/april/me0421b.html

Transcript: Senior Official Briefs On Clinton-Arafat Meeting - April 20
http://www.usembassyisrael.org.il/publish/peace/archives/2000/april/me0421c.html

U.S. Has Its Warmest Spring And Year-To-Date On Record, Noaa Reports - 2000 http://www.noaanews.noaa.gov/stories/s443.htm

Event #28

The Middle East Peace Summit at Camp David - July 2000 http://www.mfa.gov.il/mfa/go.asp?MFAH0hls0

Camp David timeline – July 2-25, 2000 http://news.bbc.co.uk/2/hi/world/middle_east/848968.stm

As Barak goes abroad, his coalition collapses – July 10, 2000 http://www.jewishworldreview.com/0700/collapse1.asp

Climate of 2000 - June-August: U.S. Drought, Heat Waves, and Wildfires - http://lwf.ncdc.noaa.gov/oa/climate/research/2000/sum/us_drought.html

2000 Fire Season Most Expensive In History Http://Www.Taxpayer.Net/TCS/Pressreleases/12-14-00 fromtheashes.Htm

Hot Spots: Forecast: Bad Year For Wildfires In Northwest http://abcnews.go.com/sections/scitech/DailyNews/wilfire010527_forecast.html

The Year of the Wildfires http://www.riverdeep.net/current/2000/09/091800t_wildfires.jhtml

U.S. Drought Monitor – October 10, 2000 http://www.drought.unl.edu/dm/archive/2000/drmon1010.htm

Event #29

Latest attempt to form Israeli emergency government fails – October 29, 2000 http://www.cnn.com/2000/WORLD/meast/10/29/mideast.violence.03/

Amid Florida presidential tumult, GOP can still count on House and Senate – November 8, 2000 http://www.cnn.com/2000/ALLPOLITICS/stories/11/07/campaign.wrap/index.html

Blow-by-blow account of Gore's concession — and retraction - November 8, 2000 http://www.cnn.com/2000/ALLPOLITICS/stories/11/08/gore.election/index.html

U.S. names Mitchell to head Mideast fact-finding commission – November 8, 2000 http://www.cnn.com/2000/WORLD/meast/11/07/mideast.02/index.html

After meeting with Clinton, Arafat's next stop is UN - November 10, 2000 http://www.cnn.com/2000/WORLD/meast/11/09/mideast.06/index.html

Jerusalem explosion starts new day of Mideast violence Arafat to push UN for security force - November 11, 2000 - http://www.cnn.com/2000/WORLD/meast/11/10/mideast.02/

Bush and Gore marshal legal forces for the Battle of Florida - November 13, 2000
http://www.swdtimes.com/swdtimes/html/Daily1/MONDAY/nov13/002.html

Legal big guns for Bush and Gore head for showdown at Florida high court- November 20, 2000
http://www.cnn.com/2000/ALLPOLITICS/stories/11/19/president.election/

'I'm ready for elections,' says Barak - November 29, 2000
http://www.jpost.com/Editions/2000/11/29/News/News.16464.html

Bush goes to U.S. Supreme Court to counter effects of Florida ruling - December8, 2000
http://www.cnn.com/2000/ALLPOLITICS/stories/12/08/election.wrap/

Barak resigns in move to sidestep push for new elections - December 9, 2000
http://www.cnn.com/2000/WORLD/meast/12/09/barak.resigns.02/

Sharply divided U.S. Supreme Court stops Florida recount - December 10, 2000 http://www.cnn.com/2000/ALLPOLITICS/stories/12/09/president.election/

Gore concedes presidential election - December 13, 2000
http://www.cnn.com/2000/ALLPOLITICS/stories/12/13/gore.ends.campaign/index.html

Sharon defeats Barak in a landslide - February 6, 2001
http://www.zipple.com/newsandpolitics/israenews/20010206_landslide-victory.shtml

Chapter 2
Event #1

Remarks by President Bush and Egyptian President Hosni Mubarak in Photo Opportunity - April 1, 2001 -
http://www.whitehouse.gov/news/releases/2001/04/20010402-4.html

U.S. aircraft collides with Chinese fighter, forced to land - April 1, 2001
http://www.cnn.com/2001/US/04/01/us.china.plane.03/

Statement by the President on American Plane and Crew in China- April 2, 2001
http://www.whitehouse.gov/news/releases/2001/04/20010402-2.html

Remarks of the President and His Majesty King Abdullah of the Hashemite Kingdom of Jordan in Photo Opportunity- April 10, 2001
http://www.whitehouse.gov/news/releases/2001/04/20010410-1.html

Remarks by the President on Release of American Servicemen and Women in China - April 11, 2001 -
http://www.whitehouse.gov/news/releases/2001/04/20010411-3.html

Event #2

Text: Powell Endorses Mitchell Report on Mideast Violence - May 21, 2001
http://www.usembassyisrael.org.il/publish/peace/archives/2001/may/0521a.html

Bush Discusses Mitchell Report with Leaders of Egypt and Jordan - May 22, 2001
http://www.usembassy.it/file2001_05/alia/a1052201.htm

Bush Calls Sharon, Arafat About Mitchell Report - May 23, 2001
http://www.usembassy.it/file2001_05/alia/a1052305.htm

President Bush Meets with the Dalai Lama - May 23, 2001
http://www.whitehouse.gov/news/releases/2001/05/20010523-3.html

Jeffords leaves GOP, throwing Senate control to Democrats - May 25, 2001
http://www.cnn.com/2001/ALLPOLITICS/05/24/jeffords.senate/

Catastrophe #3

CIA's Tenet Meets Sharon, Arafat - June 8, 2001
http://www.newsmax.com/archives/articles/2001/6/7/190806.shtml

Bush Hails Israeli-Palestinian Cease-fire Agreement - June 13, 2001
http://www.usembassyisrael.org.il/publish/peace/archives/2001/june/0614a.html

Noaa's National Weather Service Releases Service Assessment Report For Tropical Storm Allison Texas / Louisiana Flood Event, October 31, 2001
http://www.noaanews.noaa.gov/stories/s797.htm

Allison's Impact: A Look Back at a Killer Storm that cost $4 billion in damage http://www.disasterrelief.org/Disasters/010622AllisonReview/

Tropical Storm Allison Floods
http://www.srh.noaa.gov/hgx/projects/allison01.htm

Catastrophe #4

September 11: Chronology of terror
http://www.cnn.com/2001/US/09/11/chronology.attack/

Statement by the President in His Address to the Nation- September 11, 2001
http://www.whitehouse.gov/news/releases/2001/09/20010911-16.html

Marriage of Convenience: The U.S. - Saudi Alliance - February 10, 11, and 12, 2002:

Three-part article that Bob Kaiser and David Ottaway published in the Washington Post http://www2.aya.yale.edu/classes/yc1964/activities/kaiser.htm

Review of the Studies of the Economic Impact of the September 11, 2001 Attacks on the World Trade Center - http://www.gao.gov/new.items/d02700r.pdf

How much did the September 11 terrorist attack cost America? http://www.iags.org/costof911.html

Catastrophe #5

Bush: Palestinian state 'part of a vision' if Israel respected - October 2, 2001
http://www.cnn.com/2001/US/10/02/gen.mideast.us/index.html

Before Attacks, U.S. Was Ready to Say It Backed Palestinian State - October 3, 2001
http://www.globalpolicy.org/security/issues/israel-palestine/2001/1003uspal.htm

Chronology of anthrax events
http://www.sun-sentinel.com/news/local/southflorida/sfl-1013anthraxchronology.story?coll=sfla-home-headlines

Anthrax Threat - October 31, 2003
http://www.pbs.org/newshour/bb/health/july-dec01/anthrax_10-30.html

Catastrophe #6

President Bush Speaks to United Nations - November 10, 2001
http://www.whitehouse.gov/news/releases/2001/11/20011110-3.html

Powell: Bush's use of `Palestine' deliberate - November 12, 2001
http://www.haaretzdaily.com/hasen/pages/ShArt.jhtml?itemNo=93580&;subContrassID=1&;sbSubContrassID=0&;listSrc=Y

American Flight 587 crashes into residential Queens; 260 dead - November 12, 2001
http://www.uwire.com/content/topnews111301002.html

Catastrophe #7

President Bush Meets with Crown Prince of Saudi Arabia - April 25, 2002
http://www.whitehouse.gov/news/releases/2002/04/20020425-4.html

Statement by the President on the Middle East and Arafat's Release - April 28, 2002
http://www.whitehouse.gov/news/releases/2002/04/20020428.html

F5 Class Tornado Strikes Southern Maryland on April 28, 2002
http://www.somd.com/news/2002/04/tornado/

Killer tornado becomes one for the books in Maryland - April 29, 2002
http://www.cnn.com/2002/WEATHER/04/29/storm.deaths/
Tornadoes rip through towns from Missouri to Maryland, killing at least six - April 29, 2002
http://www.ardmoreite.com/stories/042902/new_tornado.shtml

Catastrophe #8
President Bush Meets with Egyptian President Mubarak- June 8, 2002
http://www.whitehouse.gov/news/releases/2002/06/20020608-4.html
Hayman Fire Was Unstoppable: 137,000-acre blaze out of control as soon as it started, report says -
http://www.fs.fed.us/rm/main/pa/newsclips/02_11/1114_hayman01.html

Catastrophe #9
Hell comes to the White Mountains - June 18-26, 2002
http://www.azcentral.com/news/specials/wildfires/
President Bush Calls for New Palestinian Leadership - June 24, 2002
http://www.whitehouse.gov/news/releases/2002/06/20020624-3.html
President Visits Displaced Families in Arizona- June 25, 2002
http://www.whitehouse.gov/news/releases/2002/06/20020625-4.html
WorldCom admits massive fraud: $3.8 billion scheme inflated profit; financial exec fired - June 25, 2002 -
http://www.siliconvalley.com/mld/siliconvalley/3545267.htm
Adelphia is filing for Chapter 11 - June 26, 2002
http://www.forbes.com/2002/06/26/0620adelphiapackage.html
President Reiterates Path for Peace in Middle East - June 26, 2002
http://www.whitehouse.gov/news/releases/2002/06/20020626.html

Catastrophe #10
Bush Hesitates on Moving U.S. Embassy to Jerusalem - October 1, 2002 -
http://www.foxnews.com/printer_friendly_story/0,3566,64565,00.html
Bush, Congress clash over Jerusalem status - October 2, 2002
http://www.jewishsf.com/bk021004/us11.shtml
Chronology: Sniper attacks Began October 2, 2002
http://www.cbc.ca/news/features/sniper_victims.html
Lili damage estimated at $600 million - October 5, 2002
http://www.cnn.com/2002/WEATHER/10/05/lili/
Hurricane Lili NOAA Report
http://www.nhc.noaa.gov/2002lili.shtml

Catastrophe #11

President Hosts Iftaar [Ramadan] Dinner - November 7, 2002 http://www.whitehouse.gov/news/releases/2002/11/20021107-11.html

Twister: A Case Study of the 10-11 November 2002 Tornado Outbreak http://www.personal.psu.edu/users/j/l/jln177/Twister/

November 10, 2002 Tornado Outbreak: Overview and brief look at SPC forecast decision process - http://www.spc.noaa.gov/staff/evans/talk1/talk1_frame.htm
Boucher Says Mideast Peace Roadmap Not "Frozen," November 13, 2002 http://www.usembassy.it/file2002_11/alia/a2111302.htm

Catastrophe #12

President Commemorates Eid al-Fitr: Remarks by the President on Eid Al-Fitr

The Islamic Center of Washington, D.C. - December 5, 2002 http://www.whitehouse.gov/news/releaes/2002/12/20021205-5.html

Winter comes early to Carolinas: Forecasters say 1 million could be without power - December 5, 2002 - http://www.cnn.com/2002/WEATHER/12/04/wintry.storm/

Duke Power Responding to Worst Storm in History - December 5, 2002
http://www.prnewswire.com/cgibin/stories.pl?ACCT=105&STORY=/www/story/12-05-2002/0001852841

Catastrophe #13

Address at the National Conference of World Affairs Councils of America

Secretary Colin L. Powell - Washington, DC - January 31, 2003 http://usembassy.state.gov/seoul/wwwh43fy.html
President Bush Meets with Prime Minister Blair - January 31, 2003 http://www.whitehouse.gov/news/releases/2003/01/20030131-23.html

President Addresses Nation on Space Shuttle Columbia Tragedy - February 1, 2003 http://www.whitehouse.gov/news/releases/2003/02/20030201-2.html

Again on TV, riveting scenes and gathering of grief - February 2, 2003
http://www.boston.com/news/packages/shuttle/globe_stories/Again_on_TV_riveting_scenes_and_gathering_of_grief+.shtml

Catastrophe #14

'Road map' to pact in Mideast is delivered - May 1, 2003 http://www.iht.com/articles/94928.html

Second Oklahoma City twister caps nation's worst tornado week -

May 10, 2003 http://www.usatoday.com/weather/news/2003-05-10-stormyweek_x.htm

Record Number Of Tornadoes, NOAA Reports – May 11, 2003 http://www.noaanews.noaa.gov/stories/s1144.htm

May tornado count sets record – May 11, 2003 http://www.usatoday.com/weather/news/2003-05-11-tornadoes-may_x.htm

Catastrophes #15

EU says Mideast 'road map' does not belong to U.S. http://middleeastinfo.org/article.php?sid=2519

New study finds Europe's severe heatwave during the summer of 2003 was a 1-in-46,000 event - http://eces.org/articles/000741.php

Europe's hottest summer for 500 years – September 24, 2003 http://eces.org/articles/000741.php

Behind this summer's wild, tragic weather http://www.csmonitor.com/2003/0815/p01s02-usgn.html

London breaks record for heat, wildfires plague Europe - August 8, 2003 http://www.smh.com.au/articles/2003/08/07/1060145794919.html

Have Apocalyptic Weather Changes Begun? - Hal Lindsey - August 18, 2003 http://www.hallindseyoracle.com/articles.asp?ArticleID=3243

Climate of 2003 - Annual Review U.S. Drought http://www.ncdc.noaa.gov/oa/climate/research/2003/ann/drought-summary.html#natldrot

Catastrophe #16

Powell In Mideast, Pushing 'Roadmap' – May 11, 2003 http://www.cbsnews.com/stories/2003/05/11/world/main553333.shtm

Secretary Powell's Visit to the Middle East Photo Gallery: Meets Egypt's Mubarek and Jordan's King Abdullah II - May 12, 2003 http://usinfo.state.gov/regional/nea/summit/sectrip2photos.html

Bush Denounces Terrorist Attacks in Saudi Arabia, May 13, 2003 http://www.usembassy.it/file2003_05/alia/A3051301.htm

U.S. worried about more al Qaeda attacks: U.S., Saudis suspect terror group in Riyadh bombings – May 13, 2003 - http://www.cnn.com/2003/WORLD/meast/05/13/saudi.blast/

Bombings Show 'The War on Terrorism Goes On,' Rice Says – May 14, 2003 http://www.defenselink.mil/news/May2003/n05142003_200305144.html

Catastrophe #17

Palestinian Officials Meet With Congress - July 17, 2003

http://www.guardian.co.uk/uslatest/story/0,1282,-2916166,00.html
Hurricane Claudette moves inland after lashing Texas coast - July 17, 2003
http://www.augustachronicle.com/stories/071603/nat_claudette.shtml

Events # 18

Blair addresses US Congress: UK Prime Minister Tony Blair is addressing the United States Congress at the start of a visit to Washington, dominated by Iraq and the Middle East peace process - July 17, 2003 -
http://news.bbc.co.uk/2/hi/uk_news/politics/3073193.stm
Remarks by Palestinian Authority Prime Minister Mahmoud Abbas to the Council on Foreign Relations - July 24, 2003 -
http://www.cfr.org/publication.php?id=6156
President Bush Welcomes Prime Minister Abbas to White House - July 25, 2003
http://www.whitehouse.gov/news/releases/2003/07/20030725-6.html
Navy Secretary Nominee's Death Ruled Suicide - July 25, 2003
http://www.foxnews.com/printer_friendly_story/0,3566,92896,00.html
Abbas Seeks U.S. Assistance in Prodding Israel - May 25, 2003
http://www.foxnews.com/printer_friendly_story/0,3566,92909,00.html

Catastrophe #19

Abbas resigns as Palestinian prime minister - September 6, 2003
http://www.washtimes.com/world/20030907-124732-9980r.htm
Bush briefed on hurricane; White House battens down - September 17, 2003
http://www.hamptonroads.com/stories/br0917bush.html
Isabel Essentially Shuts Down Capital Region - September 18, 2003
http://www.news8.net/news/stories/0903/103048.html
Bush, Jordanian King Continue Work on Mideast Peace - September 18, 2003
http://www.foxnews.com/printer_friendly_story/0,3566,97681,00.html
President Bush, King Abdullah of Jordan Meet at Camp David - September 18, 2003 http://www.whitehouse.gov/news/releases/2003/09/20030918-4.html
Statement on Federal Assistance for Maryland - September 20, 2003
http://www.whitehouse.gov/news/releases/2003/09/20030919-5.html

Catastrophe #20

President's Ramadan Message - October 24, 2003
http://www.whitehouse.gov/news/releases/2003/10/20031024-10.html

The White House Ramadan 2003 Section
http://www.whitehouse.gov/infocus/ramadan/index.html

'The Perfect Non-Storm': Why Southern California Is Burning-October 27, 2003
http://abcnews.go.com/sections/wnt/SciTech/fires031027_why.html

Remarks by the President at Iftaar with Ambassadors and Muslim Leaders - October 28, 2003
http://www.whitehouse.gov/news/releases/2003/10/20031028-9.html

Bush: Fence will impede emergence of Palestinian state - October 28, 2003
http://www.haaretzdaily.com/hasen/spages/354749.html

One of the largest known solar flares erupted - October 29, 2003
http://www.cnn.com/2003/TECH/space/10/28/solar.flare/

Fire Roars Through San Bernardino Mountains - October 30, 2003 http://www.foxnews.com/story/0,2933,101512,00.html

Second huge solar storm hits Earth - October 31, 2003
http://www.theage.com.au/articles/2003/10/31/1067233358702.html

Sun on Fire, Unleashes 3 More Major Flares, November 3, 2001
http://www.space.com/scienceastronomy/solar_flares_031103.html

President Bush Thanks Firefighters and Volunteers in California - November 4, 2003
http://www.whitehouse.gov/news/releases/2003/11/20031104-4.html

Chapter 4

1 Bob Kaiser is Associate Editor of the *Washington Post.* He co-authored with David Ottaway and published in the *Post* a three-part article on February 10, 11, and 12, 2002.
http://www2.aya.yale.edu/classes/yc1964/activities/kaiser.htm

September 11: Chronology of terror
http://www.cnn.com/2001/US/09/11/chronology.attack/

Remarks by the President After Two Planes Crash Into World Trade Center
http://www.whitehouse.gov/news/releases/2001/09/20010911.html

Statement by the President in His Address to the Nation
http://www.whitehouse.gov/news/releases/2001/09/20010911-16.html

The Milken Institute
http://www.milkeninstitute.org/

Remarks by the President in Address to the Nation - Homeland Security Department Funding http://www.whitehouse.gov/news/releases/2002/06/20020606-8.html

President Bush Signs Homeland Security Appropriations Bill - October 1, 2002 -
http://www.whitehouse.gov/news/releases/2003/10/print/20031001-4.html

FY 2004 Budget Fact Sheet - Homeland Security http://www.white-house.gov/news/releases/2003/10/20031001-7.html

Thompson Releases Report on Fiscal Impact Of 9/11 on New York City - September 4, 2002
http://comptroller.nyc.gov/press/2002_releases/print/02-09-054.shtm

Bill Koenig's Biography

Bill began his business career in 1978 with Coldwell Banker (now CB Richard Ellis) a major-international real estate company. He began work in Phoenix, Arizona transferring to Dallas, Texas in 1979. He was associated with two other commercial real estate companies in Dallas before starting his own brokerage and investment company in 1984.

In a career change, in the summer of 1996, Bill began publishing Koenig's Watch" a weekly summary of important Middle East news from Dallas. He moved onto the Internet in 1997, expanding the coverage to international news and changing the name to "Koenig's International News" (http://watch.org).

The news ministry, which now includes "WorldWatchDaily" with constantly updated stories from a large variety of news sources, today has readers and e-mail subscribers in all 50 states and 79 countries around the globe.

In early 1999, he produced the audiotape, "Countdown 2000," discussing ten major events to watch moving into the new millennium.

In late 2001, Bill co-authored with John McTernan, *Israel: The Blessing or the Curse,* a book on the history of Israel's land, a history of the peace process, the consequences to those who have participated in the "land for peace" process and political insight.

Bill was a member of First Baptist Dallas and the Dallas Theological Seminary's Presidents Council, before moving to Washington D.C. He has been very active in both local and national Christian activities. He has attended four National Religious Broadcaster (NRB) conventions, two in Washington, D.C. and two in Nashville.

He graduated from Arizona State University, with a B.S. in Communications.

Bill and his wife Claudia reside in the Washington D.C. area where he is a White House Correspondent.